Corp. Hosea W. Rood

The Marching Twelfth

The Story of the
Twelfth Wisconsin
Volunteer Infantry Regiment
As Told by the Men
Who Served in It

Edited by
Peggy M. Singer

HERITAGE BOOKS
2007

HERITAGE BOOKS
AN IMPRINT OF HERITAGE BOOKS, INC.

Books, CDs, and more—Worldwide

For our listing of thousands of titles see our website
at
www.HeritageBooks.com

Published 2007 by
HERITAGE BOOKS, INC.
Publishing Division
65 East Main Street
Westminster, Maryland 21157-5026

Copyright © 2002 Peggy M. Singer

All rights reserved. No part of this book may be reproduced or transmitted in any form or by any means, electronic or mechanical, including photocopying, recording or by any information storage and retrieval system without written permission from the author, except for the inclusion of brief quotations in a review.

International Standard Book Number: 978-0-7884-2018-4

TO
Sergeant Walter Scott Whitcomb
and his comrades in arms

TABLE OF CONTENTS

Preface		ix
CHAPTER I,	Enlistment Begins	1
CHAPTER II,	Camp Randall to Kansas	9
CHAPTER III,	The Army of Tennessee	15
CHAPTER IV,	The Vicksburg Campaign	25
CHAPTER V,	Jackson to Natchez	31
CHAPTER VI,	The Meridian Campaign	37
CHAPTER VII,	Kennesaw Mountain	43
CHAPTER VIII	Nickajack Creek	53
CHAPTER IX	The Battle for Atlanta	59
CHAPTER X	The Battles of Ezra Church, Jonesboro, & the Pusuit of Hood.	73
CHAPTER XI	The March to the Sea	81
CHAPTER XII	The Carolina Campaign	89
CHAPTER XIII	Conclusion	99

ROSTER

Field and Staff	111
Company A	114
Company B	121
Company C	127
Company D	133
Company E	140
Company F	147
Company G	155
Company H	161
Company I	168
Company K	176
Index	185

Col. George E. Bryant

ILLUSTRATIONS

Corp. Hosea W. Rood	Frontispiece
Col. George E. Bryant	p. vi
Col. James K. Proudfit	p. viii
Map-From Atlanta to the Sea	p.80
Map-From Savannah to Goldsboro	p. 88

Col. James K. Proudfit

PREFACE

On the rare occasions when the Civil War was a topic of conversation as I was growing up, my mother remarked that her, "grandfather marched to sea with Sherman." A fact of which she seemed quite proud. The March to the Sea was certainly a dramatic event that captured the imagination of the nation, but it was relatively uneventful in comparison to some of the other marches he had made. And then, of course, there were the battles of Vicksburg, Meridian, Kennesaw Mountain, Atlanta, and Bentonville in which his regiment was involved.

I contacted as many relatives as I could find, but no one knew if his letters had survived or, if so, who had them. I obtained his military and pension records from the National Archives and so knew when he was with his regiment and could assume which events he took part in. But I decided the best I could do was write a short history of the Twelfth Wisconsin Volunteer Infantry Regiment and include it in my family history so that others in the family would know and take pride in his service to his country.

In the process of researching this regimental history I utilized the resources of the Wyles Collection in the Special Collections Department of the University of California at Santa Barbara (UCSB). It was there I discovered a book entitled: "The Story of Company E of the Twelfth Wisconsin Regiment of Veteran Volunteer Infantry in the War of the Rebellion", Beginning with September 7, 1861 and ending July 21, 1865." Written by "One of The Boys." There was no publisher, no copyright. There were probably just enough books printed for those who wanted one.

It was, however, a fair sized book with over 500 pages. Books in the Special Collections Department cannot be checked out and they allow only ten percent of the book to be photocopied. I wrote to the Historical Society of Wisconsin and the University of Wisconsin and asked cousins living there to check library holdings hoping to find another copy and someone who would give me a photocopy of the whole book. But none had ever heard of the book or possessed a copy.

To drive back and forth to the University, spend hours enclosed in the reading room of Special Collections reading and making notes, then going home to type up the material I'd gathered seemed like a rather daunting task at the time so I contented myself with the short, rather factual history of the Regiment.

That was twelve years ago. And for all those years that book haunted me. I could not forget there were stories written by the men who had served with my great grandfather; experienced the hardships he must have experienced; seen what he must have seen.

In the forward of the book, the author told how a few of them had gotten together at a reunion and decided to write the book. They described how important they felt it was their children and grandchildren and children yet to come, should know what they went through; to know what it was like. By accident or by fate I had found their stories. Well cared for and preserved by the staff of Special Collections; but essentially out of sight and out of reach of the very people for whom they were intended. I don't mean to fault the system. The book may never have survived without it.

So, in the summer of 2000, I decided I must do what I could to bring these stories to light. Since I could only photocopy ten percent of the book, I had to choose carefully which 50 pages were the most important. I chose the ones describing the march from Clifton, Tennessee to Kennesaw Mountain and Nickajack Creek, the battles for Leggett's Hill, Ezra Church and Jonesboro near Atlanta, and the Grand Review in Washington, D.C. These were dramatic events best told by the men who experienced them I copied them as written in the book.

I managed a few pages concerning the March to the Sea and the Carolina Campaign, but for these and other events I had to rely on my notes, the history I'd written earlier, and a few excerpts from the diary of Maj. George Ward Nichols, General Sherman's aide-de-camp. The reports of various officers were copied from <u>The Compendium of the War of the Rebellion,</u> a multi-volume set which contains all the official reports, orders, etc., of both Union and Confederate Armies and Navies. Available in many public and university libraries.

Most of the men responsible for the book were all in Company E, and many of the stories concerned the men of that company, but the experiences were virtually the same for all the men in the regiment and men from other companies contributed as well. The committee responsible were as follows:

H. S. Beardsley, was responsible for collecting stories.
S. Glyde Swain, was to gather statistics and reports.
Hosea Rood, was to organize the matrial and write it up.
John G. Ingalis, was to take subscriptions for the book.

Mr. Rood was chosen for this task probably because he was a high school English teacher. I have assumed that he is the primary author and I have used his name to precede any direct quotes from the book where no other contributor is named. The book is well written and took over two years in the writing.

Other contributors are listed as:

Col. George Bryant   John Griffin
Lt. Alpheus E. Kinney   H. S. Beardsley
Lt. Lewis T. Linnell   N. D. Brown
Henry H. & Edmond F. Bennett   S. Glyde Swain
Nathaniel Darrow   Lt. Harlan P. Bird
Seneca Briggs

The Wisconsin Historical Society sent me a few letters written by Pvt. William Enderby who served in Company H. They were all letters to his parents and mostly personal in content. I did, however, include part of one letter describing their march to Humboldt, Tennessee. It was written in the vernacular of the day and I copied it as written. It made me realize that Hosea Rood had probably corrected the grammar, puncuation, spelling, and perhaps, syntax of the diaries, letters, stories, etc., that he had received. Since many of the men were still alive when the book was printed, I'm sure they appreciated it.

In two or three places in the book Mr. Rood mentions that others may not remember a certain event the same way he does. Or, perhaps not at all; or complain that he should have added other incidences; or told it differently. His answer was that had the men of the regiment been a "bit more liberal" in submitting their stories, he could have done a better job. "Stories" were probably rampant at the reunions. Getting the men to write them down was another matter. He had, therefore, to rely on his own observations and memories of many of the events.

The first reunion of Company E was held in June of 1880. In 1887, Col. George Bryant called for a reunion of the 12th and 16th Regiments at Madison, Wisconsin. A second reunion of Company E was held September 26, 1888. In August of 1889, the National Encampment of the Grand Army of the Republic was held at Milwaukee, Wisconsin.

On the last page of the "Forward", Hosea Rood wrote, "Presented to my old comrades by the author". Written at Milton, Wisc., June 8, 1893. I assume that was about the date the book was printed.

CHAPTER I
Enlistment Begins

Years after the Civil War most units of the Army held reunions. At one of the reunions a woman, looking around the room at the graying heads and middle-aged physiques, asked one of the men why they always referred to themselves as, "boys?" He answered, "Well ma'am, if you went to your local high school and picked out the biggest boys, lined them up and made them toe the mark and stand up straight you'd have a pretty good picture of what half of the regiment looked like. The other half was a bit older. Some of them had started to shave."
The average age of the Civil War soldier was eighteen. They were just boys. Their officers addressed them as "boys", and the public referred to them as "boys"; the boys in blue or the boys in gray, and so the term stuck.
At the beginning of hostilities there were only 36,000 men in the United States Army. Forts were manned by small maintenance crews and most of the soldiers were scattered along the vast western frontier. With the secession of the Southern states many of the regular officers and men transferred their allegiance to their particular state. The North was left with the bare nucleus of an army and the South had to start from scratch to set up a government and build a military force.
The first federal recruiting effort enlisted men for a period of three months, after which they were released. This minimal amount of training was often enough to elevate a man to officer status when, later, a longer term of enlistment was begun. This was the case of John Gillespie who was made a lieutenant in the Company recruited in and near Delton, Wisconsin and he was put to work drilling the new recruits.
The boys were recruited by a Captain who was usually a resident of the community. The goal was to enlist approximately 100 boys sufficient for a company. Captain Abraham Vanderpoel, a man somewhat over-age for military duty, was responsible for the enlistment and training of recruits in the Delton, Sauk County area of Wisconsin. Following is an account of the experience of some of the boys recruited by him and who would later all be assigned to Company E of the Twelfth Wisconsin Volunteer Infantry.

1

The small town taverns of the day usually had a ballroom, either upstairs or down. In Mr. Freer's tavern in Delton it was upstairs. They placed twenty beds, ten on each side of the room, and created accommodations for twenty boys. Presumably, they did occasionally get some sleep, but it is doubtful that any of them had the good fortune to retire at nine in the evening and sleep in peace 'till daylight of the next morning.

The first group that moved in formed themselves into a "society" of sorts, hence it became a necessity to initiate every newcomer into the profound mysteries of the "order". Not every candidate, of course, was willing to submit and sounds of combat filled the room, disturbing the slumber of the neighboring villagers, to say nothing of the Freer family housed downstairs. However reluctant the candidate, he had to be put through the whole performance according to ritual. Once completed, of course, he was entitled to all the benefits of the order.

The "order" was naturally of a military nature. Exercising and disciplining the prospective member in the arts of war. Sham battles between the occupants of one row of beds on one side against the row on the other side. The implements of war were pillows, boots and shoes and any other projectiles that came to hand. Prisoners would be captured and recaptured. Unable to sleep, Mr. Freer would march upstairs threatening dire vengence on the first one he caught. What he would find, of course, were twenty boys sound asleep and snoring. On his way downstairs he usually had a pillow thrown in the general vicinity of his head. He was scarcely in bed again before the battle would continue. When the company finally left Delton for Madison, Mr. Freer reported there wasn't one bed left standing. The boys had spent the last week or so sleeping on the floor.

The "Dutch Company" was recruited by Charley Briggs and Erastus Cospes. They were enlisted from the regular company. Briggs proceeded to, "schwear him mit der schtate." An obligation that none of those of the best mettle would dare take, and so the "Dutch Company" never became very large. Their drills were a burlesque of military proceedures and decorum to the merriment of all who watched.

At least one day a week the company would take part in a "War Meeting". These were usually held in the local schoolhouse in Delton or one of the nearby towns and were well advertised. On the day of the meeting Captain Vanderpoel, Lieutenant Gillespie, the flag bearer and the "Band" would all load into the first wagon and the rest of the company, or as many as could fit, loaded into the second wagon. The band consisted of a fifer, a snare drummer and a bass drummer. On the way to the schoolhouse the band would strike up a patriotic air and there would be much "hallooing" from the boys. The townspeople congregated at the schoolhouse and would give the boys three cheers when they arrived. The boys would follow with three cheers for the townspeople. The band would give a concert; the shrill fife nearly blowing out the schoolhouse windows. When the band finally needed a rest the audience would give them another noisy three cheers.

Capt. Vanderpoel would then make a stirring and patriotic speech to which the boys of the company gave enthusiastic support with much cheering and clapping. His speech was spirited and full of patriotic zeal. It would always end, however, with the Captain making an appeal to all the young men in the audience to join the company. This appeal was usually followed by dead silence.

Now and then a young lady would add her power of persuasion to that of the Captain and urge boys to enlist. This could be a trying ordeal for a young beau to hear his best girl express such convictions. He must have wondered how receptive she would be to his kisses if he failed to enlist. Or, he may also have wondered just how important her kisses were to him. It was one thing to exercise their lungs, but actual enlistment was a more serious matter.

Mr. Freer had contributed two of his sons to the company and so when it was time to harvest his corn he was short handed. The captain mustered the company, explained the situation, and by mutual agreement the boys marched to Mr. Freer's field. There, with military precision, they formed a skirmish line across the field then rallied by two's upon the rows of corn stalks. Harvested the corn and bundled the stalks. But when the boys tried to leave they found the gates locked and a Freer wagon blocking their path. The Freer family ambushed the soldiers and bombarded them with apples and donuts.

It took Captain Vanderpoel a little over a month to recruit 100 boys; enough to form a Company. This must have been about the average time for all companies to form as they converged on

Camp Randall within a short time of each other.

On the 31st of October the boys were mustered and marched down the main street of Delton. By Tobey's store were drawn up thirteen farm wagons and teams to take them to Camp Randall in Madison. Eight boys in each wagon. The village preacher talked to them about state and country, self-sacrifice, danger and temptations. He exhorted them to keep good courage and "never doubt--on the battlefield, in sickness, in death,--that the prayers of loving and faithful hearts are ascending for us to the kind Father in heaven who takes note of the fall of a single sparrow."

Parents and friends lingered over the farewell. Clinging to the sons and beaus who were going off to an unknown future. Soon the order came. The wagons were loaded and the teams moved forward. It is always harder for the ones who stay behind. But for the young men the ride was genuine fun and merriment. The rough boards laid across the wagon boxes for seats had (by some mistake or other) been placed with the hard side up. Several boys took to their feet and cultivated an acquaintance with those who lived along the highway. Asking after the health of the family and keeping an eye out for the local lovelies.

The town of Baraboo heard of their coming and hung flags down the main street and fired off the 4th of July cannon amid a great deal of waving flags and handkerchiefs and hallooing. It was just beyond Baraboo where they had their first roadside meal. They crossed the Wisconsin River at "Mott's Ferry" and by dark had reached the town of Lodi, just 20 miles from Madison. Where they spent the night.

Daniel Titus was digging potatoes when he heard the band playing and saw the colors flying. He was a friend of Lt. Gillespie and ran after the wagons begging them to stop while he went back to the house to change his clothes. He was sworn in on the spot and found a seat in the wagon next to his friend. One wonders how eager he would have been had he known that on July 28, 1864, he would lose his life.

While the above adventures were largely the experiences of the boys who had been recruited in and around Delton, Wisconsin and would later be assigned to Company E, all the young recruits received their first training in or near their home towns from the captains who recruited them and who would accompany them to Camp Randall and beyond.

By the middle of the afternoon the company passed through the streets of Madison and on to Camp Randall about a mile beyond the City. It was known at that time as the "Fair Ground." The stables were being converted to barracks; a big building called "Floral Hall," became the hospital and rows upon rows of conical tents filled the west side of the grounds. There were hundreds of men in uniform; two or three companies marching across the grounds; officers in bright uniforms; and guards straight and soldierly. What impressed the new arrivals the most was the sight of the Eleventh Wisconsin Regiment in full dress parade.

The Eleventh Regiment was up to full compliment. The Twelfth was just forming. It would consist of ten companies; each about 100 men; thus 1000 men to the Regiment. The officers assigned to command the Twelfth were:

    Col. George E. Bryant, Madison
    Lt. Col. Dewitt C. Poole, Madison
    Maj. William E. Strong, Racine
    Adjutant James K. Proudfit, Madison
    Quartermaster Andrew Sexton, Madison
    Surgeon Dr. Luther H. Cary, Greenbush, Sheboygan Co.
    1st Asst. Dr. E. A. Woodward, Sun Prairie, Dane Co.
    2nd Asst. Dr. F. St. Sure Lindsfeldt, Sheboygan
    Chaplain Rev. L. B. Mason, Madison
        Captains:
    Co. A: Norman McLeod, Prescott, Pierce Co.
    Co. B: Giles Steven, near Reedsburg, Sauk Co.
    Co. C: Charles F. Loeber, near Dodgeville, Iowa Co.
    Co. D: John M. Price, near West Bend, Wash. Co.
    Co. E: Abraham Vanderpoel, near Delton, Sauk Co.
    Co. F: George C. Norton, Onconta, Onconta Co.
    Co. G: Daniel Howell, Grand Rapids, Wood Co.
    Co. H: Milo C. Palmer, Green Bay, Brown Co.
    Co. I: H. L. Turner, Iowa & Richland Counties
    Co. K: D. H. Sylvester, Grant Co.

The conical tents were set on raised wooden floors and the canvas fitted over a wooden framework. Twenty men were housed in each of the tents. They arranged their beds with their feet towards the center, but room was at such a premium that they slept curled up like so many nested spoons. When one man had the urge to turn over he would call, "Attention squad! Make ready! Spoon"!

The tents did not have individual stoves or heaters. Instead there was a hole in the center of the tent, bricked at the bottom and four sides and covered with a sheet of iron. On each side and underground a flue was built. One for a draught of fresh air, the other for heat. But if someone were burning green wood in the central furnace both flues would produce an abundance of smoke driving the men from the tents into the cold air outside. There was no way to control the heat (or lack of it). Often the men would perspire in an overheated tent and then go into the frigid air outside to drill or perform guard duties. Many of them developed a condition that was diagnosed as, "rheumatism." Painful swollen and inflamed joints. Years later in applying for disability pensions many of the men from Camp Randall sited the heaters as the beginning of their health problems.

The men drew uniforms not long after they were in camp. They were handed whatever size was next in line with no consideration for the size of the man. Twenty men in a tent trying to make everything fit and trading britches for jackets, etc., was a ludicrous sight.

The new recruites spent four to six hours each day in ranks drilling by company or battalion. The young ladies of Madison visited the camp frequently to watch. One day as a bevy of beauties watched the men of the Twelfth the Colonel dressed them in line of battle facing the young women and then ordered them to march "double quick." The ladies scattered in all directions on the dead run as the men charged their ranks.

Col. Bryant was less than thirty years old and described by one of the men as, "scant physically--both in latitude and longitude--but had plenty of vigor." Although "scant" in stature his voice was apparently anything but "scant." As one of the boys put it, "the whole regiment could hear it and maybe even those a mile or two away." He rode a large black horse and the men soon dubbed him, "The Little Corporal." It was a title given in jest, for they had great respect and affection for their Colonel.

The men also performed light guard duties. Eight hours on post and sixteen at rest. Four hours on nights and since temperatures in November often plummeted, guard duty was a cold, and unpleasant duty.

Civilians could come and go into the camp without challenge. Soldiers received only one-day passes occasionally. Some of the men kept civilian clothes in a separate knapsack and would pass in and out of the camp along with the civilians. Others who received a pass would double back to a pre-determined spot along the fence and pass it through to a friend. Passes were not always collected by the guard when the men returned so it was quite easy to alter the date on the pass from a "2" to a "12", etc. Like soldiers the world over, in war or peace, the Civil War soldiers found ways to circumvent authority.

Their morning started with the military band (ten snare drums, ten fifes, and three or four bass drums) playing reveille at sunrise. They had but a few minutes to dress and report for roll call. Then they had a half hour of drill. Usually at double quick time over the frozen ground until they were all puffing and blowing like so many porpoises. Their mornings were spent on a variety of drills and duties. From two until four in the afternoon they had battalion or regimental drills. Then an hour of company drilling before dinner. At five they fell in for dress parade. The military band would take up their position at the foot of the flagstaff. They played retreat and three or four other pieces. The cannon would boom and the colors came down and the men were marched to dinner.

Their evenings were spent mostly in their own quarters; telling stories, discussing politics or religion, talking of home and the tricks they played in school. Sometimes they sang songs or played cards. The atmosphere was often bluish with tobacco smoke, that great comfort of all soldiers. At 9 p.m., the band played "tatoo." The men fell in for evening roll call and then to bed.

The first deaths in the regiment occured at Camp Randall. Edwin Tubbs of Company A, and William Oliver of Company D both died in December of 1861, of disease, and the boys were initiated into the ritual of a military funeral.

On one of their marches out of Camp Randall they were marched through a field of millet. The men all picked up a millet stick and shouldered it like a rifle. One of the young captains ordered the men to drop the sticks, but they would not do so. Finally, the captain reported to Col. Bryant. The Colonel halted the men, formed them in ranks, and gave the order to, "ground millet sticks." The men obeyed. At Camp Randall the men of the twelfth felt not only respect, but genuine affection for their Colonel. My great grandfather, a private in Company H at the time, named his first born son, George Bryant Whitcomb. There were probably many more children bearing his name.

In December they were finally issued muskets. The type called, "Belgian Rifles." As one of the boys put it, "There was no doubt they would do good execution in front, and we found out by painful experience they were able, also, to do tolerable execution in the rear."

Their first payday was in January and they received their pay in "greenbacks" (Treasury notes). The first money of the kind they had ever seen. Privates were paid $13.00 a month and were given $52.00 a year for clothing. There were usually three or four sutlers in camp who carried sweets as well as more useful articles. "Concerts" were organized by the men for the benefit of the poor sutlers. Every kind of musical instrument, pots, pans, kettles, rattles, spoons, etc., were gathered together for the event and the more the merrier. The din was enormous. When the sutler could stand no more of the cacaphony he would shower the men with sweets. Usually, just to have the band show up was sufficient for the treats to be handed out.

The men were given one furlough to go home for a visit. There were, of course, a few who took "French leave" to see their families. In those cases the Corporal's Guard went in search of the missing men, but rarely found them as they usually used the opportunity to see their own families. The Corporal's Guard's traveling expenses, however, would be deducted from the miscreant's next pay check.

The men of the Twelfth along with the 15th and 16th Regiments, took part in the inauguration ceremonies of Governor Louis P. Harvey on the 7th of January 1862.

CHAPTER II
Camp Randall to Kansas

The Twelfth left Wisconsin a little after daylight on the eleventh of January 1862 in a blinding snow storm. They mustered for the last time in Camp Randall and with packs on their backs marched to the depot and boarded the cars of the Chicago Northwestern Railroad.

When Harlan Squires, one of the men in Company E, went home on furlough he returned to Camp Randall with his sixteen-year-old son and the son's pet bear. The Regiment inducted the son and adopted the bear as their mascot. He was securely staked and the men built a raised platform for him so he could watch the goings-on at the camp. Considering the time of year, he also slept a lot.

When the Regiment arrived in Chicago they formed in ranks and prepared to march across town to the Chicago, Burlingon & Quincy Railroad Depot. Col. Bryant suggested that they put the bear at the head of the column. Father and son demurred, claiming the bear would not do anything he didn't want to do and would be upset by the band and the tramp of feet behind him. The Colonel insisted they give it a try. Perhaps with more insight into the bear's personality than the father or son. Young Squires with the bear on a lead marched off at the head of the column. The bear fully appreciated the role he was playing and pranced and cavorted. Thoroughly enjoying the applause and delighted squeals of the crowds lining the streets. The bear, whose name I could not find in any record, did not become as famous as "Old Abe", the eagle who went to war with the 8th Wisconsin Regiment and whose stuffed remains still honor the Court House in Madison. When the Regiment was ordered to march from Fort Riley, Kansas to New Mexico, a distance of 800 or more miles, the Squires decided the bear would never survive such a march and sold him to a farmer in Fort Riley, Kansas for seventeen dollars.

The men described the trip to Quincy, Illinois as travelling through a sea of prairie white with snow. The train stopped at the town of Galesburg and the women in the town, knowing of the coming of the troop train, brewed several wash tubs of coffee which they generously passed out to the men.

It took them all day to cross Illinois and didn't arrive in

Quincy until early the next day. Due to an ice jam the men were unable to cross the Mississippi. The decision was made to march to Douglasville, opposite Hannibal, Missouri. The officers hired wagons to carry the baggage, but the boys marched the twenty-two miles to Douglasville in the intense cold. Many of them had frostbitten ears and hands. It took them six hours and then found out the small steamer that was to transport them across the river was frozen in ice on the Missouri side. It had to be chopped out and a channel cut in the ice. Their rations were frozen, but some of the boys had seen a beehive a mile or so back and returned to harvest the honey. They returned, not only with the honey, but with several turkeys as well. They tore down some old sheds for fire wood and managed a feast of sorts in the frigid air. The temperature was recorded as 20 degrees below zero.

The steamer made it across the next day and by late afternoon all the men and their equipment had been ferried across the River where they were quartered in the Hannibal Court House. The following day they were loaded into "hay cars" on the Quincy & Weston Railroad and began the long cold trip to Weston near the Missouri/Kansas border. The cars were fitted with wooden planks for seats and there was little shelter from the elements. At one place where the train stopped for water the boys pulled the planks loose and threw them off the train. In a nearby field were stacks of hay and the boys left the train and brought in arm loads of hay for bedding. It was much softer to sit on and they were warmer and somewhat sheltered from the elements.

They arrived in Weston on the 15th of January, cold, dirty, tired, and hungry. Over a hundred men were on the sick list. Some so sick they had been left at stops along the way. They were lodged in several buildings throughout the town whose population was largely pro-slavery so the boys never felt overly welcome. They remained there just a month and were on picket duty, but saw no Rebels. The 18th Missouri Regiment was also stationed there and they were joined by the 9th Wisconsin which was an all German regiment and the men of the other regiments could seldom communicate with them.

There was trouble on the Kansas/Missouri border even before the Rebels fired on Ft. Sumpter. In 1819, Missouri asked to be admitted to the Union as a "slave state." The Northerners wanted it admitted as a "free state." It's hard now to imagine the depth of feeling this controversy generated, but challenges were made and duels fought between prominent men in Washington and in St. Louis. The pro-slavery people prevailed, but were upset at the large number of Northern farmers, Germans, Irish, English, Swiss, and Central Europeans who were moving into the state--all adamently opposed to slavery. Both sides formed guerrilla bands and kept up a reign of terror along the border.

It was to forestall these terrorist activities that Union troops, including the Twelfth Wisconsin, were ordered to the area. In some respects they were not a lot better than some of the guerrilla bands since their foraging often targeted Southern sympathizers and the locals referred to them as "Jayhawkers" (bandits).

One group of foragers were entertained by one of the farmers and just as they began to relax and enjoy the hospitality they were suddenly surrounded by men in gray uniforms and the boys figured they had been captured. It was a joke played on them by men of the Missouri regiment who also happened to wear gray uniforms.

The Twelfth stayed in Weston only a month and then marched the eight miles to Fort Leavenworth, Kansas. There their duties were few. The most exciting occurrance was an outbreak of measles which put many of the boys down.

On the 28th of February they received orders to march to Fort Scott, Kansas. The march began the next day, the 1st of March. The men referred to it as the "Tanglefoot March" since many of the boys had filled their canteens with whisky. They only made eleven miles that first day in rain, cold, and eventually snow, and a howling gale. They chose their campsite well, but the wagons didn't come up with them until after dark. The ground by this time had turned to mud; the wind was howling and they learned how difficult raising a tent could be. When they finally turned in the only choice was to lay down on the cold muddy ground. By morning the place where they slept was a frozen mold of mud in the shape of their bodies. After a breakfast of coffee and hardtack they were glad to start marching just to warm up.

Their route at first was through heavy timber bordering the Missouri River. They camped the next night on the banks of the

Kansas River near Wyandotte. The third day the march took them through Shawneetown, Olathe, and Paola. By then many of the boys were so stiff and sore some crawled on hands and knees to their tents. At least they had found an abundance of hay and straw for bedding. They arrived at Fort Scott on the 6th of March; 160 miles from Fort Leavenworth. They spent twenty uneventful days there with little to do except learn the game of Cricket. A sport at which Col. Bryant displayed considerable ability.

On the 27th of March they were ordered to march to Lawrence, Kansas. Approximately 125 miles from Fort Scott. They arrived there on the 2nd of April where, again, they camped on the banks of the Kansas River at Camp Halleck.

On one very rainy night they were surprised to be called out and formed up in front of Col. Bryant's tent. The Colonel stood in the doorway of his tent with a newspaper in his hand and inspite of the pounding rain told the men there had been a great battle at a place called Pittsburg Landing in Tennessee in which several Wisconsin units were engaged with the loss of many men. He went on to read the account in the newspaper and then the names of the men who had been killed or wounded. The list was long and many names all to familiar to both the Colonel, who had served with some of them, and also the boys who learned the fate of brothers, fathers, and friends. Tears ran down the Colonel's face and his voice choked many times as he read the name of a friend. The battle today is more commonly referred to as the "Battle of Shiloh." The Confederates also suffered dearly. For most of the men on both sides it was their first battle and they fought with exceptional bravery. But both armies, officers and men, were inexperienced and poorly trained. Their willingness to stay and fight it out was a lesson to all the generals who learned just how formidable their opponent could be. It was a learning experience for both sides, but at a terrible cost.

Again, there was little for the men of the Twelfth to do in Lawrence. In the middle of April they were ordered to Fort Riley. They were ostensibly scheduled to continue on to New Mexico, but this expedition was cancelled. On the way Col. Bryant rode passed each Company and told of the drowning death of Governor Harvey at Savannah, Tennessee, 10 miles down river from Pittsburg Landing. He was there to distribute articles to the wounded men, but stepping from one steamer to another he fell between the two boats and was drowned. The Governor was a man greatly liked and respected by the troops from Wisconsin and they were saddened by his loss.

They marched to Fort Riley by way of Tecumseh, Topeka, and crossed the River at Manhatten, Kansas. One day they rested near a school ground. The children, at first, were timid and held back, but soon the braver ones came forward and started singing "Three Cheers For The Red White And Blue." Soon all the children and the boys joined in the singing.

They arrived at Fort Riley on the 25th of April and were joined by the 13th Wisconsin Infantry and the 8th Wisconsin Battery. Again, camp life at Fort Riley was quiet and uneventful. One enterprising farmer brought a wagon load of apples into camp and was selling them to the boys. Two of the boys crawled under the wagon and with their knives dug a hole in the floor of the wagon. They then convinced the farmer that he could probably sell more apples on the other side of the camp and so the farmer headed his team in that direction. The wagon full of apples was covered with a tarpaulin so the farmer didn't notice the rapid decline of his load or the gathering of the harvest that fell through the hole as the wagon bounced across the campground.

Although the Twelfth saw no fighting in their tour of duty in Missouri and Kansas, they suffered their share of casualties. Twenty-two boys died of disease and sixty-six were discharged, largely due to disabilities brought on by exposure and the arduous marches.

With the cancellation of the New Mexico expedition the Brigade, which included the Twelfth, was ordered to join General Grant's army at Corinth, Mississippi. On the 18th of May they left Fort Riley for the 125 mile march to Fort Leavenworth. They raced the 13th Wisconsin and won; accomplishing a one-day march of 40 miles. Throughout their tour of duty in Kansas the Twelfth had marched an aggregate distance of 515 miles in about three months time. They participated in a grand review at Fort Leavenworth and then the Twelfth and Thirteenth Infantry Regiments, the Eighth Wisconsin Battery and the Third Wisconsin Cavalry boarded a steamer on the 29th of May. They traveled down the Missouri and Mississippi Rivers to Columbus, Kentucky.

CHAPTER III
The Army of Tennessee

The troops landed at Columbus, Kentucky on the 2nd of June, 1862, and became part of the Army of Tennessee and in which they would remain for the balance of the War. They were promptly put to work repairing and guarding the Mobile & Ohio Railroad. In the process they had to march to Union City and from there to Troy in the Northern part of Tennessee. They camped for awhile on the Obion River and there rebuilt a bridge that had been burned by the Rebels. The water was bad and caused quite a little ill health for the boys, but the blackberries were plentiful and they built several small brick ovens and became quite adept at making pies. They were then ordered to Humboldt, Tennessee.

William Enderby of Company H in a letter to his parents writes: "You must excuse me for not writing sooner, but I could not for we left Camp Leach on the 2nd of July and started for Humboldt. The distance was 75 miles. It took us 8 days to march it for the roads were very bad and the weather was very hot so we had to get up at 3 o'clock in the morning and start before it got very hot. But that wasn't the worst for us boys for we had been working on the railroads and fixing bridges so as to get the cars arunning and to take us to Humboldt, but not as we expected. Just as quick as the cars got arunning, we was ordered to march it and the Illinois soldiers could ride and we had to march beside the track and it made our boys grin some when the cars passed us and was loaded with other soldiers, but we got there all right...better to travel than be still.

"The City of Humboldt is pretty large. There is 2 dwelling houses and a depot station and 1 or 2 stables and that forms a "city" in this part of the country. But there is some cotton plantations and tobacco farms. There is some very nice orchards of peaches and apples and there is plenty of blackberries around here. It is very hard times for the farmers. There isn't any money around here at all and some of them is starving."

Humboldt, Tennessee was the junction of the Mobile & Ohio Railroad and the Memphis & Nashville Railroad. The Twelfth would remain there until October '62. Humboldt was almost beginning to feel like home. Company I, on a foraging excursion, seized at Gadsden, not far from Humboldt, $11,000 worth of sugar and molasses and $60,000 worth of cotton.

The nearest they came to the war was the "The Humboldt Scare." Rebel General Jackson with 1,000 cavalry and a battery were in the vicinity. For the first time the men heard the "long roll" drum beat--fall in for battle. They built breastworks and prepared for battle, waiting long hours for the enemy to attack. They slept at night with their muskets loaded and at their sides, but Jackson chose not to attack Humboldt.

The boys in the western army were fresh off the farms where resourcefulness is a necessity. Whether it was building a bridge or repairing a locomotive there was always someone with the know-how or the ingenuity to do the job. George Sager of Company H and Albert Blodget from Company C found a printing press and combined their talents to establish a regimental newspaper, called, "The Soldiers Budget." It not only kept the boys informed to the extent they had news to report, but also amused. Reporting the antics of their fellow soldiers.

Picket duty at Humboldt was a pleasure. The fields and orchards were full with ripe fruits and vegetables. Even the corporals and sergeants begged to stand picket duty in place of the privates so they could share in the bounty. One sergeant, while on picket duty, captured a black man. He had traveled thirty or more miles to gain his freedomn and left his wife and children, hoping to establish a new home for them where they could enjoy freedom. This particular black became the cook for Squad Seven of E Company. His name was Tom Allen. He was twenty-nine years old, six feet four inches in height. A man who commanded respect and was soon liked by all the men of the Company.

Mail call in the army during the Civil War was much as it is in any army today. The Chaplain picked up the mail and gave it to a sergeant who in turn assigned an orderly to stand on a box or some other elevation and call out the names.

At 8:00 a.m. every morning there was "surgeons call." The main complaint was diarrhea and the procession to surgeons call was described as "a gaunt parade of men with sunken bellies and wobbly legs". Some so "wobbly" they had to be supported by their friends. About the only medication available was quinine. The main means of diagnosis, described by one of the boys, was for the surgeon to look at their tongue. He described the experience of one fellow with blistered feet who asked the surgeon if he might ride in one of the wagons. The doctor looked at his tongue and said, "Your tongue looks fine" and denied his request.

In order to adequately protect the railroad from marauding bands of rebels, ten men in each company were mounted on horseback. The mounted unit was under the command of Capt. Maxson of Company A, and would range far and wide to forestall surprise attacks by the enemy. Col. Bryant would also order a mounted lieutenant and a squad of men on foot to forage for horses. While they started on foot they usually returned well mounted. One squad returned with 80 horses. The lieutenant gave receipts to the owners who could be reimbursed by the adjuntant general.

One clever woman, whose husband was probably serving in the Confederate Army, invited the foraging party to dinner. She captivated the men with her charm and graciousness and they were about to partake of the meal when one of the negro slaves alerted the men that some of the best horses in the county were being run off while they ate. The men abandoned the meal for the horses and then returned to thank the woman whose response was less then "genteel."

As the boys continued to guard the railroad there were scattering bands of Rebels that attacked the trains on the road to Corinth, Mississippi. It was 80 miles from Humboldt to Corinth and the guards rode down one day and back the next. During the battle for Corinth the guards had come close to being captured.

By October of 1862, many of the original recruits had been discharged due to disabilities and new recruits had taken their place. The end of their first year of service was September 19th. The Twelfth was not involved during the Battle of Iuka, 20 miles east of Corinth where Rebel Generals Price, Van Dorn and Villipigue were defeated by Union forces. Corinth was attacked on the 2nd of October, and the Rebels withdrew to the vicinity of Holly Springs, Mississippi, hotly pursued by the Union forces. There was severe fighting on the 4th and 5th of October near Pocahontas, called the "Battle on the Hatchie".

General Grant dispatched to the Post Commander at Humboldt: "How many men could be spared for defense of Corinth?" Maj. Strong replied that the Twelfth Wisconsin, 1,000 men, could be ready in 30 minutes. They were, and then loaded into a train which took them to Bolivar, Mississippi by the next morning. They were marched to the front, a distance of 30 miles, in ten hours, but the Rebels had already retreated. After a days rest they were marched back to Boliver with General Hurlbut's forces.

The men were exhausted by marching and lack of sleep and at one point fell out in a wooded area and fell sound asleep. A carriage came by and suddenly a booming voice, "Boys, what in hades are you doing here." The only person they knew with the "voice to wake the dead" was their beloved commander, Col. Bryant who was just returning from leave in Madison. The men forgot their fatigue and jumped up to greet the Colonel. Later they went into camp at Boliver and remained there until the third of November when they were assigned to the 3rd Division, 17th Army Corps.

The Army marched southward and encamped in the vicinity of Grand Junction and La Grange, Mississippi. On the 8th of November, Gen. James B. McPherson with a large force, including the Twelfth which formed the advance, went on reconnaissance in the direction of the Coldwater River. They marched 25 miles and camped for the night. Cavalry scouts ascertained there was a considerable detachment of Rebel horsemen in the vicinity, believed to be Jackson's Cavalry. The following day they made a slow cautious advance. In the afternoon the battery was ordered forward and stationed on a hill by the roadside. The Twelfth was ordered forward to support the battery. Supporting troops usually lie on the ground behind the battery. On this occasion, however, they lay in front of the guns, firing a mile to their right front. It was not a large force of Rebels and 16 of their number were killed by Union forces who also took 150 prisoners, some of whom were wounded. On the 10th of November they returned to La Grange.

The next move was south along the Cairo & New Orleans Railroad. They camped for a while at Holly Springs, 25 miles south of La Grange. It was here in the woods some of the boys disturbed a shoat and her piglets. The scramble was on until all of the pigs were captured, dressed out, and served up for dinner. Some of the boys also found ammunition left by the Rebs. There were conical shells for large field pieces. Some were brought into camp.

One Company of the Twelfth had a young negro, about

fourteen years old, cooking for them. His name was Caesar. One day while cooking his beans Caesar thought it would greatly add to his pleasure to see, "one of 'dem tings bust". He set it up on end by his fire, got a large coal and put it on top of the business end of it. Then went down on hands and knees to blow the fire. At the sound of the explosion the whole regiment turned out assuming they were under attack. Especially with the bean pot hurtling through camp spueing beans as it went. As for Caesar? He lost his eyebrows and much of his hair and his face was badly burned, but he survived the shock.

They continued south. The advance ran into a few Rebels and drove them back with slight loss. They went into camp at Waterford, near Lumpkins Mills, 9 miles south of Holly Springs. There they remained until the 10th of December. It rained most of the time, turning the red clay into a slimmy, slippery mess.

The Army left Lumpkin's Mills on the 10th, passed through Waterford, Abbeville and Oxford and camped at Yocona Creek 35 miles south of Holly Springs. By the 20th of December they were camped in Water Valley another 8 or 10 miles south of Yacona. In the meantime, Rebel Gen. Van Dorn circled Grant's Army and attacked Holly Springs which Grant was using as a depot for supplies. Van Dorn's forces captured 1800 men and 150 officers and destroyed rations, clothing, and ammunition. This left the Union Army on short rations. They ate mules and corn.

They camped again at Lumkin's Mills and remained there until the 8th of January, 1863. They continued to suffer from short rations and had to depend on forage. The men tried to grind the corn brought in by foragers, but Lumkin's Mill would only "bruise" the corn.

On the 8th they marched north to Moscow, Tennessee and once again were guarding and repairing a rail line. This time the Memphis & Charleston Railroad. They arrived at Moscow on the 11th of January, the anniversary of leaving Camp Randall. On the 15th of January they marched to Memphis then on to Lafayette where they camped briefly. On the 20th they marched to a town called Collierville, 23 miles from Memphis. It was only a 15 mile march, but one of the most disagreeable marches they made. At the start the weather was warm and sultry. Then came the heavy rain which flooded the roads in low lying places and ran in torrents down every river. It next turned to snow which soon became slush and mud, but not for long. Soon it was cold enough to freeze the mud into slippery, ankle wrenching mounds. The men's clothing, already wet from rain and perspiration, froze stiff upon their bodies. Fire wood was in short supply and the men could do little, but stand around with their teeth chattering.

It was Ed Robinson who took up an axe and began operating on a big white oak tree. Pretty soon the blood began coursing through his body, his teeth quit chattering and he was the happiest he had been in many hours. By the time the tree came down he was in a sweat and the others were begging for a chance with the axe to lop off branches and split logs. The result was a huge fire that, according to first-hand accounts, "made everything torrid for 20 feet in every direction."

As along the other railroads they had guarded, the Memphis & Charleston was plagued by Rebel guerrilla bands attempting to disrupt communications and supplies. Several men on picket duty around Collierville were shot at and some wounded.

The foragers brought in hogs, sheep or calves. Sometimes only as much of a beast as they could carry. One poor family with young children living in a log cabin on a bare subsistance farm begged the foragers not to take what little they had. The boys could show compassion and as long as they were in Colliersville that family was well supplied with meat by the foraging parties.

On the 6th of February the Corps moved to Camp Butler near Germantown Station, 9 miles nearer Memphis. They stayed there until the 14th, guarding the railroad and on picket duty.

For most of the first year of their enlistment the Twelfth Wisconsin Regiment had a twenty piece brass band of which they were very proud. But in August of 1862, the members of the band were mustered out of the service. The instruments, however, were the property of Uncle Sam. Only one man who had been in the original band was still in the Regiment. He offered to give lessons and lead a new band. Men who had never played any instrument or ever thought they would, volunteered to try. The practice sessions of this new band were ear shattering and discordant, but the men persevered and the music began to improve. In time, it approached the excellence of the original band.

On the 14th of March, they marched to Memphis and went into camp about a mile east of the city. The boys were delighted to discover their neighbor was a large tent of play actors and circus performers. The tickets cost half a dollar, but it was more fun to outwit the ticket takers and find ways to sneak into the tent. An art at which they became quite adept.

The worst enemy they encountered at Memphis was smallpox. Many of the men became ill and the rest were encouraged to report to the surgeon for vaccination.

Col. B. F. Grierson with the 6th Illinois Cavalry, the 7th Illinois Cavalry, and the 2nd Iowa Cavalry; 1700 men in all; started from La Grange, Tennessee. Their orders were to ride as rapidly as possible through central Mississippi to Baton Rouge, destroying railroad bridges and anything else of value to the Rebels. They left on April 17th. A perilous ride 800 miles in length. It would take them 16 days.

To draw the attention of the Rebels from the Grierson expedition, Col. Bryant led an expedition from Memphis on the 18th of April, to attack Rebel General Chalmers near Hernando, 30 miles south of Memphis. General W. Sooy Smith to attack the front and Col. Bryant the rear. They had a sharp skirmish with Chalmers' pickets, capturing several of them plus 7 officers and 60 men in all. The Rebels retreated. The Twelfth lost one man who was taken prisoner.

The next day they marched south of Hernando to the Coldwater River, skirmishing with the Rebel cavalry that was guarding the ferry. Companies C. D, and H advanced near the enemy. It was the first time the boys had been under fire at short range. While marching down into the marsh they saw several dead and wounded brought up from the front. One member of the battery had predicted his own death prior to the engagement and was indeed killed. Following are excerpts from Col. Bryant's Report of the battle dated Memphis, Tenn., April 25, 1863:

"...on the morning of the 18th, in pursuance to orders from General Lauman, I moved from Memphis, on the Hernando road, with the Twelfth and Thirty-third Wisconsin, Forty-first Illinois Volunteers, and the Fifteenth Ohio Battery. At the Nonconnah, Major

Hayes, with 265 men, of the Fifth Ohio Cavalry, reported to me.

The column reached Hernando, Miss., 25 miles south of Memphis, at 6 p.m. [G.L.] Blythe, with 300 men, hovered on my rear and flanks all day, twice firing on the flankers thrown out from the column. At 6:30 p.m., the pickets on the south of town were attacked by Col. [W.C.] Falkner, with from 600 to 700 men on foot. I immediately sent Major Hayes, with cavalry, to meet them, and got my forces in position for battle. After a sharp engagement of thirty minutes, and killing and wounding 30 of the enemy, the enemy fell back, leaving in our hands 72 prisoners, including 7 commissioned officers. I immediately sent the surgeons of the command with their ambulances...to look after the enemy's dead and wounded, but they were fired upon, and returned with only 4 of the wounded. In this skirmish we had 2 men slightly wounded.

The command was under arms at 3 a.m., Sunday morning, and at sunrise started for the Coldwater, met the enemy's pickets 2 miles south of Hernando. The column moved swiftly on. When 4 miles out, our rear was attacked by Blythe. I sent Companies B and K, of the Twelfth Wisconsin, with 18 cavalrymen, to repel them, and they soon scattered them. About the same time I received a message from Major Hayes that he had reached Perry's Ferry and driven the enemy across; that he was badly wounded, and the men getting out of ammunition. I immediately put the battery (Fifteenth Ohio), the two leading regiments, the Thirty-third Wisconsin, and the Forty-first Illinois, upon a very swift double-quick, which, through mud ankle-deep, they kept up for 4 miles, Lieutenant-Colonel Poole, with the Twelfth Wisconsin, in rear of the train with prisoners, was instructed to move steadily on, with flankers thrown out on either side, and bring forward all the men who might fall out from fatigue, that might be caused by our rapid advance. Arriving at the river, found the cavalry dismounted and holding the ferry...

In the meantime the Thirty-third Wisconsin had formed in the swamp on the right of the road, and the

Forty-first Illinois, with Companies C, H, and E, of the Twelfth Wisconsin, on the left of the road, close by the river bank. The enemy advanced nearly to the brink of the river, where, under cover of felled trees and a gully, they poured in a perfect shower of balls. The brave Captain Spear, as they [the battery] advanced down the road within 40 yards, commanded, "Cannoneers to your guns; canister". The men worked with a will, and it was only when he found that their sharpshooters, under cover of large cypress logs, were picking off his men and horses, that he fell back. On our side was a thick, wooded swamp, which, from the last night's rain, was full of water. The two regiments and three companies [of the Twelfth] on either side remained in their position from 9 a.m. 'till 5 p.m., lying flat on the ground, and keeping their sharpshooters, five companies from a regiment, close to the bank, under cover of trees. A continuous fire was kept up from both sides all day. Seven companies of the Twelfth Wisconsin guarded the prisoners and the hill, in our rear. I posted the cavalry up and down the river, to find another crossing... At 4 p.m., the enemy were again re-enforced, and commenced shelling us from the hill opposite, to which we replied with our artillery, but we could get no range on them. The ground was so watery that we could only get position for one gun..."

    Col. Bryant was expecting help from General Smith, but Smith with troubles of his own was unable to come up with him. Bryant withdrew his troops back to Hernando and continued to manouver in the face of the enemy until the 24th when they were ordered back to Colliersville, then to Camp Butler and finally, Memphis. Their mission accomplished, namely causing a diversion to draw attention from Col. Grierson's expedition.
    Hosea Rood writes: "I include just here a short extract from a letter from Charley Fosbinder, written in the summer of '89, twenty-six years after the skirmish on the Coldwater:"
    "On the 18th of April ('63), about ten o'clock in the forenoon, I came off picket to find most of the regiment gone down toward Hernando, Miss., to look after some Rebels who were doing mischief in that section. I bantered some of the boys

who had been on picket with me to follow the regiment, for, if any fun was to be had, I wanted my share of it; but none of the fellows wanted to go. So I filled my gun, cartridge-box, haversack and canteen and started off alone. I caught up with the regiment sometime in the afternoon, having, probably through fear of being gobbled, marched faster than they. The captain reprimanded me for my rashness, or foolishness, as he termed it, and that was all the punishment I got at the time; but you remember what I got on that, to me, memorable Sabbath, April 19, '63. You know something of the ride of the two and half days I had in an ambulance back to camp, and the time I had to save my arm, which was not set for good until eighteen days after it was wounded. My father came down to Memphis after me, and, as soon as I was able to go, he got a furlough of twenty days for me, and we started for home. The trip, in my weak state, nearly used me up, but I got home alive, and *such a meeting can never be forgotten!*

"I remained at home until in the fall, when I reported at Madison and applied for a discharge, as I felt sure I was not going to be able to do any more service in the field. But the surgeon said that I could not do anything at home, and that I would better serve out my time. He said that he would give me some light duty in the hospital there; so I stayed, and had charge of one of the wards until my term of service had expired.

"While there, and about a year after I was wounded, the doctors cut open my arm and took out several pieces of bone, making, with those that had come out before, seventeen in all. My arm is now one and a half inches shorter than the other, and, though not much account for work, is worth a dozen arms cut off. I came home in the fall of '64".

On the 11th of May, the Twelfth and other units boarded the steamer, "The Continental," and proceeded to join Grant's main army.

CHAPTER IV
The Vicksburg Campaign

During the winter and spring of 1863, General Grant, with the bulk of his army, was headquartered at Young's Point on the west side of the Mississippi River a few miles north of Vicksburg. The batteries at Vicksburg, Haynes' Bluff, and Warrenton, Mississippi commanded the river. The Yazoo delta north of Vicksburg was two hundred miles of wet, swampy ground through which no army could pass. Grant and Admiral David Porter, who commanded the gunboats assembled on the river north of Vicksburg, tried every means possible to find a way to cross the river and reach high ground east of Vicksburg, but without success. Sherman's Corps was put to work digging a four mile canal from one bend in the river to another to bypass the batteries at Vicksburg, but only one shallow draft steamer got through before the level of the river dropped making the canal unuseable. The land on the westside of the river was also low, wet and crisscrossed with rivulets, inadequate to support an army and its wagons. Finally in desparation Grant decided to commit his forces. McClernand's Corps was put to work, corduroying roads, building bridges, filling in swamps, and in a few weeks these westerners had built a road seventy miles long winding down from Milliken's Bend to a riverside hamlet named Hard Times, both on the Louisiana side of the river. Grant notified Porter to run past the batteries, first with the gunboats and then with transports. On the night of April 16th, Porter successfully passed the batteries and Grant's Army was moving down the McClernand road. Now with the transports the army could cross the river to dry ground.

The Twelfth Wisconsin landed at Milliken's Bend on the 13th of May, then dropped down to Young's Point six or seven miles above Vicksburg. They marched across the Point three or four miles and camped opposite the lower Vicksburg batteries. On the 14th they marched five miles down toward Carthage and camped in an open field where Union soldiers had worked to establish a new landing place twelve miles below Vicksburg. They remained in that camp until the 18th. Fished lobster and crayfish from a nearby brook. Raided a bee tree and suffered multiple stings. The weather was hot, sultry and showry. Roads were muddy. Finally the steamer, "Forest Queen" took them down river to Grand Gulf on the Mississippi side, 25 miles below Vicksburg. There they remained on provost duty until the 9th of June.

Confederate General John Pemberton, who commanded the Rebel forces at Vicksburg, moved south to intercept Grant. They fought at Port Gibson May 1st, at Raymond on the 12th, Jackson on the 14th, and a place called Champions Hill on the 16th, where the Union forces lost 2400 men and the Confederates lost 3800.

On the day after Champion's Hill was fought, Grant's vanguard came up to the Big Black River and overwhelmed Pemberton's rearguard with little difficulty. Then with Sherman's Corps in the lead, the army marched towards Vicksburg as fast as it could, and before nightfall on the 18th of May reached the heights that ran north from Vicksburg to Haynes' Bluff, overlooking the Yazoo River.

On the 19th of May Grant ordered Sherman's Corps to attack the left end of the Confederate trench line, but Pemberton's soldiers had reorganized themselves behind good fortifications and Sherman's assault was repulsed with more than a thousand Union casualties. Hoping to avoid a long siege, Grant ordered a larger attack by the entire army on the 22nd of May, but the attack fared no better than Sherman's and they were beaten back with heavy losses.

Grant's army dug in, encircling Vicksburg with trenches. They couldn't get in, but Pemberton couldn't get out, and the long siege of Vicksburg began.

The boys of the Twelfth could hear the bombardment and see smoke of the battle, but they remained on provost duty at Grand Gulf and were not engaged in the battles.

The weather was extremely hot and the boys built shelters by driving posts in the ground and attached a framework which they covered with bark. They foraged the countryside and kept cows in camp. Beyond picket duty their chores were light and mosquitos were the enemy.

Now deep in the South the negros began to attach themselves to the Union forces. Though the Confederates had told them, and the poor whites, that the "Yankees had horns and were devils capable of all sorts of atrocities they sensed that "Linkum's sogers" were going to set them free. And no risk was too great to achieve that goal. They followed and camped near the Union forces. The troops could employ a few of them as cooks, teamsters, or laborers, and they did their best to supply them with food, but little else could be done for them. Their camps lacked sanitation, shelters, and medical care. The men of the Twelfth were assigned guard duty at these makeshift camps.

Hosea Rood of Company E, describes his experience: "Not used to camp life, and having no one to control them, the condition of some of them became wretched. Crowded together, with no sanitary regulations, they sickened in large numbers and died off like sheep. When death is a constant visitor either in home or camp the very atmosphere becomes freighted with gloom; so it was in this camp of contrabands, and the condition of things was a pitiable one.

"Two or three guards were sent up there daily to see that order was maintained in the camp. It came my turn to spend one twenty-four hours there, and no day in my service has been more firmly fixed in my memory than that one. In one part of the camp a large space had been set apart for a burial ground, and during that day several of the poor creatures were laid away in the only freedom that Mother Earth had to give her dark-skinned children--rest in her own loving bosom. This was all Mother Earth could do, but the Father of us all can do more; he can give their emancipated souls the freedom of all heaven, where they will shine as white and as bright as the purest angel there.

"As I stood during the day and watched a little group coming from this or that part of the camp and slowly bearing all that remained of someone who was just as dear to them as our friends are to us, saw them halt at a shallow grave, heard the sad prayer of some one of them who had access to the Throne, listened to the plaintive song, sung only as the down-trodden and oppressed can sing, watched them tenderly lower the uncoffined body into its final resting place, heard the moaning and sobbing as the grave was filled and the little mound rounded up, and saw the group sadly move back to care for others who were dying. I was strangely wrought upon by the simple touching scene.

"It was their custom to hold prayer meetings every evening. As soon as the twilight became dusky, a large company of them gathered silently about the corner of the camp in which I stood, where they seated themselves on the ground under a group of trees. A man who seemed to be something of a leader among them, began to sing a plaintive, camp-meeting melody; he was joined by the audience, and the place became tremulous with a strangely pathetic music. I beg you not to think of it as being like the jargons of the burn-cork minstrels who sing for money. I cannot describe the pathos of the melody nor the sweet tenderness of the words as they arose on the night air, and--who does not believe it?--were wafted like sweet incense up to the God who loves his black children as well as those who are white.

"After the singing came earnest, pleading prayers to the Father in heaven, "to set his people free; to bless General Grant, and 'Massa Linkum,' and 'Massa Linkum's sogers,'" and they did not close without a plea that God would lead sinners to the Cross of Christ.

"Then came the 'testimonies' of those who were, in this time of trial, clinging to that Cross for help and guidance. Then more singing, more prayers and testimonies, until the evening was far spent, and they dropped off one by one to their various sleeping places.

"Never shall I forget the prayer-meeting on the bluff by the Mississippi River. No light,--none was needed--they could not read the Scripture--the breese coming down the broad river just stirring the leaves of the trees--a hushed stillness all around--the ground covered with dusky forms, some of them motionless, others swaying back and forth--the plaintive music--the prayer, eloquent in its intensity--the 'Christian experience'--the low moaning now and then of the worshippers--all impressed themselves on my young mind. As I leaned against a tree and saw, and heard, and felt, my own heart, which had so far resisted the prayers of many dear friends for my conversion, was strangely softened; and now after all these years, some things I heard from the lips of those poor half-freed slaves, seem sweet and encouraging to me; they have helped me through some trials in my past life."

On the 9th of June the boys boarded the steamer, "Cheesman" at Grand Gulf and sailed up river to Warrenton, seven miles below Vicksburg. They were attached to General Lauman's Division and took up residence in a deep ravine 1/2 mile from the front and thus joined in the siege of Vicksburg.

They dug rifle pits on the highest places on the ridges above the ravines which characterized the whole countryside. There were six to ten men in each pit at all times with the enemy in view. There were no trees on the Rebels side, but there were on the Union side. The siege guns were behind them and kept up a steady shelling of the City. In spite of the noise the boys managed to sleep. After the surrender with the guns quiet, they could not.

There was always danger with the two sides in such close rifle range of one another. It was at night that the Union forces advanced and established new rifle pits closer and closer to the enemy. Three or four men would construct the pit. Others would stand guard. During the day the Rebels might sally forth only to be driven back after a sharp skirmish. During the daytime it was not unusual for the men to use from 50 to 100 cartridges a day. The rations were more than sufficient, but the water was bad.

By the first few days of July the rumors began to fly. Surrender seemed imminent. On the 3rd of July as the boys of the Twelfth peered out of their rifle pit they saw to their surprise a large number of Rebels standing up and milling about. One of the Yanks shouted,

"I say, Johnnies, what's up?"
"Nothing as we know of Yanks."
"What are you standing up for?"
"'Cause you are."
"How's the thermometer over there on your side?"
"Up to the top notch and still arisin'. Say, you got any coffee to swap for terbacker?"
"Lots of it; come over and trade."
"Come over yourself and see how you like it."
"You're too close shut up; 'fraid we'd smother."

Both sides had ventured out to pick blackberries. Finally, one fellow from the 11th Wisconsin Regiment said, "I'm going down in the ravine and shake hands with them Rebs."

To the many suggestions of what they might do to him or make him prisoner, he replied, "Who's afraid to, I ain't." And he joined the Rebs. They met him and shook hands and soon a hundred men from both sides were shaking hands, trading coffee and tobacco and souvenirs and discussing the war in general. No one knew what caused this freak meeting and why enemies by some common yet unspoken consent would meet and shake hands. It was a colonel from the Vicksburg side who discovered them and ordered his men back to their rifle pits. The Yanks returned to theirs and the firing commenced.

The following day was the Fourth of July. Some batteries fired a National Salute and some thought the siege was continuing, but they actually fired blanks, for Gen. Pemberton had surrendered Vicksburg to the Union forces that morning. The men were hilarious with joy. They had not yet heard of the victory at Gettysburg the day before or the victory gained that same day at Helena, Arkansas.

Port Hudson, below Vicksburg surrendered and the Mississippi was in control of the Union forces.

A total of 27,000 Rebels, including 15 generals were parolled and allowed to return to their homes. The Yanks had also captured 128 pieces of artillery, 80 siege guns, arms and ammunition for 60,000 men. Less than a dozen men of the Twelfth had been killed or wounded during the siege.

The Union soldiers, knowing how hungry the Rebs were, invited them to their camps and shared their hardtack, swapped coffee for tobacco, and gave them any surplus rations.

CHAPTER V
Jackson to Natchez

At 7 a.m. on the 5th of July, 1863, the Twelfth Wisconsin, now attached to the Third Brigade, Fourth Division, Sixteenth Army Corps, but temporarily attached to the Thirteenth Army Corps, began the expedition to Jackson, the capitol of Mississippi. The division being commanded by Brig. Gen. J. G. Lauman, and the Corps commanded by Maj. Gen. William T. Sherman.

The boys had been on guard duty all of the preceding night. The weather was hot and sultry; the road very dusty, and many dropped out of the march with heat exhaustion and were sent back to camp at Vicksburg. They finally stopped late in the day to camp along the roadside and were just getting settled in when they were ordered to "fall in" and marched another 8 miles. It rained in torrents and the boys were as, "wet as drowned rats." By the time they made camp it had become uncomfortably cold and they spent a miserable night in their wet clothing.

The advanced units reached Jackson on the 9th of July and invested the City by the 12th of July. Much of the city had been destroyed during Grant's pursuit of the Rebel forces under Gen. Pemberton earlier. The Rebs had destroyed some of it themselves. By the time the Union forces left the City much more of it had been destroyed. The cavalry was busy destroying railroads and other property.

Gen. Lauman ordered the brigade to charge a fortified enemy position over an open field exposed to enemy musketry, grape shot, and canister. About 500 Union soldiers were killed, wounded or taken prisoner. The Twelfth had, fortunately, been detailed to guard the supply train and thus was not engaged in the disastrous charge. It largely involved men of the 28th and 41st Illinois and 53rd Indiana Regiments. Gen. Lauman was soon after relieved of his command.

There were 50,000 men in the expedition and they were running out of ammunition. The supply wagons didn't arrive until the 16th of July, which gave Confederate General Joe Johnston time to retreat. He marched eastward toward Meridian.

The brigade remained at Jackson until the 20th of July, and then returned to Vicksburg where they arrived on the 23rd of

July. They set up camp inside the Rebel fortification in the City. It was a bare, tree-less hill where the Rebels had camped before them. The temperature was 100 degrees with no shade, and the boys had the choice of frying in the sun or boiling inside the tents. Many of the men were already ill with "La Grippe" (diarrhea) or the "Ague" (malaria). The hospital was full to overflowing. The sickest men were transported to St. Louis and put into hospitals there.

On the 30th of July the regiment was ordered to take passage to Natchez, Mississippi, sixty miles south of Vicksburg. The wagons that transported them to the landing were full and the boys had to get to the river any way they could. Some so sick they could barely walk and gaunt to the point their stomachs nearly shrunk to their backbones and were little more than skeletons. Some used a staff; others had to be helped by friends, but sick or well they were on their way.

They landed at what was called, "Natchez Under The Hill." An area of docks and warehouses and negro shanties. The arriving steamer was immediately surrounded by small boats manned by "darkeys" and filled with fresh peaches, apples, tomatoes, cucumbers, sweet potatoes, and melons-- especially watermelons. Soon each squad's commissary was filled with sweet, fresh fruit. They disembarked and marched two miles to "Natchez On The Hill." A charming town of neat houses and tree lined streets. The effect of the fresh fruit on the sick men was immediate. They began to feel better and soon regained their strength.

Health and spirits began to mend. Fresh fruit and vegetables were plentiful as long as the money held out. The negros kept raising the price so the boys began to steal about as much as they paid for. The negros complained to the "cunnel," but Bryant liked watermelon as well as the boys. He posted a scale of fair prices and that pretty much resolved the problem.

On the 1st of September they were ordered to Harrisonburg on the Black River in Louisiana. Their camp was on a large plantation with rows of chicken coops. Chicken became a regular part of the menu. The plantation bordered beautiful Lake Concordia and it was a bivouac long remembered. They next camped near the junction of the Tensas and Washita Rivers; the two forming the Black, a tributary of the Red River. They crossed to Trinity in the afternoon and marched to

Harrisonburg on the Washita. Their camp was a rather swampy place and about the only thing memorable was that they had sheep for dinner. The next day enemy cavalry were discovered manouvering to attack their rear. The men took up position in a cornfield and set up a breastwork along a fence, but the cavalry never came. There was artillery firing near Harrisonburg, but the Rebels soon left the area. The Union troops stayed long enough to destroy the artillery they found and then returned to Natchez.

They established a semi-permanent camp with tents neatly layed out along "streets," dug cesspools and swept a parade ground. Except for a brief return to Vicksburg from November 22nd to December 5th, they remained at Natchez. Their duties were light, consisting of standing guard and picket duty and building a fortification. They were on duty about every third or fourth day.

It was at Natchez that "Maggie" joined on as an additional cook. The men described her as "black as a well polished shoe, but good looking with regular features and a shapely figure." The boys called her, "a real clipper." She bubbled with merriment and was a delight to have around and the boys treated her with respect. She and Tom Allen shared the cooking duties at the same campfire and they soon became friends. The boys watched with interest, and perhaps a little envy, as the romance proceeded. Old Tom smiled at her "chin music" and said little. Apparently forgetting the wife and children he had left behind. He enlarged his sleeping quarters and Maggie soon moved in.

The Twelfth had just returned to Natchez from a couple of weeks in Vicksburg and it was reported that a force of 6,000 Rebels was in the vicinity. They formed battle lines in the suburbs of Natchez under command of newly appointed Lt. Col. Proudfit. They remained in formation until daybreak, but no enemy appeared. The following day they marched out Washington Road and into the country. Gen. Gresham spoke to the men, telling them there was a large force near. The next morning they were within skirmishing distance with the Rebels rear guard, but most of the enemy were mounted and thus escaped. The boys arrived back in camp on the 8th of December. The weather had turned cold and rainy.

Their baggage from Vicksburg arrived the following day.

They had been issued new tents, 8 feet square and 8 feet high. They set up camp about half a mile from their previous camp on the Quitman plantation. They built fireplaces from old bricks they had found; used mule teams to haul in firewood, and managed to remain reasonably comfortable in spite of a very cold and rainy New Year.

Uncle Sam offered a bounty of $402 to every man who had been in service two years or longer if he would re-enlist for another three years or the duration of the war. Those that re-enlisted would be given a furlough of at least thirty days in his own state and would there after be called a "Veteran" as a token of special honor. Although the draft had begun it was still difficult to get enough men the manpower shortage was so grevious. The veterans of the Twelfth's time expired at midnight, January 5, 1864. Gen. Gresham, their brigade commander, and Lt. Col. Proudfit announced that the 512th man who re-enlisted would get a $5 greenback. About 10 p.m. on the 5th, Corporal J. W. Root of Company B won the $5.00. The regiment actually exceeded the required enrollment and the Twelfth remained whole. The officers sent each company headquarters a large barrel of Natchez Ale and the boys celebrated by getting grandly drunk.

Hosea Rood writes: "It seemed a bit unfair to some of the boys that the corporals and sergeants who did not "veteranize" were reduced to privates for the balance of their enlistment. The rationale being to promote the men who would continue with the regiment.

"Our re-enlistment and the celebration of it over, our camp life settled down to its old routine, sometimes becoming very monotonous. An old faded diary written in part at Natchez by H. H. Bennett of Company E, tells it pretty much like it was:

'Friday, Jan. 8, '64. No doubt there are many who think that every day of a soldier's life has in it some exciting or interesting incident. It might seem so to one not in the army, but to a person who has passed two or three years in camp it is not so. I well remember the time when I thought that a soldier must be one of the merriest fellows on earth, leading a life of pleasure and devoid of care and trouble. Two years in the service has somewhat changed my mind in regard to that. Many of our days pass by slowly, and I may say that, for all there are so many of us together, we sometimes get lonesome. With me, today has been so. The excitement of re-enlisting has passed away, and we have settled back into the old dull routine of camp life:--get up in the morning--eat breakfast--sit around 'till noon--eat dinner--sit around 'till suppertime--eat that. And so it goes day after day except when we are detailed for fatigue or picket duty.'

"Of course, the season for the melon trade was over, still there was something to buy. People both white and black, young and old, frequented the camp streets with all sorts of things tempting to the inner man. One had milk, another "cawn" bread, another peach pie, another "pok" (pork) pie, another ginger bread, another cakes. Occasionally, a sweet looking pie girl from the city brought along with her a bottle or two--maybe three--hidden away in some part of her drapery, from which hiding place she dexterously brought one forth whenever a knowing chap gave her the wink.

"Another excerpt from Bennett's diary is a fair sample of many picket post incidents. Bennett describes his efforts to halt what at first appeared to be a stump, but which on closer observation, seemed to be moving toward him. He was two or three times on the point of firing, but thought it best to be sure what sort of game he was about to bring down. After getting behind a log, and crawling up very close to his midnight visitor, he found it to be just what he took it to be at first--a stump."

On the evening of the 22nd of January, they got orders to be in readiness at daylight the next morning to go aboard the boats. Accordingly, they were up very early, ate their hard-tack and coffee by the light of their camp fires, and had everything in readiness for moving before sunrise. But, for all that, they were not marched down to the boat landing 'till 10 o'clock. And did not swing out into the stream until a couple of hours before sundown. Scores of people from the city came down to see them off. They had been in Natchez so long that some associations had been formed not easily to be broken.

A goodly number of the crowd that came to say goodbye were negros. They knew intuitively that every man who wore the blue was in a certain sense a friend to them. And so it was that most of the handkerchiefs that fluttered from the shore as the boat steamed away were waved by black hands.

Slowly the pretty city on the hill faded from their sight. Most would never see it again. It had been a pleasant camping place and they left it with real regret.

CHAPTER VI
The Meridian Campaign

The Twelfth left Natchez and arrived in Vicksburg on the 25th of January 1864. The Rebels still held most of the railroad east of the Mississippi River and could move troops and supplies pretty much at will. Sherman developed a plan to destroy the Southern Mississippi Railroad from Vicksburg to Meridian near the eastern boundry of the state, and the Mobile and Ohio Railroad from Columbus, Kentucky by way of Corinth and crossing the Southern Mississippi Railroad at Meridian and terminating at Mobile.

Sherman commanded two division of McPherson's Corps, two of Hurlbuts, and marched to Meridian. Gen. William Smith, Grant's chief cavalry officer, accompanied by the famous Gen. Grierson and his cavalry, moved from Memphis with all cavalry to strike the Mobil and Ohio RR at Okalona, destroy the railroad and join Sherman at Meridian. The Twelfth was part of McPherson's 17th Corps. There were about 25,000 men employed in this expedition.

They spent the first night at Edwards Station then met the enemy at Champion's Hill, the scene of the former bloody battle. Here their right of way was mildly disputed by the Rebels whom they managed to drive back. The second night was spent camped at Baker's Creek where the Twelfth maintained the picket line that night. The regiment had three men killed (all of Company I) during this march.

The Rebels attempted to defend a bridge. Gen. Leggett, commanding the 3rd Division, took the lead; crossed the bridge and deployed right and left. Gen. McPherson then brought his battery forward. The Rebels opened fire, but a few well placed shots from the rifled guns sent them packing.

The troops passed through Clinton and reached Jackson, the State Capitol, the following day. Crossed the Pearl River on pontoons. They moved so fast the Rebels had no time to set up and defend Jackson. The City, already largely destroyed, was left in flames.

East of Jackson the cavalry skirmished with the Rebels at Morton; left the railroad and curved toward the north passing through Hillsboro and Decatur. The Rebels took up one position behind a house. The family had little choice, but to stay inside.

The woman of the house, a mother of five, was killed. Hundreds of negros joined the column, feeling it was their best chance for liberty. Not untypical was an old man in a cart with one foot missing and with him three young girls, "Goin' wid Massa Linkums sogers to be free."
Many dwellings were burned and public property destroyed. They reached Meridian on the 14th of February, eleven days of marching and 140 miles east of Vicksburg. Grierson's cavalry was attacked by Rebel Gen. Forrest who beat them quite badly at Okalona. Grierson's unit was sent back to Memphis. In Meridian they destroyed stores of provisions, and tore up railroads in every direction. The Twelfth and the rest of the Division went south on the Mobile road to Quitman, 25 miles from Meridian. On the 20th of February they started their return to Vicksburg by way of Decatur and Hillsboro, then bore off toward Canton, 23 miles north of Jackson. Growing short of provisions some units were sent on to Vicksburg. The Twelfth waited at the Pearl River for the cavalry. On the 28th they marched to Canton where the Rebels attacked the Union pickets. The Twelfth and the rest of the 3rd brigade were sent out to meet them. They skirmished with the Rebels for the next ten miles. The Rebel cavalry attacked the brigade's flank and the Rebs lost forty men and their colonel. The Union brigade crossed the Big Black River and were back in camp at Hebron. Following is the report of Brig. Gen. Walter O. Gresham who commanded the 3rd Brigade, dated March 5, 1864, Hebron, Miss.:

"...I have the honor to submit the following report of the operations of my command on the recent expedition through Mississippi.
On the 4th ultimo, being the second day out, the Second Brigade, Colonel Hall, encountered the enemy's cavalry on the eastern slope of Champion's Hill, and advanced skirmishing to within 1 1/2 miles of Baker's Creek, when I received orders from General Crocker to send a regiment to the front and relieve the 15th Illinois.
The Twelfth Wisconsin, Lieutenant-Colonel Proudfit commanding, was ordered up and moved forward promptly and cheerfully and relieved the 15th Illinois and drove the enemy up to and across Baker's Creek, with a loss of 3 men killed and 3 wounded. In this charge the Twelfth

Wisconsin captured 1 lieutenant and 5 men. The enemy left on the field 4 men killed and 1 major mortally wounded. At the same time and place the Fifty-Third Indiana had 2 men wounded. Near Decatur the Twelfth Wisconsin had 1 man killed and 2 wounded while on duty with a forage party, and near the same place 4 men straggled from the Fifty-third Indiana and were captured. No casulties in either of the other regiments.

On the 16th ultimo, in pursuance to orders from Brigadier General Crocker, with my own brigade, the Eleventh Illinois Cavalry and one section of Spear's battery, I proceeded from Enterprise to Quitman and destroyed a large railroad bridge over the Chickasawah, 2 miles south of the town. The bridge was covered and 210 feet long. Immediately north of the bridge I effectually destroyed 600 yards of trestle, from 10 to 30 feet high. We also destroyed the railroad depot at Quitman, the large and elegant hospital buildings, recently erected, one large steam flouring mill, and one large steam sawmill. The railroad bridge was guarded by the Ninth Alabama, but on our approach they abandoned their stockades and fled in the direction of Mobile.

Having accomplished the object of our expedition to Quitman, I moved my command back to the head of Alligator Swamp and bivouacked for the night, having marched from 7 a.m. to 8 p.m., 27 miles and worked four hours.

On the morning of the 17th, we destroyed the trestle-work over Alligator Swamp, 1 1/2 miles in length, and from 9 to 30 feet high. We also destroyed 2 and 1/2 miles of railroad north of the swamp, burning the ties and heating and bending every rail.

During the expedition my brigade marched 375 miles, destroyed 4 1/2 miles of the Mobile and Ohio Railroad, 2 miles of which were bridges and trestle. Although the march was fatiguing, both officers and men bore it with cheerfulness and without a murmur."

Their uniforms had become shabby even prior to this expedition and after almost 400 miles of marching, fighting, and destroying railroads many of the boys were without shoes;

some without trousers. It was February and very cold. About 5,000 negros had fallen in with them on the march. Women, some with small children, older people, and some with disabilities. Many of the younger men enlisted in colored regiments. Most of the people had to fend for themselves. They were pathetic, poor, tired, and hungry and many died rather then return to their former masters.

Furlough

Finally, new recruits arrived to replenish the ranks of the Twelfth and the Veterans were sent on furlough. They boarded the steamer, "Continental," the same one that had carried them south before the Vicksburg campaign. It was crowded and cold with a drizzly rain. A couple of the men cut the ropes on a bail of cotton and buried themselves in its downy interior. Emerging later looking like walking snow men. Others found whiskey and most of them ended up in the guard house.

They arrived at Cairo, Illinois on March 18th and were housed in what they described as a, "well ventilated building". Some of the men found a theater where the acting was deplorable, but at least the building was warmer so they suffered through the performances. The following day they were loaded aboard freight cars of the Illinois Central and transported to Chicago where they arrived on March 20th. They were marched through cold which was even more intense as they moved further north, but their destination was "Soldier's Home." A large building with heat, a dining room with tables that could accommodate the whole regiment and young ladies in pink gowns and white aprons serving pitchers of hot coffee and tea. The women heard the Regiment was coming and had worked all day preparing hot food for them. Col. Bryant called for three Wisconsin cheers and the men enthusiastically got up on their chairs and gave a "hip, hip, hurrah, hurrah, hurrah, and a tiger." The band came in on the last refrain and the ladies were serenaded. Some wiped tears from their eyes.

From Soldier's Home they marched to the depot and boarded passenger cars for the ride to Madison. Upon their arrival they were greeted by the Governor of Wisconsin and members of the Legislature who waited upon them serving coffee and donuts. They then marched off to Camp Randall.

The camp had been transformed since their training days there. The countless rows of conical tents had been replaced by barracks. Even the heating system had been improved. They remained there from March 21st to 31st, being outfitted with new uniforms and equipment and the surgeons doctoring any physical complaints. They were then given their pay and they dispersed to their various homes and the happy welcomes awaiting them. They had not seen their families or friends for over two years. These happy reunions would provide food for conversation for the months ahead around many a campfire.

By the 22nd of April they were back at Camp Randall and on the 30th again left Wisconsin. At Chicago they were put into freight cars on rough board seats. The officers rode in passenger cars at the end of the train. Somewheres near Kankakee someone managed to remove the coupling pin connecting the officers car and the train pulled out without them. It was many miles before the engineer realized part of his train was missing. The train was parked on a siding and the engine returned for the missing car.

The townspeople along the way always seemed to know when a troop train was passing through. Young girls in Illinois met the trains and provided reading material for the soldiers. The men responded by whittling arrows from lath or shingles, attached messages or addresses at which they could receive mail and tossed the arrows at the feet of the fair sex at each town they passed through. Many of the girls responded to the messages and wrote the soldier who threw the dart.

It was on this return trip an unfortunate railroad accident occurred. Most of the men just felt a strong jolt, but two or three of the passenger cars carrying a Michigan battery, derailed. Two young brothers were killed and another man injured so severely he died later.

When they arrived at Cairo they learned that Rebel General Nathan Bedford Forrest and his cavalry had raided Paducah, Kentucky. The non-veteran men of the Twelfth had reinforced the garrison there and helped repulse the attack. Forrest next attacked and captured Fort Pillow. He murdered in cold blood as many negro soldiers comprising the garrison as he could get his hands on and earned the sobriquet, "Butcher Forrest."

On the 5th of May the non-veterans were employed to drive

10,000 head of beef cattle to Sherman's army in Northern Georgia. They arrived in Athens, Alabama via Pulaski on the 11th of May, a march of 100 miles, then on to Decatur 16 miles to the south. On the 19th they moved the cattle to Huntsville. There they halted and ramained until the 23rd of May to await the arrival of the veteran contingent of their regiment.

Grant had been promoted to the command of all the Union forces and Sherman took command of the Western Army. Grant wired Sherman to head for Atlanta. Sherman had 100,000 men at his disposal; the Rebels about half as many under the very able generalship of Joe Johnston.

CHAPTER VII
Kennesaw Mountain

When the veterans of the Twelfth returned from furlough they detrained at Cairo, Illinois and were assigned to the 1st Brigade, 3rd Division of the 17th Army Corps. About 10,500 men under the command of General Frank P. Blair. They were transported up the Ohio River to Paducah, Kentucky then up the Tennessee River to Clifton, Tenn. From Clifton they marched to Huntsville, Alabama where they arrived on the 3rd of May 1864. There they joined with the non-veteran contingent and once again were a complete regiment. Then over the mountains to join Sherman's Army at Big Shanty, a town near Marietta, Georgia.

The Twelfth had already earned the title, "The Marching Twelfth," but from Clifton to Big Shanty, a distance of about 300 miles, was the most difficult and arduous march in their military career. The portion from Huntsville, Alabama to Big Shanty, Georgia is best described by the following diary written by John Gaddis, dated June 9, 1864, at Ackworth, Georgia:

"On the 25th of May, we left Huntsville and marched twelve miles; very pretty country, weather warm but pleasant. We camped near good water.

"On the 26th, we marched twelve miles; pleasant country--good farming land planted principally with corn and wheat--not much cotton. Arrived opposite Decatur [Ala.] on the Tennessee River.

"27th. Crossed to Decatur on a pontoon bridge, and marched about six miles out of town; 'till midnight getting into camp; night dark, roads bad. An artilleryman was killed by the upsetting of a gun carriage.

"28th. Marched fifteen miles. Country uneven--traveled over some high and rocky hills; water scarce, weather hot; men getting very tired. Camped at Somerville, a dilapidated village--ruined and deserted because of the war; good spring of cool water near our camp.

"29th. Marched twelve miles. Country mountainous--many difficult places in the road. The center of our column was attacked--two pieces of cannon and twenty-four prisoners, including one Lieutenant Colonel and one Captain, captured from the enemy. Column delayed until midnight getting into camp--troops very tired. Camped near a spring of excellent water large enough to supply a city.

"30th. Marched twenty miles. Climbed mountains; weather very warm; plenty of dead horses and mules strew the way; troops very tired; water scarce. General Blair cursed by all the troops. Camped at midnight at Warrenton, wreck of a town. Terrible work descending the mountains after dark; wagon upset and a colored woman and two soldiers killed; men all worn out for want of sleep and proper nourishment, as we are marching on one-third rations. Country very poor, inhabitants all showing extreme poverty. Plenty of good timber--chestnut and pine of the best kind; huckleberries growing in the woods. Blair receives plenty of curses from all lips.

"31st. Marched fifteen miles. Country very poor, inhabitants poorer; strict orders against taking anything from the poor people--provost guard detailed to prevent its being done. Many rocky hills to climb, men very much exhausted; encamped early in the afternoon beside a rocky stream of good water.

"June 1st. Marched twelve miles--good roads most of the way; terrible work descending from the mountains into a low valley--frightful place for teams to get down with loaded wagons. Camped in a valley surrounded by mountains, near Will's Creek, a good sized stream; rear of column until midnight getting into camp.

"2nd. Weather very warm and dry. We lay over today for rest. Four wagons and two hundred men from each brigade detailed for a foraging expedition. Heavy rain towards night. Troops greatly refreshed by the day's rest, and by bathing in the stream. Rained again during the night.

"3rd. Marched sixteen miles. Rained during the day; country mountainous, roads very bad, troops very tired after marching through the mud. Camped in the mud after dark, and in much confusion.

"4th. Marched sixteen miles. Roads very bad. Forded the Coosa River, men up to their waists in water, and wagons in over the axles. A novel sight to see an army of men on undress parade, clothing and trappings on the top of their head to keep them dry, wading a river, shouting and plunging through the stream, all eager to gain the opposite bank, some crowding others down overhead in the water, mule drivers swearing and whipping up their teams. Some men hang upon the wagons thinking to get over dry shod, but several are shaken from their places and get a ducking. Much difficulty in marching, having to wait for pioneers to put the road in condition. Our road was rough; plenty of the best of water all along the way. Got into camp after dark.

"5th. Marched sixteen miles over very bad roads, but not quite so mountainous; ranges of mountains on either hand look very picturesque in the distance. Cleared off at noon. Camped near Rome, Georgia, a very pretty town about the size of Baraboo [WI], country beautiful.

"6th. Marched fourteen miles over good roads, but the weather is so warm that the troops suffer from heat. Arrived at Kingston at one o'clock P.M. One year ago today I left home, after a furlough, to rejoin the regiment at the siege of Vicksburg. More rain in the night.

"7th. Marched fourteen miles. A pleasant morning. Today the national convention meets for the nominations for the presidency. The day with us was very warm in the forenoon, but cloudy and cooler toward night. Some rain, but the roads are good. Passed by Rebel fortifications that Sherman flanked, and they are therefore of no avail to the said Rebs. Passed through Cartersville, a railroad station on the road leading from Chattanooga to Atlanta, and encamped by the side of the Etowah River, and near the railroad crossing. The bridge, as large as three of that at Kilbourn City, was burned by the Rebels, but nothing is too much for Yankee enterprise and perseverance; the bridge is being quickly rebuilt, and the road will soon be in running order clear to the front. Such things must surely discourage the Rebels. To us, it is amusing to see such formidable works as they have constructed all flanked by our army and rendered useless to them.

"8th. Marched twelve miles over hard gravelly roads, but sometimes very steep. Country is broken and hilly--mountainous in the distance. The road is lined with troops, some in camp, some on the way back to the railroad station with wagon trains after supplies. Saw many wounded men lying in the shade of trees, and under the care of surgeons. During the day we arrived at the front. Our Corps occupies the extreme left of our army. The enemy is said to be three miles ahead of us.

"General McPherson and staff visited our Corps. As he

passed along, each regiment cheered him loudly, flinging their hats high in the air.

"It rained again at night. None of us, except the officers, have any tents; tents take up too much room in the baggage wagons, so we must do without. We do the best we can to fix some sort of shelter from the storm.

"9th. I feel somewhat rested this morning. Three army corps move forward today, but we are resting. I am well, but much worn down by the long and tedious march of three hundred miles--the hardest we ever had. We are blessed here with plenty of good, pure water."

Hosea Rood continues the account: "I am very glad to be able to present the above diary, for it gives a detailed account of one of our most notable and most trying marches.

"Comrade Gaddis mentions the fact that all the men were cursing General Blair. I must write more concerning this matter:

"General Blair was a new man to us. We had heard of him in a political way, but had known nothing of him as an army officer. Our march from Clifton, Tennessee, by way of Huntsville, Alabama, to Sherman's army near Atlanta, was an unusually hard one all through. The distance was nearly three hundred miles, and a part of the road was over mountains, while the weather was hot and sultry. We always spoke of it as a forced march. We had a notion that Blair was in some way to be blamed for our hard marching and short rations. We said then, though I do not recollect that we had any reason for doing so, that he put off starting on the journey from Cairo until a forced march became necessary in order to get through at a given time. However that may be, we felt a bit spiteful when we got tired and wet, and hungry, and sleepy, and we took occasion to vent our spleen upon our new general. In order that he might know the state of our minds, we fell into the habit, whenever he had just ridden past us, of drawling out in a very *vealy* sort of way, "*Bla-a-a-ir*", dwelling at great length on the middle of the name. Once started, this came to be a constant means of letting our discontent be known. Before long the whole line took up the refrain, and *Bla-a-a-a-ir!*" followed the general where ever he went. The boys used to put their hands to their mouths and shout it after him with all sorts of variations. At first he did not seem to mind much about it, but after a while we got orders through our officers that our "*blatting*" must be stopped. We did stop it to a certain extent, in daylight, but we made up after dark for all such delinquencies. The old woods fairly rang with the doleful sound; and, as we did so much night marching, we had abundant opportunity to remind the general that he was still in our minds.

"I recollect that late one very dark night a hundred or more stragglers lay about on the ground in a little roadside clearing. It was raining heavily, but some of the boys who were near the road had managed to get a fire started under some sort of cover, and they were trying to extract a bit of comfort from its light and heat. Horses' hoofs were heard in the mud and water at a little distance. The splashing and clattering came nearer and nearer, and soon a dozen horsemen galloped along the road by the fire. "Who is it?" Asked a dozen voices. Then someone near the fire sent out on the night air the old familiar sound, "*Bla-a-a-a-a-ir!*" And they kept it going until the general and his staff were well out of hearing.

"One day a straggler, who belonged, I believe, to the 16th Wisconsin, becoming satisfied that *blatting* was not equal to the proper expression of his feelings toward the general, sent a *shot* at him in broad daylight! The fellow was put under arrest. That night he was kept in a tent under guard. I have heard it said that Blair called to make him a visit. The General said, "Did you shoot at me today?" The straggler answered promptly, "Yes, sir, I did, and I'll do it again if I get the chance!" I never heard the rest of the conversation reported, and so I do not know what else was said. Neither have I any knowledge of what was done about the matter."

Sherman wanted to break through between Pine Mountain and the Kennesaw Range. The Twelfth had been assigned to McPherson's Division which took up a position on the extreme left, just in front of Big Shanty. Here they built breastworks and rifle pits. Working only at night in two shifts; one shift from dark to midnight and the next from midnight to dawn. It was a particularly tiring duty after their arduous march and lack of sleep. They felled trees and then carrying the logs they stumbled and grumbled as they tried to find their way in the dark to the breastworks. All the time there was constant firing from both Rebel and Union rifle pits.

On the 14th of June, Rebel Generals Johnston, Hardee,

Polk and others could be seen on the summit of Pine Mountain. Sherman told a nearby battery to direct their fire to the summit. Although the range was extreme it was very effective. General Polk was killed and the rest scattered.

The Union soldiers left their rifle pits and charged the enemy. Several men were shot. The young drummer boys and the black cooks left the safety of the rear area and risking their own lives ran onto the field with stretchers to bring off the wounded to safety and medical care. The Twelfth was on the extreme left during this battle and not in the heaviest fighting and did not have to charge the enemy.

Hosea Rood continues: "The enemy being driven back, our next move was to construct a new line of works some distance out in the field. This had to be done in the night, when we could not be seen by the enemy, but it was easy digging, and the line was completed a couple of days after that exciting 15th of June. The weather was rainy, and our position in the field was muddy. To show how muddy it was I copy a paragraph from a letter written by General Sherman on the 21st of June:

'This is the nineteenth day of rain and the prospect of fair weather is as far off as ever. The roads are impassable; the fields and woods become quagmires after a few wagons have crossed over. Yet we are at work all the time. The left flank is across Noonday Creek and the right is across Nose Creek. The enemy still holds Kennesaw, a conical mountain with Marietta behind it, and has his flanks retired to cover that town and the railroad behind. I am all ready to attack the moment the weather and the roads will permit troops and artillery to move with anything like life.'

"During these days there was almost incessant firing from the hundreds of rifle pits on either side, and a pretty steady booming of artillery in our part of the lines. This death grapple between the two armies was relaxed neither day nor night; it was a continual battle. We had gone into the works on the 10th of June and were on duty a part or whole of every night for more than a week. Men would fall asleep even on guard, and some had repeatedly to be aroused in order to keep up at all.

"One of the recruits, who shall be nameless, had his right forfinger nearly shot off by his own gun on the night of the 18th of June. The accident occasioned some expression of opinion among the boys at the time. The chap took his sore finger back to the hospital the next day, and they never saw either him or his finger again.

"About the night of the 20th of June the enemy evacuated his line in front of Big Shanty, and retired to the Kennesaw Range, about three miles to the south. This range is, perhaps, five miles in length. At the northeastern extremity it terminates in a peak rising quite abruptly about 700 feet above the surrounding country. Being only a peak, it was not a very fit place for the posting of large bodies of troops; but a few men could easily repel the attack of a large force. To the southwest there is another dome on this range of a lesser altitude, but it is about a thousand feet long. This was known as Little Kennesaw, the other Big Kennesaw. The smaller hill was a capital place for the Rebel batteries, and they had it well fortified with cannon. The range as a whole made a very strong position. A mile to the north, and running almost parallel with the east end of this range, is another, but lower one, which was known as Brush Mountain. When the enemy left our front at Big Shanty, we advanced and took position along the crest of Brush Mountain. A deep valley separates the two ridges and it was along this valley that the railroad extended southward towards Marietta and Atlanta.

The general situation at this time was summarized by General Sherman in a letter to General Halleck, as follows:

"We continue to press forward on the principle of an advance against fortified positions. The whole country is one vast fort, and Johnston must have at least fifty miles of connected trenches with abatis and finished batteries. We gain ground daily, fighting all the time. ....Our lines are now in close contact, and the fighting is incessant, with a good deal of artillery fire. As fast as we gain one position the enemy has another all ready, but I think he will soon have to let Kennesaw go, which is the key to the whole country. The weather is now better, and the roads are drying up fast."

Following is a list of the battles fought from the 13th to the 27th of June. It may be seen that it was, indeed, one long battle around old Kennesaw:

June 15, Noonday Creek, Pine Mountain and Gilgal.
June 17, Mud Creek
June 18, Kennesaw Mountain
June 20, Kennesaw Mountain--to the southwest.
June 20, Kennesaw Mountain--Cavalry battle.
June 21, Kennesaw Mountain--to the southwest.
June 22, Kulp's Farm.
June 24, Kennesaw Mountain.
June 25, Kennesaw Mountain.
June 27, Kennesaw Mountain--the great battle.

Twelve battles in twelve days! The great battle of the 27th was the most stubbornly contested one on both sides. Sherman undertook to drive the enemy from Kennesaw Range, but this he found himself unable to do, and the Rebels scored a victory.

Hosea Rood continues: "Our regiment, being toward the extreme left of our lines, was not brought into the heaviest of any of this fighting. On the morning of the 27th we were ordered into line, and were told that in an hour we were to charge against Big Kennesaw. As we stood looking up at that gloomy hill we did not feel very happy, for it had been said that the enemy intended to defend himself there by rolling stones down upon the charging column. We felt, somehow, as if we'd rather face cannon ball than masses of rock. It used to be a common saying among the boys that they did not want to go to war to be kicked to death by a mule, and they might have added, or to be mashed flat by a stone rolling down hill.

"For all that, we tried to prepare ourselves for climbing the mountain at the end of the hour. In the meantime, there was a constant roll of musketry and a boom! boom! boom! of cannon off to our right.

"When the hour was half gone Sergeant McVey said, 'Boys, I'm ready to go, and now the sooner the better; I don't want to wait another minute. I don't care now what is to be done; I'm ready for it'. In the meantime, the rest of us tried to work ourselves into the same state of mind that Jem had reached; yet I recollect it was pretty hard work for this particular soldier."

Following is an excerpt from the report of Col. W. L. Sanderson, dated Kennesaw Mountain, June 28, 1864:

"...The enemy's skirmishers were soon encountered

and driven back to their rifle-pits, where three regiments of the rebels were held in reserve and so completely concealed by bushes and undergrowth as to be unperceived by our men. The enemy evidently expected to capture the entire line, as they did not fire until our men reached in some instances the parapet of their works, when they opened a murderous fire of musketry, compelling our men to fall back with a loss of 65 killed, wounded and missing". [Col. Bryant reported 25 killed, wounded and missing from the Twelfth.]

After falling back the boys were pinned down for some time by enemy artillery. Only four or five shots were fired and did little harm except that one of the balls carried away the hind feet of the old cream-colored mule owned by Jackson, one of the wagon-masters. The faithful old fellow had been so long with the regiment that the boys all felt a genuine sorrow when he had to be shot and put out of his misery.

When General Blair arrived at Kennesaw with his command the carpenters were just finishing the rebuilding of the railroad bridge across the Etowah River. The track had been repaired and supplies from Chattanooga were beginning to arrive near the camps. One of the engineers decided to come down and greet the Rebels on the mountain. Just before sundown one evening the boys heard a train coming toward the front. The rolling of the trucks over the rather rough track awoke the echoes among the hills and they met with hearty responses from the boys. The train thundered along the track until it was brought to a stand still just under the brow of Old Kennesaw, and close to the Rebel lines. Here it began to toot its respects to the Johnnies on the mountain. It sent forth long toots, short toots, straight toots, crooked toots, and all sorts of toots, until it seemed as if the echoes would surely tear rocks loose from the hillside. All the fellows on the Union side of the lines tooted an accompaniment to the locomotive, and, take it all around, there was considerable noise going on for several minutes. But the fellows entrenched on the hill kept silent. As dusk deepened the engineer backed his train slowly to the rear of our camps.

Both the Union and Confederate picket posts were down in the valley between the hills, and they were very close together. They could not be reached in safety during the daytime, hence the boys had to go to them before daylight in the morning and return before light the next morning. Once in the pits they had to "keep shady", as the sight of a head above the works would surely bring a shower of bullets. Many of the boys in those pits had narrow escapes, but none were hit.

On the night of July 2nd, the pickets were relieved by cavalry at dusk and the Twelfth was ordered to quietly pack up and form a line of march. They moved silently around the Kennesaw Range in the darkness then headed southwest. The next day they found themselves clear to the right of Sherman's late line, and there went on picket duty. That day Marietta was captured by Union troops with many provisions and considerable stores of supplies.

CHAPTER VIII
Nickajack Creek

Nickajack Creek was an important, but not a major engagement, and therefore, tends to get rather short shrift in the official records. Once again I'm relying on Hosea Rood to give us an account.

"On the 4th, Independence Day, we lay in a quiet camp resting up after the fatigue of our all night march and picket duty. It was a lovely day. On the 5th we were in line of battle all day and skirmished over hilly, wooded country which was very tiresome. Most of the time we were close upon the heels of the enemy. Once we overtook him, and a lively skirmish ensued; a few of the regiment were wounded.

"Late in the afternoon our line emerged from the woods upon a large open field. It was much easier advancing in line of battle in this broad clearing than it had been in the forests through which we had struggled during the day, and we made good headway. But we soon saw there was something ahead worse than a forest, for a heavy fort, with strong works stretching away on either hand, skirted the further edge of the field. These works were on the further bank of the Nickajack creek. and very near the Chattahoochee River. They looked rather formidable to us as we moved forward toward them, but we saw no sign of hostility. Some of our boys said, "The Rebs must have vacated those forts". Soon a small flag was seen floating from the large fort. Someone suggested that it might be a white flag, and ventured the opinion that as like as not the enemy meant to surrender.

"Directly we noticed little clouds of dust arising here and there a foot or two from the plowed ground in front of us, and we found that a line of skirmishers were sending the leaden hail that raised the little dust clouds.

"But we eyed the fort in front of us more closely than we did the skirmishers that were disputing our progress. Again some of our boys declared that the works must be deserted. But just then there flew out from one of the embrasures a long horizontal column of white smoke, and then another and another. Then quickly followed deafening explosions as the shells screamed along over our heads. There was no further discussion as to whether the fort meant business.

"We set our teeth together and moved forward to settle the question as to the possession of those fortifications. The little clouds of dust rose thick and fast all about us; the bullets whizzed by us making most disagreeable music. One of them struck with a dull, sickening *thud!* just at my left, and my dear comrade Henry Fluno, my mate, who, on all the marches we ever made, walked elbow to elbow with me,--my room mate at Delton and my friend always afterward, uttered a short, quick agonized "Oh!" and dropped back. I never saw him again; none of us ever saw him after that. He was shot through, and he died the next day. I believe, however, that Rufus Johnson was with Henry at his death; but Rufus, too, is now dead, and I cannot ask him about it.

"The death of comrade Fluno came to me as a personal loss, for I loved him as a brother. After this we spoke his name tenderly, lovingly, and our hearts went out in sympathy for his friends at home, especially for the young wife he had married just before leaving home.

"Henry was quiet, always prompt to do every duty, and a good soldier in every way. He was the first one of Company E to give up his life in battle. We had thus far been very fortunate, indeed.

"As night was fast approaching, General Gresham thought it best not to charge at once the works of the enemy. And so, after advancing to within easy range of his lines, we formed in line on a high ridge extending parallel with the creek, and that night threw up strong defenses. Here we remained several days. Our position was a tolerably safe one in spite of the incessant musket firing on both sides, and the occasional attention paid to us by the batteries over the creek.

"I suppose that our line here was about half a mile from the creek at the bottom of the field. The pickets of the enemy were stationed just on the other side, while ours occupied pits pretty well down the slope. It was worth one's head to make much of a show of it above the bit of earthwork by which each post was protected. Close by our regiment there was stationed a battery, and it was a favorite pastime of ours to watch the daily duel between this battery and the fort over beyond. Considerable noise was made, but not much execution done, at least by the Rebels. Our cannoneers enjoyed taking deliberate aim at some picket post across the creek and then sending a shell into it--if they could. When the shell burst and threw rails and sand high in the air, we used to laugh ourselves hoarse to see the frightened Johnnies streak it in every direction to find a place of safety.

"Our works on this ridge were heavy--the embankment high, and the ditches deep. They were made so as a protection against cannonading from the fort over the creek. The enemy did not do any unnecessary firing, as he was short of ammunition. But one night well after dark a battery situated away to our right, and which seemed to have our range, began throwing shells across our lines and pretty close down to the top of the works of our regiment. We huddled into the deep ditch and "lay low" whenever a shell came our way. ...in looking over the works in the direction from which the shells came, whenever a gun went off we could see a flash; it looked like a faint bit of sheet lightning well down to the horizon. Since light travels much faster than cannon balls, we were safe in looking 'till we saw the flash; but then it behooved us to get down upon our stomachs. We had time to get pretty well fixed before the shell would come tearing along over us. Then we would all climb up at once and watch for the next flash; then down again. On this occasion there was a typical Irishman, from another regiment among us. He seemed to fear serious consequences from the "dhirty bomb-shells," and he amused us mightily with some of his sayings. After the flash had been seen he would fairly dig himself into the dirt at the bottom of the ditch, exclaiming in a rich brogue, "Howly Moses! byes, lie down! lie down *flat..*" By the powers o' mud! byes, lay low, lay low, byes!" "Bedad, byes, get down! *get down!* the murtherin' thing will be afther killin' every wan av us if you don't get *close down!* Oh, hear the murtherin' thing a -screamin.'" But for all Pat's solicitude, no one was killed. One shell burst near us, however, and a piece of it, after striking a post in our works, glanced off and hit George Freer on the back of the neck and shoulder making an ugly bruise.

"One of our guns, belonging to a battery on a hillside in our rear, threatened to do us more damage than all those on the Rebel side. The shells had an unpleasant habit of exploding just as they left the muzzle of the gun, and there was not much telling just where the pieces would strike. When they came down among us a yell of indignation from the men would go up to that battery that would persuade the gunners to give the slobbering old gun a rest for awhile. If I remember rightly, the troublesome piece was taken down to one of the picket posts nearest the enemy, and there allowed to spew its ammunition about just as it chose, as there were nothing but Johnnies in front of it. It would have been a blessing to us and a damage to them had they captured it; but they did not.

"I think it was on the evening of July 8th, that some of us had a bit of an experience that makes me laugh now every time I think of it, and I fancy many of the boys have had more than one laugh over it. I have said that the Nickajack Creek flowed between our lines and those of the enemy; but it was much nearer their works than ours. Our picket posts had been advancing until they were pretty close to this creek, and our officers became desirous of establishing some rifle pits across the creek, and very close to the Rebel outposts. Though such a position would be dangerous to our men who should occupy the pits, they would be able to do much damage to the enemy, and so it was decided to make the attempt to throw our line across the creek.

"Of course, the only time to do such a thing must be after dark. Accordingly, one night just at dusk a detail of several men was made to carry the plan into execution. Some sort of long timbers would be needed to build a foot bridge across the creek, also in the construction of pits on the other side. In order to get the necessary timbers, a log house by the side of the road, a little to our right, was torn down. This road led straight down to the creek, and we were ordered to carry the timbers down the road until we should get near the creek, and then, turning to the left, carry them up the stream about thirty rods to the point where it had been decided to build the bridge. About a dozen of us formed a squad to work together. I think there were two or three such squads. We formed six pairs, each couple having a short stick on which we bore the timbers down the road. The night was dark but pleasant, and the timbers being light, we rather enjoyed the job. But we knew that when passing along the creek we were close by the enemy's pickets on the other side. Because of this, we had been ordered to keep very quiet, not to speak a loud word, for fear of drawing their fire. For some reason our crowd felt lively, and we *whispered* pertty loud; and *giggled* and *snickered*. When we were putting the timbers across the creek, Lt. Colonel Proudfit scolded us for our levity in whispers that were so emphatic that he made more noise than we did.

"As we brought timber after timber our ill-suppressed merriment increased, until we became quite jolly. On one of our trips we stopped alongside the creek to rest. Sitting in a row on our log we whispered and giggled considerably, being out of Colonel Proudfit's hearing. In the midst of our fooling we were surprised by a *bang! bang! bang!* The Johnnies across the creek had located us by our noise and let fly at us. We stopped our giggling, there was a bit of a "whish," and every man of us had disappeared--each doing what seemed to him the safest thing to do. I know of what only one did. He ran like a racer at right angles with the creek to get out of that. He soon struck the plowed ground and began to run up the side hill. He would make good time for a few rods, and then, finding the bullets flying about in delightful recklessness, would flatten out on the ground for safety. A minute of lying down did not lessen the number of bullets, and then he would run a few rods further and conclude to flatten out again. It was amusing to him to see others darting by him on the gallop, and others flattening out on the ground for a minute, but concluding to jump up and run again. Finally, with a hop, skip, and a jump he landed inside the works up near the road, glad enough to be alive and well, though quite out of breath. And he was not alone in this self congratulation; others rejoiced likewise. After a few minutes the firing ceased, and all was calm. The gallant chaps who had beaten such a lively retreat then timidly made their way back to the creek. When this one arrived at his log he found his mates just gathering in from the surrounding darkness. Some had been only a few steps from the log and had lain flat to the ground all the time, while several had stretched themselves alongside the piece of timber, thereby having an excllent protection. It was no doubt true that the fellow who ran the furthest up the hill got into the greatest danger, for the balls went high and quite above those who stuck to the log. So it often is; those who run away from danger are the very ones to run into it. It is commonly better to stick to one's post through thick and thin.

"We took up our log and carried it to the crossing, but we *kept still* after that. The bridge was built, a few pits were constructed across the creek, and the Rebels in that particular viciniy were made thereby pretty uncomfortable.

"For the next day or two our batteries kept up a pretty steady fire on the enemy's works. On the morning of the 10th we found that the works in our front were empty, the Confederates had evacuated them in the night, escaped across the Chattahoochee and taken refuge in Atlanta.

"The next day we were transferred from the 4th Division under General Gresham, to the 1st Brigade of the 3rd Division. In this brigade we found the 16th Wisconsin, a regiment that was with us in the fall of '61, in Camp Randall. Our new brigade commander was General Manning Force, and the division commander, General M. D. Leggett. We had known "Pap" Leggett before, and we were not at all displeased to be placed under him. Still, we had liked General Gresham, and we regretted to leave him..."

The regiment then marched to Roswell's Mills on the Chattahoochee, 12 miles east of Marietta. They crossed to the Atlanta side of the river, 20 miles to Decatur [Ga.] on the Augusta railroad where they arrived on July 19th. They were put to work tearing up the railroad. They could hear the sounds of battle taking place at Peach Tree Creek.

CHAPTER IX
The Battle for Atlanta

Hosea Rood writes: "We were, on the 20th of July, 1864, marching from Decatur [Ga.] towards the works on the southeast of Atlanta. During the afternoon, firing began in or own front, and we plainly saw that we, too, must soon be drawn into the general battle. While resting near a farm house, during a blockade in the road ahead of us, ambulances came back from the front with several wounded men. General Gresham's division, the one from which we had recently been detached, was already in action, and we were following them. Soon we moved forward and, emerging from the cover of timber, we found ourselves forming in line of battle in an old field.

"There was no very heavy firing going on, but a number of the Fourth Division had been killed or wounded. It was at this time that we heard that General Gresham himself had just been severely wounded in one of his legs. We felt very anxious about the good General, for we had been in his brigade ever since the fall of '63, and we held him in high esteem.

"We passed on through this old field, and then began advancing in line of battle through a strip, perhaps half a mile wide, of timberland covered with a growth of rather small oaks. Just as the sun was setting in front of us, we came to the further edge of this timber, and saw just before us a small creek running about parallel with our line; and beyond the creek a sloping cornfield reaching fifty rods, perhaps, up to a scattered growth of timber along its farther edge.

Though we had encountered little or no opposition in our progress through the woods, the bullets began whizzing over our heads now and then with much of the spirit of mischief in them. At the low land near the edge of the woods, we were halted. Most of us lay down on the ground and many were dropping asleep, when Captain Gillispie told us that we could go to sleep for the night; but he directed us to keep our knapsacks, cartridge boxes, etc., strapped on, and our guns in our hands ready for immediate action if anything should demand such a thing of us during the night. The ground being covered with leaves, and we being pretty tired, sweet sleep soon came to us and held us in loving embrace until sunrise the next morning,--the 21st of July '64,--a memorable day to many of....our regiment.

"When we arose and began to look about us, we found ourselves in line of battle, joining the 16th Wisconsin on our left, and having in line in our rear the four Illinois regiments of our brigade--the 20th, 30th, 31st, and 45th. As we looked up across the cornfield in our front, we could see at the farther edge of it the Johnnies working hard to strengthen their works. They evidently expected us to charge upon them.

"We had a line of pickets a few rods in our front, and they were exchanging occasional shots with the pickets of the enemy, and at pretty short range. As the sun arose the shots became more and more frequent, and now and then a man was hit. Most of the balls, however, passed over our heads and struck the trunks of the trees, or snipped off twigs here and there. James Miles of Company B was wounded at this time on the picket, or skirmish, line.

"It was plain enough to us all that something serious was about to happen, and it is my recollection that we all felt just a little serious. Captain Gillispie had the one or two spades that belonged with the company brought forward and put to use in building breastworks. Some of the fallen trunks of trees lying about were laid up in the fashion of a backwoods farmer's straight log fence, and a ditch was begun on our side of the fence, the earth that was removed being thrown over on the side toward the enemy. Our spade or two were doing pretty quick work; a man would seize a spade and shovel for dear life for a minute, the captain keeping time, and then another man would dig his minute, and so on in turn. The other companies were doing much the same thing, and we soon had a good line of works well under way.

"While this was going on, 'Billy' Stevens, our Commissary Sergeant, came along the line bringing orders from the Colonel. We heard him say, 'Captain, we move forward in an hour.' Gillispie's only remark was, 'Men, throw down those spades!'

"We knew pretty well what 'moving forward' meant. We were to charge the enemy on the hill in our front, for the purpose of taking his line of works.

We had been in the service nearly three years, yet we had been so favored by circumstances that we had never before been called upon to make a deadly charge upon the enemy's works; and so an entirely new experience lay just before us.

"It was seven o'clock, I think, when these orders came to us, and the charge was to be made at eight. I think it is easier going into battle when it comes on at once, and one is hurled almost before he knows it into the very thickest of the fight. When one has an hour to think it all over, he is beset with all sorts of conflicting emotions. He knows that many men must be killed outright, that many others must be so wounded as to lie a long time dying, while a great many more must go maimed to the hospital to suffer more than death for weeks and months--perhaps for years--until death finally comes to bring a tardy relief for pain. He knows all this, I say, and he wonders which lot is in store for him. He feels a little like taking counsel of his heels, as did poor Launcelot Gobbo, the servant of Shylock; but conscience, manhood, patriotism, combine to lead him in the path of duty, come what will. Home, father, mother, brother, sister, wife or sweetheart fill one's thoughts, perhaps for the last time on earth. One feels that he loves all these better now than ever before, and that it is very hard to give them all up. But he feels, also, that all the ties binding him to his home are, in fact, the very ties that bind him to his country; his loyal service is for them. He fights for his country that they may enjoy the blessings of liberty in a home made safe by the majesty of law. If he has not often prayed before he will not be neglectful at such a time of pleading with the patriot's God for a gracious forgiveness of human sins and frailties.

"I suppose that serious and tender emotions moved the hearts of all of us that beautiful, bright and sunny July morning in '64, as we waited for the hour to pass before 'moving forward;' but outwardly all were cheerful. I recollect that one of our younger boys sat apart from the rest, leaning against a tree, and that, quite unconsciously, I suppose, he was humming to himself that touching little song,

'Just before the battle, Mother,
I am thinking most of you,
While upon the field we're watching,
With the enemy in view.'

"All hours come to an end, and that one did too. We were directed to put our packed knapsacks into a pile, and then the low-spoken order came, 'Fall in, men, outside the works.' Our line was quickly formed, the 16th Wisconsin being at our left, and the four Illinois regiments in our rear. Our flags were unfurled to the light morning breeze, and it seems to me now that they looked brighter and more beautiful than they ever did before. I believe that our men, as they saw the colors almost sparkle in the morning sun, while we all stood in line with faces to the front that brief moment, and realized that in them was symbolized everything we held dear in government, hightly resolved to count their lives as nothing that the dear old flag should that day move on to certain victory. They held their muskets with an iron grasp, set their teeth together, and their features took on an expression of frigid resolution.

"Soon General Force, our brigade commander, came riding along the rear of our line, saying in low and quiet tones, 'Boys, now be cool and firm; don't waver, don't falter; just make up your mind to drive the enemy from yonder hill, and you'll do it. Be cool and determined, boys, and it will be all right.'

"Though we had not been long in General Force's brigade, we had learned to have entire confidence in him and his quiet talk made us more determined than ever to plant our colors on the hill in our front.

"A minute later the command came along the line from captain to captain, 'Forward, men, forward!' Slowly we moved down through the trees to the narrow strip of grass land skirting the little brook in our front. We crowded together slightly, and the brook so hindered us that in trying to jump it, and in splashing through it, we got considerably confused. The center of the line fell a little behind, and as the right and left swung around forming a curve, the center was badly crowded. After getting across the brook, the order came, 'Give off to the left!' We did crowd to the left to get more room, still we were huddled. Again, and louder, came the order, 'Give off to the left, men! Give off to the left!' Although we kept pushing in that direction, we did not break the jam.

"Captain Gillispie seeing the condition of things shouted above all the growing clatter and confusion, swinging his sword, as he did so, along the line in unpleasant nearness to our noses, 'Give off to the left, men! Give off to the left!' There was something in his way of doing this that meant business, and we turned and fairly ran to the left until, just at the right time, he commanded, 'Forward, men!' Nothing could have been done better; we were in order again.

"Just before us a steep bank arose about twenty feet high. Climbing this bank, we found ourselves in tall grass just at the lower edge of the sloping cornfield that reached to the hill top, and a few rods beyond which the Rebels had built their breastworks. Just then the order came, 'Lie Down!' It was, indeed, refreshing and comforting to 'lie down' at such a time,-- especially so when we heard the little leaden messengers of death whizzing over us on their way to our rear. The next order came,--'Fix bayonets!' A sharp clicking ran along the line for two or three seconds, and then all was still except the indescribable 'ping' of the bullets speeding along overhead. Then we heard General Force shout the order,'Forward, men!' A long line of bayonets flashing in the morning sun arose from the grass and began to move. Then came the final and supreme command, 'Charge bayonets! Forward, double-quick, March!'

"The time of suspense is over, and that brigade of men spring forward. Yells rend the air, bayonets clash together as, in the mad rush toward the front, every man runs a race with his comrades through a perfect shower of lead and iron toward the top of the field. Bullets come tearing down the rows of corn laying low many a poor fellow beneath the feet of those rushing up from behind towards the works of the enemy.

"Coming to the top of the hill, the surging column goes tearing over the rickety old rail fence, out through the scattering bushes, till they come square upon the line of Confederates, who are stubbornly defending their position.

"But this onslaught is too much for them; they fire their parting shots at short range and take to their heels. And now there is, indeed a race for it. On rush the Blue coats after the Gray coats, pell-mell, helter-skelter, hurry-skurry, yelling and firing through the woods, leaving the ground strewn with dead and dying. In the mad chase many prisoners are captured and sent to the rear.

"Soon a second line of works is reached, and the advance is checked. A heavy firing breaks out from a poiint to the right and in the rear of the men in the charge, and they are ordered to fall back into the works first taken, and this command is quickly obeyed.

"This position is held during the day, though several countercharges are made by the enemy with the intention of taking back what they have lost. When night comes on the companies are so scattered that no captain knows how many men he has left. After dark there is a general gathering in of the unhurt and slightly wounded. It is found that of our regiment one hundred and fifty-nine are either killed, wounded or missing,--other regiments having suffered proportionlly; and the most of this loss has occurred within about fifteen minutes after the order to charge bayonets.

"I have given the bare facts concerning our part in the battle of July 21, '64, or, as it is sometimes called, the 'Battle of Leggett's Hill' [aka 'Bald Hill']. But there are many details and incidents that ought to be recorded. I am not able to give all that should be given, for each of us saw only the things that took place close by him; and, besides, each saw with his own particular eyes. It is pretty well understood by old soldiers that no two of them sees the same thing quite alike in a battle. Moreover, in spite of a person, his memory of such events becomes in time tinged by the peculiar coloring of the mind that treasures them through the years. And I may say in this connection that I fear the old boys will say of much that is written in this sketch of our service, that they have no recollection of it; but that they do have in mind many other things that should have been recorded and of which no mention is made. If such things are said, the only answer the writer hereof can make is, that he must of necessity put down things as they seem to him; and perhaps, he may add that, if his comrades had rallied a little more freely to his aid in furnishing details and incidents, he could have done better.

"But let us return to the battlefield, all strewn with our dead and dying comrades. The following is the list of the losses of our company:

Killed: Corporals John Stults and Charles Fields

Wounded: Captain John Gillispie; Sergeants Henry W. Stutson, and Michael Griffin; Privates James M. Clement, James Camp, Edwin M. Truell, Wm. L. Mosier, Orson Wright, H. W. Rood, Jacob Lawsha, William Stowell, Clement Broughton.

"We were scattered considerably when we got back to the line of works against which we first charged. Here we found the Illinois regiments of our brigade in possession, they having, as before stated, formed a second charging column in our rear. We sought the shelter of trees, constructed barricades of rails, or crowded into line behind the works with the Illinois boys,--anything, so as to get somewhat of a protection from the flying bullets, and have a chance to return the fire.

"The wounds of Rood, Moshier and Lawsha were slight, and did not remove them from duty for many days; some, I think, did not lose a day.

"Some of the best known men of the other companies were either killed or wounded during that day and the next, among them Sergeants Libby, of Company B; Henry, of Company B; and Wood of Company C; Privates Henry Keeler of Company H; H. Wempner, of Company I; E. H. Hagaman, of Company B; Sergt. Miles of Company B.

"At nightfall the firing ceased, and there was a general time of "gathering of the clans." All the men were tired enough to sleep soundly though surrounded by dead and dying comrades; but details were made to work all night at bringing together the dead for burial, and the wounded for hospital treatment. Also, a detail of men was made to build upon the ground just captured, a strong line of works in order that it might be successfully defended against any attack the Rebels might make for the purpose of recovering the position.

"I do not know just what officer ordered the position to be thus fortified, but we who were there do know that that particular line of works saved us from utter defeat the next day, July 22nd. That morning found us tolerably quiet in camp. Our regiment occupied the heavy line of works mentioned; to our left lay the Fourth Division--Gresham's--constituted the extreme left of our army. During the morning we were drawing rations and were preparing for a good solid breakfast, when, somewhat to our surprise, we heard away back in our rear two or three shots. We did not think the enemy could be back there, yet those shots were followed by half a dozen others, then a dozen--twenty--a hundred--volleys--volley after volley,--then boom! boom! rang the artillery reports over the noise of all the rest.

"Our boys looked their astonishment into one another's eyes, dropped their hard tack and coffee and rushed for their guns. In the meantime Colonel Bryant was shouting as only he could shout, 'Fall in, men! Fall in!'

"The firing in the rear grew heavier, and soon the smoke of battle arose in a long, billowy cloud over the woodlands in that direction. Nearer and nearer the dense cloud came rolling toward us, indicating that the enemy were driving our men before them. In almost less time than it takes to write it, the surging tide of battle swept out of the timber and into the long stretch of open ground reaching a mile or two along the immediate rear of our lines.

"Such a scene as that was, one does not often behold, even in active service. When the long tidal wave of battle beat against the higher open ground our army occupied, and felt the full force of our regiments and brigades and divisions, their onward rush was checked, and then came the struggle for the mastery. As old Ocean beats against his rocky shores, rushing up with terrific force and then, though compelled to roll back for a few seconds, comes on again with renewed vigor, determined not to give up the strife, so did those confident Rebels charge and recharge. As we looked down upon the fighting, struggling mass of horses, wagons, cannon, ambulances, men, mules,-- now hidden in part by the clouds of dust and powder smoke, then in plain view,--and listened to the horrid din of battle, and then reflected that we were right between that desparate struggle and Atlanta; and when we found that at the same time the Confederates were attacking us from the front as well as rear, we truly felt that the outcome of the battle so suddenly thrust upon us was of considerable consequence to us. If ever we were in a position to fight like madmen we were then. Colonel Bryant was shouting at the top of his voice, 'Get into the works, boys! Get into the works!' We got into the works, but we found the balls coming from both front and rear. Some of the men shouted back to the colonel, 'Which side, Colonel, which side?' 'I don't care which side,' fairly yelled the excited commander, 'but, Get into the works! And do it quick!'

"We did 'get there' and mighty quick, too, but we were still greatly puzzled to know which side of the embankment would do us the most good.

"The struggle during the entire day was a fearful one,-- one that I cannot undertake to describe in detail. The Rebels made half a dozen violent assaults upon our position from the rear, and at the same time they kept up a terrific fire in our front and to our left. They came into hand to hand conflict with our Fourth Division and both sides fought desperately. Little by little the Fourth Division yielded the ground, until the enemy gained the position. As they were slowly beaten back they came into our works and we all fought together.

"At the left of our regiment a battery had been planted during the preceding night, and this held the Rebels in check. But one by one the horses were killed off, and then, for fear that the guns would be captured, they were drawn back out of the way. It seemed then as if we, too, must yield, but, because of our excellent works, we were able to hold our position, and when night came on the enemy gave up the fight. The next morning we had no foe in our immediate front, and we were the victors. But, oh, what a fearful loss of life there had been! The ground over which the Rebels had charged was thickly strewn with dead and dying; and along the line occupied the morning before by the Fourth Division, both Yankee and Rebel lay so close together that one could walk for long distances stepping from body to body. In some instances two men lay dead still clutching each other as they were doing when both were killed by the same shot.

"The 23rd was spent in exchanging and burying the dead, an armistice having been entered into for the purpose. The Rebel dead within our lines were carried to the line between the two armies, and our own dead within the Rebel lines were brought to the same place. Here the poor fellows were exchanged, carried tenderly away, and buried as decently as men could be buried on the battlefield.

"This was a sad day, for in some respects the horrors of the battlefield are much greater after the strife is over than during the combat. There is no excitement to keep up the nerves; dead friends are found here and there; the dead are bloated to twice their natural size; faces are so blackened by decomposition that one can scarcely recognize his own tent mate; the stench is terribly offensive;--but I must not say more of it.

"Strange as it may seem, Company E had no loss in either killed or wounded on that fearful day of battle, July 22nd. Our excellent works did us the best of service. We could fire without exposure to the fire of the enemy. Companies B and G to our left, and next to the battery of which I have spoken, suffered heavy loss.

"Soon after the attack, and when in the midst of the hottest firing, we heard someone shouting, 'Colonel Bryant! Colonel Bryant! Where is Colonel Bryant? General Force has been wounded, and Colonel Bryant is wanted to take command of the brigade!'

"The colonel was soon doing his best to get a good hold of the duties thus suddenly thrust upon him, and he succeeded so well that we scarcely noticed the change in commanders. About the same time Force's Adjutant General, Captain Walker, was severely wounded and borne from the field.

"But the saddest event of that day was the death of General McPherson, which occurred about noon. He had just been in consultation at the Howard House with Generals Sherman and Schofield and was riding back to deploy his troops in accordance with Sherman's orders. While passing along a path through a belt of woods, having sent all his staff officers off on various missions, some passing Rebels discovered him and shot him.

"I can not do justice to the manliness and soldierly qualities of General McPherson in any words of my own, and so I will quote a few words that General Sherman said of him two days after his death:

'General McPherson fell in battle, booted and spurred, as the gallant knight and gentleman should wish. Not his loss, but the country's; and this army will mourn his death and cherish his memory as that of one who, though comparatively young, had risen by his merit and ability to the command of one of the best armies which the nation had called into existence to vindicate its honor and integrity.

History tells of but few who so blended the grace and gentleness of the friend with the dignity, courage, faith and manliness of the soldier. His public enemies, even the men who directed the fatal shot, never spoke or wrote of him without expressions of marked respect; those whom he commanded loved him even to idolatry; and I, his associate and commander, fail in words adequate to express my opinion of his great worth. I feel assured that every patriot in America on hearing this sad news, will feel a sense of personal loss, and the country generally will realize that we have lost not only an able military leader, but a man who, had he survived, was qualified to heal the national strife which has been raised by designing and ambitious men.'

Hosea Rood continues: "I have read somewhere that when General Grant, quiet, self-possessed soldier that he was, heard of the death of gallant General McPherson, he went to his tent and wept. General Oliver O. Howard was appointed to succeed McPherson.

Following is an excerpt from the report of the above action by Colonel George Bryant, Near Atlanta, Ga., dated September 11, 1864:

"At 7 a.m. on the 21st the brigade was ordered to charge and hold the hill in its front. The Twelfth and Sixteenth Wisconsin Regiments formed the advance of the charging column, supported by the Twentieth, Thirtieth, and Thirty-first Illinois Regiments. The charge was made under very heavy musketry, the enemy being protected by intrenchments on the crest of the hill. The works were taken at the point of the bayonet and held, with aggregate loss to the First Brigade of (except Twentieth Illinois Regiment) about 258 killed, wounded and missing. The steady and unwavering advance of the columns under the terrible fire from the enemy's line (Cleburne's famous division), advantageously posted behind intrenchments, was such as to merit for both officers and men the highest record for courage and skill. In this charge the Twelfth Wisconsin Regiment lost out of less than 600 men engaged 134 men killed and wounded. It captured more small arms that it had men engaged, many of the arms still loaded and capped. It had 5 color bearers shot and 2 flag-staffs shot off. Other regiments of the brigade behaved with equal gallantry, but suffered less loss. Early in the great battle of the 22nd of July the brigade became engaged, and continued fighting until the next morning, repulsing many charges, literally piling the enemy's dead in heaps in front of the works, fighting the enemy all night with but the breastworks between them and the foe. Early in the action Brigadier-General Force was severely wounded, and the undersigned assumed command. During the fight the brigade changed fronts many times, fighting from both sides of the same breastworks, and at times it was obliged to refuse its flanks to meet the desperate and furious onsets of the enemy, so that it had to fight at the same time on two fronts and one flank. But it held the hill so dearly gained the day before, and the key to the position of the Army of the Tennessee, with a loss (excepting Twentieth Illinois Regiment), aggregate, of 329 killed, wounded and missing.

During all these two days' desperate fighting the organization and order was excellent and the men in the best of spirits. They fought to whip, and when the enemy at one point of the line had reached the outside of the breastworks, fixed bayonets and swore that they would stay or die.

From the time the command joined the grand army at Acworth, June 8, until the close of the campaign it was constantly at the front, under fire, marching, digging, and fighting. It has not failed to take and hold any position it was ordered to, nor has any part of the command moved except in pursuance of orders from proper authority. The officers and men believe they can't be whipped, and have always had perfect confidence in their officers and their final success.

The aggregate loss to the brigade in killed, wounded, and missing since June 8, 1864, is 863."

[In the Battle for Atlanta the Confederates lost between 7,000 to 8,000 men. The Union about half as many.]

Hosea Rood continues: "We remained in the position we occupied on the 22nd until the night of the 27th. Our works were made still stronger, and we kept a close watch on the movements of the enemy. General Hood, in the meantime, kept us from going to sleep by a pretty constant firing upon our lines.

"I must stop here to mention an incident or two. I do not know but I have already mentioned the fact that Clem Boughton and Will Stowell were close friends and pretty apt to be together. I had occasion to go down to the field hospital on the night of the 21st after the fighting was done. I found the wounded lying here and there on the ground under the trees, where they were being cared for by a small army of nurses, while the surgeons were busy amputating arms and legs and caring for other serious wounds. I saw a few who were already out of pain, death having come to their relief. Under one tree I found Will and Clem lying side by side. They were already in a high fever and were very weak. I was much disappointed, for I had thought that if I could find them I could talk with them. But they were both too far gone to notice anything. Deacon Sexton came along and spoke to them, asking if they would like a drink of water. They could scarcely speak, but he put a cup to their lips and they each took enough to moisten their fevered mouths, scarcely opening their eyes as they did so.

"What a change in those two boys since morning! The day found them joyous, bright and hopeful; it was leaving them in a dying condition. I was glad that good Deacon Sexton could be there to care for them so kindly and tenderly.

"On the 27th, six days later, I visited an uncle of mine in the 4th Iowa. On my way back that night to our own camp, I found a little knoll covered with new graves. I passed along among them wondering who were buried there. The last two I passed had head-boards. On one was the name of William Stowell, on the other Clement Boughton, both of Co. E, 12th Wisconsin. Together in life, together dying under the same tree, together lying side by side in death.

"Two noble young soldiers they were. Colonel Bryant was warmly attached to Clem. He speaks of him today [at a reunion] as 'the typical American soldier.'

"I have occasion for an especially grateful recollection of Colonel Bryant, and this is why: My right arm was in a painful condition because of being hit by a spent ball on the 21st. It was about the 24th that I was on 'alarm' guard on the works in front of our company. It was our business to rouse the men in case of any hostile move by the enemy in our front. I lay reclining on my elbow on the works just as daylight was coming in the east, and was looking intently over towards the Rebel lines. Being very tired and worn after our hard marching and fighting, and feeling sick from my swollen arm, I could scarcely keep awake. Once or twice I dozed just a minute, and felt afraid I should get to sleep if I did not get up and walk. But I was so worn out I thought I could not stand it to walk. As I lay thinking, and gazing across the field, my head dropped again and I dozed once more. Just then someone shook me, and said, 'Wake up, Bub, wake up!' I was, indeed, startled, and got upon my feet. A man was walking rapidly away from me on top of the works, but I did not see who it was. After he had gone on out of sight, the next guard to me said, 'Do you know who that was?' I said, 'No." 'Well, said he it was Colonel Bryant.'

"That was a pretty state of affairs. Colonel Bryant, commanding the brigade, had caught me asleep on guard right in the face of the enemy! I was anxious that day I wondered what he would do about it. But I never heard anything further concerning the matter. He had awakened me, and then got away from me as quickly as possible, so that I should not know who did it; and I should not have known had not the other guard told me. I suppose Colonel Bryant might have had me shot--had he been like some other officers. But he was not. He knew how to sympathize with one of his boys who was sick and wounded. That was a peculiarity of the man.

"Blessed are the merciful, for they shall obtain mercy."

CHAPTER X
The Battles of Ezra Church, Jonesboro, & the Pursuit of Hood

Hosea Rood continues: "On the evening of July 27th, just at dark, we received orders to pack up and be ready to move. Soon after we quietly filed out of our line of works, while some cavalry men remained to keep up the picket firing. We marched all night, making a circuit around the north side of the city, and halting in the morning on the northwest side, exactly opposite our position of the night before. The 15th, 16th and 17th Corps had all been thus changed in position, and they began to form in line, and to build works. About 11 o'clock Hood made a determined attack upon this new line, but he was repulsed with great loss,--about 5,000--General Sherman losing about 600. This action is known as the battle of Ezra Church.

"Our brigade was ordered that day to fill up a gap between the 15th and 16th Corps, a distance of two miles to the right. The success of the battle depended upon their getting there as soon as possible, and the most of the march was done on double-quick. The day was intensely hot, and some of our men were so overcome with the heat that they have never fully recovered; among these are William Mosier and John Gaddis. James H. Clement died a week afterward because of over exertion.

"The regiment lost two killed and eighteen wounded, our company losses being, Daniel Titus killed, and Cotton and Mathews slightly wounded. After charging to the top of a ridge and filling the gap before mentioned, our boys engaged in firing upon the enemy that lay close at hand. Titus had fired a shot at a Reb, and the fellow having been seen to fall, he was engaged in a bit of discussion with one or two others as to who brought him down. Someone suggested to Titus that if he did not get his head out of sight below the rail stockade they had just built, he might get hit himself. Dan turned his head to smile at the kindly suggestion and sank quickly upon his back never to move again. A ball had cut across his temple killing him instantly. After the battle he was tenderly buried by Nathaniel Darrow, his bunkmate, Ed Robinson and John Griffin; and Ed Bennett cut his name on a board to mark his final resting place.

"Daniel Titus was the support of aged parents who, with his six sisters, loved him passionately. The home seemed very desolate to them after his death and they were sorely stricken with grief; but they made no complaint. I think they loved their country all the better for the sacrifice made. He was a generous hearted young man, one who would divide his last cracker with a hungry comrade. He was always faithful in the performance of duty, and was much missed by all of us after having thus suddenly received his final discharge."

Following is a report of the above battle by Col. George E. Bryant, Near Atlanta, Ga., dated September 10, 1864:

"...I have the honor to report the following as the part taken by the First Brigade, Third Division, Seventeenth Army Corps, in the battle before Atlanta, July 28th:

"The brigade at 12 noon on that day was formed in two lines, facing westward and was engaged in throwing up breastworks, when the sound of heavy musketry on my right, in front of Fifteenth Corps, caused me to form in line my two reserve regiments, the Twelfth Wisconsin (Lieutenant-Colonel Proudfit commanding) and the Thirty-first Illinois (Lieutenant-Colonel Pearson commanding) Veteran Regiments of Infantry. Soon after forming them, I received orders from Major-General Howard to send my reserve regiments to the support of the Fifteenth Corps. They were immediately started on double quick, the Twelfth Wisconsin in advance, and proceeded more than a mile to the right of the Fifteenth Corps. The Twelfth Wisconsin formed on the extreme right of the army in a ravine and charged up a hill, from which our men had just been dislodged, thereby nearly turning our right flank, routing the enemy there from, capturing and killing some hundred of the foe. This position they held during the day and night following, during which time several charges were made by the enemy, but in each case easily repulsed. The regiment was protected by the slight rail breastworks built by our men, and by the enemy during the short time they held the hill, and improved by themselves after they retook the hill. The regiment lost but 2 men killed and 17 wounded. The Thirty-first Illinois, on its arrival at the Fifteenth Corps, was held in reserve for the same time and suffered no loss. The balance of the brigade, in common with the troops of the division, was exposed to an enfilading fire from the enemy's artillery, but lost but 1 man killed and 1 man wounded. The conduct of Lieutenant Colonel Proudfit and his regiment in promptly and quickly moving to the place of need, was highly commended by many officers who witnessed their acts. It was without doubt one of the important movements that saved our flank and gained us the victory."

Hosea Rood continues: "After this battle, Sherman had Atlanta practically in a state of siege, and he thus held it until the night of August 25th--nearly a month. Our regiment took place in the line about two miles northeast of where they fought on the 28th. During the month we changed position in the line several times, the object always being to get a little closer to the Rebel works. We were every day under fire, and not many days passed that did not take some of our comrades either to the hospital or the grave.

"The only loss to Company E was occasioned by the wounding of Lieutenant Thayer, August 14th. At that time we had a heavy line of works, and we felt as if we were pretty well protected; but we were never safe from danger. That day Thayer was sitting on John Ingalls' bunk, in a shady place behind the works, and talking with some of the boys grouped there. A bullet came across the works, glanced against the limb of a tree and struck him on the right side of his back, passing, I think, between the fifth and sixth ribs. The lieutenant was quickly removed to a place of safety and search was made for the ball; but it could not be found. He was then sent to the general hospital at Marietta, careful, faithful Will Mosier going with him as nurse.

"This sad event brought deep sorrow into our company. Lieutenant Thayer had been a model officer in every way and his loss coming so soon after that of Captain Gillispie, left us bereft, indeed, as Lieutenant Linnell was absent on detached service. Lieutenant Ephraim Blakeslee, of Company H, was by special order put in command of our company.

"The campaign was over and Atlanta was taken after four months of continual marching, skirmishing, fighting and sieging. In order to give a notion of the daily life of the Company during such a movement as this last, I copy from the memoranda sent to me by Lt. Alpheus Kinney and Nathaniel Darrow:"

"August 25th. Company E on picket a part of the day. At night the regiment moved to the right and rear a short distance, to see what the Rebs would do, or try to do.

"26th. Moved still further to the rear. Companies C, H, and E were sent on in the advance with pioneers from two Divisions. After marching all day, we halted at night and waited for the regiment to come up.

"On 27th of August. The regiment came up early in the morning and halted a short distance from where we were camped. After the men had rested a few hours, we marched five or six miles and stopped for a short time. Here we found a field of green corn and our men soon filled themselves with it. As we had not tasted anything of the kind for a long time. At night the 17th Army Corps moved forward some three miles and went into camp for the night."

"On the 28th. Ordered out at 7 in the morning and halted at noon on the Montgomery Railroad. A part of our brigade went to building works and the Twelfth to tearing up railroad. This was done by turning the track bottom side up, and tearing the rails from the ties. The ties were then piled up with the rails lying across the top and set afire. When the rails were red hot, six or eight men would take hold of each end of one, drag it to a tree and twist it around the tree trunk. They called this giving Jeff Davis a necktie.

"The Rebs had found out what we were doing and they threw a few shells over at us. One took an arm from the Adjutant of the 31st Illinois. I happened to be looking at him just as the ball struck. He fell from his horse as if shot through the body.

"The 29th. Still tearing up the track.

"The 30th. Started out late in the morning and in the rear of the line of march. Went into camp at 12 o'clock at night near the Macon railroad. Rained all the latter part of the night.

"The 31st. Left camp at daylight and marched to within a short distance of Jonesboro station where we threw up a line of works. Had just finished them when we were ordered to move to the right and support the 15th Corps. Just as we got into the position assigned us, the Rebs charged the 15th Corps. As soon as they found us there they backed off with broken ranks!

"September 1st. In the afternoon the 17th Corps was ordered to the rear and right. The Twelfth guarded the train.

About 12 o'clock at night a number of heavy explosions in the direction of Atlanta excited our attention. We heard afterwards that the Rebs were destroying ammunition preparatory to evacuating the place.

"The 2nd. The Rebels having left our front during the night, we were ordered to march after them in line of battle. We reached their rear guard after going some six or seven miles, and threw up a line of works, but soon left them for another advance. At night we halted and while we were throwing up breastworks, Orson Wright was shot through the face.

"The 3rd & 4th. Finished our works and laid out a camp in some order.

"The 5th. At 8 o'clock in the evening we were ordered to fall back to the rear toward Jonesboro. At midnight we halted for an hour and at daylight we were in Jonesboro. Stopped to take coffee and hard tack.

"The 6th. Marched three miles toward Atlanta and halted for the day.

"The 7th. Started out at 7 o'clock in the morning and halted at noon.

"The 8th. Marched till noon and halted near East Point where we went into camp. Got a large mail, the first since breaking the siege two weeks ago.

"The 9th. Continued our march toward Atlanta and went into camp four miles from the city. Here we built a good line of works and formed a permanent camp where we remained until the 4th of October, when we pursued Hood on his fatal Tennessee campaign.

"It was in this camp that tents were once more issued to our men, they having been without them ever since leaving Cairo on the tenth of the preceding May

"During all this time we had never been under a shelter that would keep off the rain. We fastened our rubber blankets together and put them up as well as we could and as for the rest, we tried to keep sweet tempered and endure it all".

If they thought they were going to settle down and get some rest they were mistaken. For on the 4th of October, along with other units of the 17th Corps, the Twelfth was in pursuit of Hood who was breaking up communications with Chattanooga. They marched 20 miles and camped north of the Chattahoochee. The next day moved to near Kennesaw Mountain and camped not far from Marietta where the battle of Altoona Pass had been recently fought. The garrison there had repulsed Hood and saved the supply depot. It was here the famous signal sent out atop of Kennesaw to General Corse at Altoona 18 miles away, "Hold the fort, I am coming." Corse replied, "I am short a cheek bone and an ear, but able to whip all hell yet."

The Twelfth remained in this camp until Sunday, October 9th, and then marched to Big Shanty and joined the main army on October 11th. The next day Companies A, B. and C were put to work to rebuild railroads the Rebels had destroyed and Company E was on picket duty. They skirmished with the Rebs to the northwest and went into camp at Carterville. On October 12th they camped 6 miles east of Rome and headed General Hood of at Resaca. They remained in Rome during the 13th, then marched all night toward Resaca and continued on to Adairsville.

This constant marching, early and late, sometimes all night, began to tell on the boys and they suffered from lack of sleep. The following is from Ed Bennet's "Recollections."

"We marched until evening, and then continued on during the night, occasionally halting to rest, or let the column close up; but never to lie down for some undisturbed sleep. My hard tack was about played out, I was weak, weary and never more sleepy than that October night while marching over hills, through valleys, through timberland and fields, on highways and byways and no roads at all, going to get somewhere as soon as the Johnnies did, if not sooner. If I'd had a deed to that part of the United States, I'd have swapped it then and there for one good long night of quiet, restful sleep. I wanted sleep that night more than ever before or since. I found myself staggering and nodding as we marched along, the scuffing of feet, the chafing of accoutrements, acting only as influences to make me still sleepier.

"No 'grand rounds' had ever made a sneak on my post and found me asleep, but this night I actually lost consciousness for awhile, yet marching, until I strayed outside the road and ran against a tree. My file follower, nearly as dead asleep as I myself, jamming up against me, so awakening us both that we kept awake afterwards.

"As soon as we stopped in the morning, the ground was covered with the boys who stretched themselves out and went to sleep and they slept as sweetly as if on beds of down."

All this marching was over mountainous roads and much of it was in skirmish line, that making it all the harder. From Lafayette the line of march curved to the south. General Sherman became satisfied that Hood could not be made to fight; and that if he did not move by way of Decatur into Tennessee, he would lead off into Mississippi. He felt sure that General Thomas had men enough to attend to him if he should move northward and so he resolved to put at once his long cherished plan into execution. Return to Atlanta, destroy all his communications with Chattanooga, and strike out for some place on the sea coast. He sent 25,000 men to General Thomas and gave him command of the Western Army. The sick and wounded were sent to Chattanooga. The railroad was taxed to the utmost to bring supplies down from Chattanooga after which the railroad was destroyed. All posts between Atlanta and Chattanooga evacuated, mills and factories burned. On November 14th the Twelfth marched down from their camp near Marietta. On the 15th they destroyed car shops, depots and foundries and arsenals.

Before this move, the non-veterans of the 15th and 17th Corps were ordered to get ready for a march to Chattanooga, preparatory to being mustered out. This order came to them rather unexpectedly, about the 20th of October. Colonel Bryant, whose time had also expired, led these 1500 men, and conducted several prisoners, on the 75 mile march back to Chattanooga.

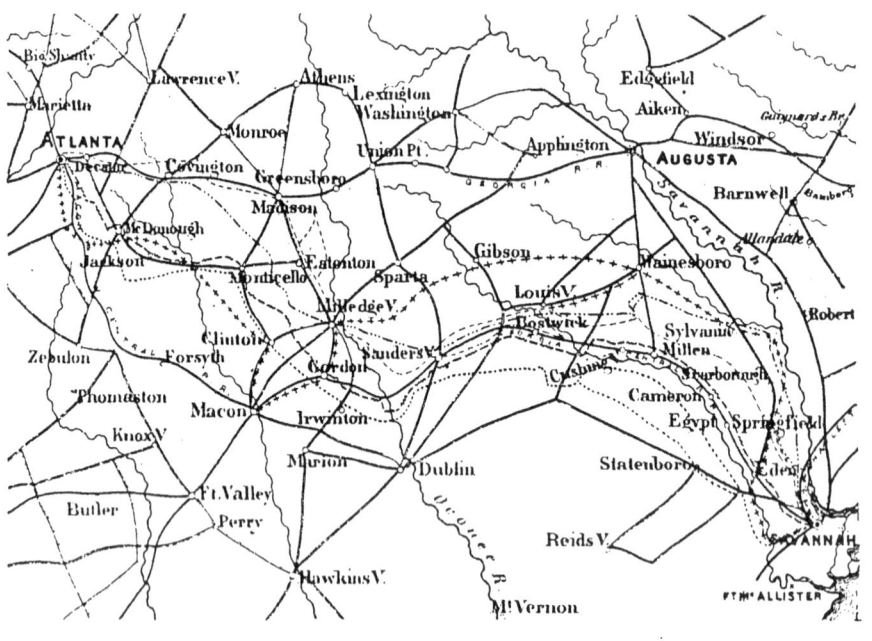

CHAPTER XI
The March to the Sea

"The mules brayed, the drivers cracked their long whips, and the boys filled what vacant space there was in the air with all the noises the human throat is capable of producing." So writes Hosea Rood.

"In the meantime the troops had been for some time moving out upon the roads leading to the southeast. The 14th Corps in the direction of Decatur [Ga.], the 15th and 17th Corps to the south of them. Soon came the order for us to fall into line. We did so quickly. Colonel Proudfit mounted his horse and shouted, 'Battalion, Right Face! Forward, March!' and we were on the 'March to the Sea.'

"We were gay that morning as we turned our backs upon the smoking ruins of Atlanta. We had been under the fire of the enemy for months. Many of our comrades who had marched out with us in the spring were sleeping under the low mounds that dotted the hillsides and valleys where we had fought the battles of the past summer, and, though we sent tender and loving thoughts back to them, we looked forward with a lively interest to the scenes before us. Of our departure, Sherman says:

'About 7 a.m. of November 16th, [1864] we rode out of Atlanta by the Decatur road, filled with the marching troops and wagons of the 14th Corps, and reaching the hill just outside the old Rebel works, we naturally paused to look back upon the scenes of our past battles. We stood upon the very ground where was fought the bloody battle of July 22nd, and could see the woods wherein McPherson fell. Behind us lay Atlanta, smouldering and in ruins, the black smoke rising high in the air and hanging like a pall over the ruined city. Away off in the distance on the McDonough road was the rear of Howard's column, the gun barrels glistening in the sun, the white-topped wagons stretching away to the south and right before us the 14th Corps, marching steadily and rapidly, with a cheery look and swinging pace, that made light of the thousand miles that lay between us and Richmond. Some band, by accident, struck up the anthem, 'John Brown's Soul Goes Marching On,' and never before or since have I heard the chorus of

'Glory, Glory, Halleluja,' done with more spirit or in better harmony of time and place.

    We turned our horses' heads to the east. Atlanta was soon lost behind the trees and became a thing of the past. Around it clings many a thought of desperate battles of hope and fear, that now seem like a memory of a dream; and I have never seen the place since. The day was extremely beautiful, clear sunlight with bracing air, and an unusual exhilaration seemed to pervade all minds--a feeling of something to come, vague and undefined, still full of venture and intense interest. Even the common soldiers caught the inspiration, and many a group called out to me as I worked my way past them; 'Uncle Billy, I guess Grant is waiting for us at Richmond.' Indeed, the general sentiment was that we were marching to Richmond and that there would be an end of the war, but how and when they seemed not to care. Nor did they measure the distance or count the cost of life or bother their brains about the great rivers to be crossed and the food required for man and beast, that had to be gathered on the way. There was a 'devil-may-care' feeling pervading officers and men that made us feel the full load of responsibility for success would be accepted as a matter of course, whereas, should we fail this 'march' would be adjudged the wild adventure of a crazy fool. I had no purpose to march direct for Richmond, but always designed to reach the sea coast first at Savannah or Port Royal, S.C., and even kept in mind the alternative of Mobile.'

    The army making this march was composed of four corps; the 15th and the 17th forming the right wing, the 14th and the 20th the left wing; also two brigades of cavalry. The right wing was in command of General Howard; the left, of General Slocum. General Kilpatrick commanded the cavalry. The artillery consisted of sixty guns.

    Everybody not able to do duty had been sent back to Chattanooga before starting. Each man carried forty rounds of ammunition in his cartridge box and the wagons contained enough to make up two hundred rounds per man. The men carried five days rations, the wagons carried twenty days and a good supply of beef on the hoof was driven along. There were 2,500 wagons, and 600 ambulances. In all, 60,598 men. Of whom 55,255 were infantrymen, 4,584 cavalrymen and 1,759 artillerymen. The Corps moved on four parallel roads if possible. The first days' march was fifteen miles. Foraging parties were made up of 30 men under a Lieutenant from each regiment and were told to take up food along the route, but not to enter houses, etc.

If inhabitants burned bridges, obstructed roads or showed hostility, Corps commanders might order devastation. Horses and mules could be appropriated (especially from the rich), able bodied negros that could be of service might be taken along. Pioneer corps were organized to clear roads and keep them in repair. Each wing of the army carried pontoon trains for crossing rivers. One assault upon a Southern woman a man would be court-martialed and shot. This proved to be a strong incentive to respect the women.

The officers issued "tanglefoot" (whiskey) after the first day of the march. It turned out to be a stronger stimulant than expected and most men regretted it on the next days' march.

The new recruits were heavily laden with all the equipment issued to them considered necessary for a day in the field. The veterans carried little more than a blanket and an oilcloth. The recruits soon learned to throw away most of the accouterments.

The tents were simple "pup tents." They'd put a bundle of hay on the floor of the tent, throw their blanket on it and considerthe bed made. At the head of the bed they generally fastened an oil cloth across the open end of the tent and built a fire of sticks or rails at the other end. This threw a genial light and warmth into their "house."

Hosea Rood: "We sat by the fire and boiled our coffee in an old oyster or fruit can to which a bail had been attached, holding it over the fire on the end of a long stick. Sometimes we set our coffee on the coals to boil; it was easier than holding it. But when something under it gave way, as the fire burned, and our delicious beverage tipped over into the coals and sent up an odor of coffee mingled with smoke, ashes, hissing cinders and 'thunder and lightning' we wished we'd tried the safer plan.

"We cooked our meat by holding it close to the fire on a forked stick, or by frying it in a frying pan made of half a tin canteen, and with a split stick for a handle. When the coffee was made and the meat fried, we lay down so as to recline on the left elbow, used our right hand to reach over after a piece of meat, a hard tack, or our coffee cup, and told stories while we ate of what happened at home 'before the war;' about our school life; discussed the causes of the war; criticized the management of our generals; speculated as to future developments; talked about the events of the day; joked one another and ate at our leisure.

"Sometimes there would be thousands of camp fires in sight, and the scene presented was a merry one. When supper was over, we sometimes sang songs and made the old woods fairly ring with music that was hearty, if not so very sweet. Some of the boys carried violins along with them for the sake of the music in camp and it was sweet enough to us poor, tired fellows. Now and then some of the lovers of the dance would clear off a spot and have what they called a 'shindig;' but such dancing parties never lasted all night. I suspect there was nothing in them that Christian people could object to. Like the dancing before the Lord of Bible times, it was done at seasonable hours and the sexes engaged in it separately,--at least one of the sexes did.

"Before long the camp fires had burned low and the great army of men lay silent in as sweet sleep as ever men enjoyed in this world. Little was heard except the tramp of the guards or the occasional braying of a mule that seemed to have troubled dreams.

"Just as we were in the sweetest of our dreams there would ring out in the distance the clear tones of a bugle. One could not help hearing it in spite of his trying not to do so. Soon another would wake the echoes in another direction and then another and another. The great camp was soon astir with life and motion. The odors of boiling coffee and frying bacon or salt pork prevaded the air and there was a clatter of tin plates and cups.

"I have said on a previous page that the march was always to begin at seven o'clock in the morning. That does not mean that all of us were to get under way at that hour. Our corps contained about 15,000 men, and these were organized into three divisions. The first division would take the lead one day, the second [division] the next, and after that the third [division]. It would take several hours to get started, especially if the roads are muddy. If the first division should start at seven o'clock, it would be nine or ten before the second could move, and noon before the third could get under way. If the roads were very bad, though the first division would camp at dark, the second division could not come up to camp before well on towards midnight, and the rear of the third might have to spend all night on the road, coming into camp about daylight. In such a case there was no chance for any sleep at all, as the division to be in advance during that day was already beginning to move. More than once we marched--or hitched along--all night, and then with scarcely a halt continued until late the following night. In general, this night marching came when there was much rain and the roads were bad; this made it all the more disagreeable."

The roads each Corps was to follow were carefully designated; as were the number of miles to be traveled each day, and the date on which they were to rendezvous. All of these conditions were fulfilled to the letter. Slocum, with the 20th Corps, arrived at Milledgeville on the 22nd, preceding Davis with the 14th Corps, by one day. On the same day Kilpatrick struck the Macon and Western railroad, destroying the bridge at Walnut Creek. The day following, Howard with the 15th and 17th Corps, arrived at Gordon, and began the destruction of the Georgia Central Railroad.

It was near here that the most serious fight of the campaign occurred up to that date. A detachment of cavalry and a brigade of infantry were sent forward to Griswoldville to make a feint towards Macon. The enemy, about five thousand strong, advanced upon our troops, who had thrown up temporary breastworks, with a section of battery in position. The Rebels were chiefly composed of militia with a few veterans of Gen. Hardee's old corps.

With the ignorance of danger common to new troops, the Rebels rushed upon the Union veterans with the greatest fury. They were received with grape-shot and musketry at point-blank range. The Rebels fell back, but then resumed the attack with the same deadly results. Our troops lost 40 killed and wounded. Their loses were 300 killed, and 2500 wounded and taken prisoners.

The following was written by Maj. George W. Nichols, Sherman's aide-de-camp who kept a diary of the march:

"This evening I walked down to the river [the Ogeechee] where a striking and novel spectacle was visible. The fires of pitch pine were flaring up into the mist and darkness; figures of men and horses loomed out of the dense shadows in gigantic proportions; torch-lights were blinking and flashing away off in the forests; and the still air echoed and re-echoed with the cries of teamsters and the wild shouts of the soldiers. A long line of the troops marched across the foot-bridge, each soldier bearing a torch, and, as the column marched, the vivid light was reflected in quivering lines in the swift running stream.

"Soon the fog, which here settles like a blanket over the swamps and forests of the river bottoms, shut down upon the scene; and so dense and dark was it that torches were of but little use, and our men were directed here and there by voice.

"Jim, are you there?" shouted one.
"Yes, I am here," was the impatient answer.
"Well, then, go straight ahead."
"Straight ahead! Where in thunder *is* 'straight ahead?'"
"And so the troops shuffled upon and over each other, and finally blundered into their quarters for the night."

As the army proceeded across Georgia an increasing number of blacks and other displaced people fell in behind Sherman's columns. Preferring the hardships and hunger and an unknown future rather than remain on the plantations where they could, at least, have had food and shelter. This rag-tag band soon amounted to over 10,000 persons who also had to forage on the Georgia countryside.

The 15th and 17th Corps camped near Millen, Ga. Again, from Maj. Nichols diary: "During our brief stay in Millen, we saw another sight which fevered the blood in our brave boys. It was the hideous prison-pen used by the enemy for the confinement of Federal soldiers who had become prisoners of war. A space of ground about three hundred feet square, inclosed by a stockade, without any covering whatsoever, was the hole where thousands of our brave soldiers have been confined for months past, exposed to heavy dews, biting frosts, and pelting rains, without so much as a board or a tent to protect them after the Rebels had stolen their clothing. Some of them had adopted the wretched alternative of digging holes in the ground, into which they crept at times. What wonder that we found the evidence that seven hundred fifty men had died there! From what misery did death release them! I could realize it all when I saw this den, as I never could before, even when listening to the stories of prisoners who had fled, escaping the villains who rushed after them in hot pursuit, and foiling the bloodhounds which had been put upon their track."

The Rebels had moved these prisoners further south on the approach of Sherman's Army. Sherman had hoped to rescue them.

There were many stragglers; men who simply took their own time. There were also men, as I am sure there have been in every army, who were opportunists. Men who could find a way to exploit almost any situation. In the Union Army they were referred to as, "bummers." They appropriated, or rather, misappropriated, every item that could be sold or exchanged for a profit. But they were equally talented when it came to acquiring needed food, horses, mules, and other supplies. They were sufficiently loyal to the cause that they could be-devil the enemy when the occasion presented itself. A few times the army found the "bummers" already occupying an objective and engaged in fighting the enemy. Because of their talents, however unscrupulous, they were pretty much allowed to operate freely while the officers looked the other way. An accepted aberation of military life.

From Millen they marched along the Georgia Central destroying it as they went. On December 7th they camped near Poolers Station, 8 miles west of Savannah. Confederate General [W.J] Hardee held the City. The Rebels made a show of defending Savannah. The 16th and 12th Wisconsin regiments formed the advance in the line of battle and moved forward, but found little opposition. Slocum's Corps pressed the siege of the city; the 15th Corps advanced on Fort McAllister; and the Union fleet was off the mouth of the Savannah River. The Fort was taken and Savannah surrendered, but Hardee and the Confederates escaped across the River into South Carolina.

The Union loss during the march to Savannah was 103 killed, 428 wounded, and 278 missing.

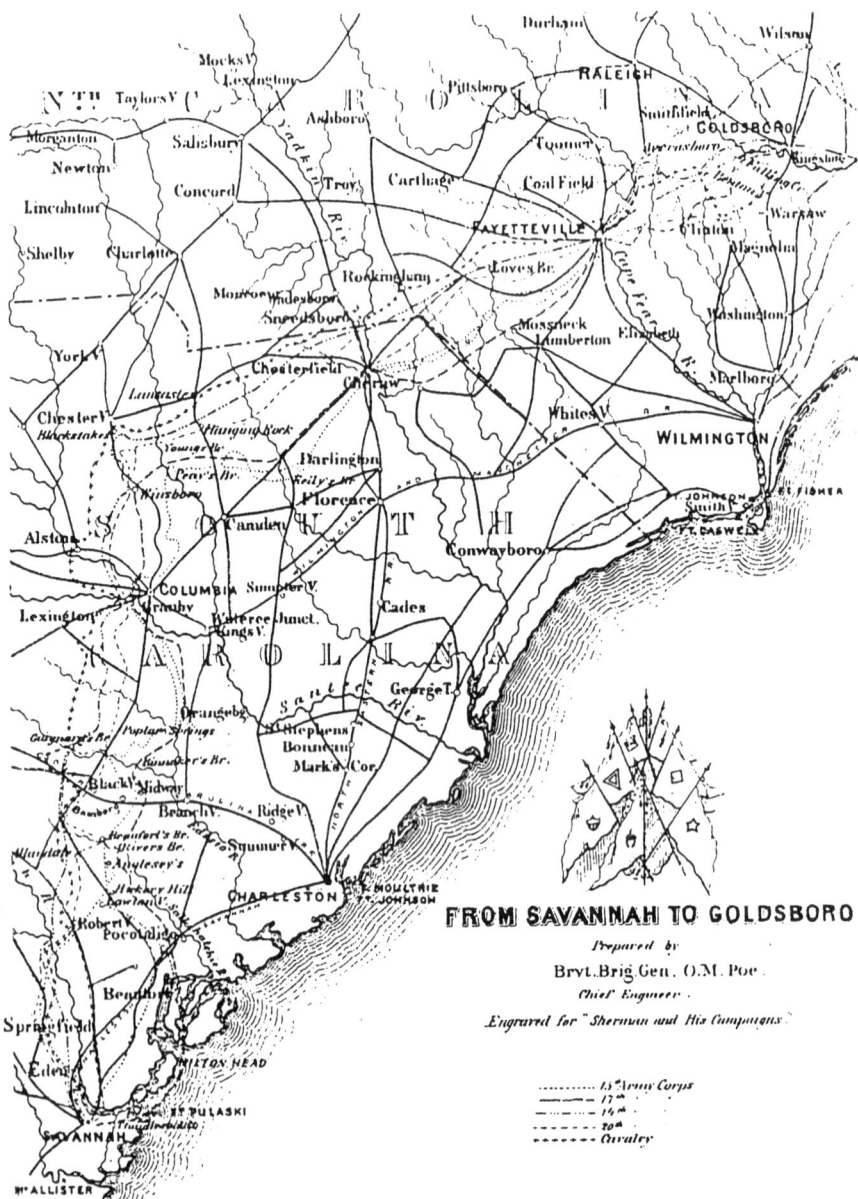

CHAPTER XII
The Carolina Campaign

The orders received by Captain Warren Langworthy [of Co. G., 12thWisc. Inf.] were as follows:

"Savannah, Ga., Dec. 21, 1864

Captain Langworthy will seize a boat and proceed down the Savannah River, and carry a verbal message to the Fleet.

By order of Gen. O. O. Howard
per Gen. M. D. Leggett"

The Union fleet lay off the mouth of the Savannah River, about twenty-three miles distant. Langworthy was to report the news of the capture of Savannah, and to order supplies to come up to Savannah instead of the Ogeechee River as previously directed by General Sherman who was now in Beaufort, South Carolina making arrangements to prevent the very movement which, on the night of December 20th, was effected by Confederate General Hardee--viz., the escape of the Confederates from Savannah by way of the railroad through Pocotaligo.

Sergeant Brown tells of their adventure: "We were fortunate in securing a fine metallic life boat, which its owner had hidden under some corn fodder in his cow-shed on the shore near where the Confederate shipping was in flames from the torch applied by its late owners.

"I confiscated a fine coil of cotton rope from the doomed ship-stores, and threw it into the boat; after which we rowed down the river, past the burning shipping, to the lower end of the wharfage. Here we landed and received final orders from General Leggett, who 'coaxed' me to surrender the coil of rope to be used for a flag-halyard at his Headquarters. He told us to stay at the coast as long as we wanted to, but to be sure to bring back some fresh oysters for him.

"Our detail consisted of first-class river men from off the Wisconsin River--(Sergeants, Elias Ticknor, and N. D. Brown; Corporals, Charles Linquist and Andrew Oleson, and Privates, Ole Albert and Thomas H. Nelson, all of Company G.)

--who cared as little for the howling of the mad waters of the Wisconsin River Rapids as for the so-called 'Rebel yell,' but here was a new experience, and the way the boys at first 'caught crabs' with their oars was amusing. They were apt learners, however, and soon profited by the skill and coaching of one of our members who had been brought up on the Niagra River. So, before the city was out of sight, we were making good progress.

"About four miles below the city we passed a Rebel fort, from which our Signal Corps had been trying in vain to communicate with Fort Pulaski. I have been told since then that J. B. Foraker, of Ohio political fame, was there when we passed, and followed us down soon after.

"About six miles below the city we suddenly found ourselves abreast of the Confederate ram, 'Savannah,' and her tender, both at anchor in a cove on the South Carolina shore. When first sighted by us there was but one man visible on her iron-clad decks; but soon the whole crew swarmed out to see what was up. With their glasses they must have seen that we were dirty and ragged enough to be their friends, and so allowed us to proceed without blowing us out of the water, which they could easily have done. We did all we could under the circumstances,--pulled our hats well down on the dangerous side, kept a civil tongue in our head, and hugged the Georgia shore.

"Soon after we passed her, the ram steamed up the river and threw shells into the city amongst their own women and children, and then dropped back to her anchorage, where, during the night, both the ram and tender were fired by their crews, thereby destroying what they could not defend.

"There were lots of old hulks sunken to obstruct the channel, but they proved no obstacle to our light craft. As we neared the coast we were met by a long, heavy swell from the ocean.

"It was getting dark when we reached Fort Pulaski, and the guards on the docks to the number of a dozen or so, mistook us for Rebels trying to run the blockade, and covering us with their muskets, called upon us to come ashore or they would annihilate us, while the heavy swells made it difficult as well as dangerous for us to land at the dock.

"Captain Langworthy, standing in the bow of the boat, and in language more forcible than polite, asked them to stop threatening to shoot, and to assist us in landing. This they did by directing us to one side of the dock, where we went ashore. When the guard became convinced of our identity they took us into the fort to the commander, Colonel Brown, of the Fifteenth New York, to whom Captain Langworthy reported the capture of Savannah with all it stores.

"Colonel Brown wrote out an order to that effect, and, calling the garrison into line, read it to them that night, setting them wild with joy. Then there was nothing too good for us. We were treated to the best to be had at the sutler's.

"There were in the fort 240 Confederate officers who had just been under fire at Charleston for retaliatory measures. They did not share the joy of the Blue-coats, but affected to doubt the truth of the news we brought.

"Captain Langworthy went aboard the fleet after supper, delivered his message and remained all night, leaving us to enjoy the boundless hospitality of the garrison.

"The next day we were put on board the small steamer 'Canonicus,' and, following General Foster's headquarters' boat, steamed up the river, leaving the life-boat with the generous garrison. On the way up the river the 'blue jackets' picked up a torpedo, and when opposite to where the ram Savannah was burned, we were fired upon by the Confederate crew, but without damaging any one, and I suppose our return fire was equally harmless.

"General Leggett ate his oysters by proxy; we were his proxies."

Hosea Rood continues: "We remained in camp at this place [Pooler's Station] from December 21st 'till January 5th, and had a much needed rest. As soon as we were settled, General Sherman wrote thus to President Lincoln:

'I beg to present you as a Christmas gift the city of Savannah, with one hundred and fifty heavy guns and plenty of ammunition, also about twenty-five thousand bales of cotton.'

"It was afterwards found that there were 250 guns and 31,000 bales of cotton--no small prize."

The army stayed in Savannah until the middle of January, 1865, held there in part by torrential rains, swollen rivers and flooded roads.

On the 5th of January the Twelfth Wisconsin, still part of the 17th Army Corps, was transported to Thunderbolt Landing about six miles south of Savannah and then transported by boat to Beaufort, on Port Royal Isle in South Carolina. It was the first time most of the men had seen an ocean. Those that knew how hunted oysters and soon taught their friends to enjoy this delicacy.

On the 14th of January, they took Pocotaligo, a town 20 miles northwest of Beaufort and along the Savannah and Charleston railroad. There was a sharp skirmish and Captain Almon Chandler of Company K was killed. On the 29th of January they began their march northward. The surrounding country was low and the rivers were high and the men were wet most of the time. The march paralled the Salkehatchie River. The pioneers were kept busy clearing roads and rebuilding bridges. The river overflowed the swamps which were 3 miles wide and one to four feet deep, interspersed with timber and under brush.

The following is a report of Brig. Gen. Manning F. Force, dated January 15, Pocotaligo, S.C.:

"I have the honor to report that Colonel Proudfit, Twelfth Wisconsin, proceeded to Salkehatchie, found the river about 100 feet wide, the turnpike bridge about 150 feet long, the bridge partially destroyed at each end, and piled with cord wood. The railroad bridge is not destroyed, but slightly damaged. The enemy have works on the other side, and opened with guns and musketry. Colonel Proudfit distinguished three embrasures, but thinks six guns were used. Negros report the force from 300 to 3,000. No one was hurt....."

The Confederates were well entrenched behind a series of breastworks with artillery to back them up, but the seasoned veterans of the 17th Corps were not to be stopped. Mower's Division literally swam or floated across the Salkahatchie amid a hail of bullets to make a frontal assault on the breastworks. More prudent units crossed down stream and were marching to flank the Confederate's position. The Rebs fled although they could have held out for days and inflicted heavy losses on the Yanks.

And thus the Twelfth Wisconsin and the rest of the 17th Army Corps, began to splash their way through the swamps and rice paddies of the one state for whom they felt genuine hatred. Maj. George Nichols writes in his diary:

"The well-known sight of columns of black smoke meets our gaze again; this time houses are burning, and South Carolina has commenced to pay an installment, long overdue, on her debt to justice and humanity."

Hosea Rood: "Came to Midway, 10 miles from Branchville on February 8th. Waded eight swamps. Very tired and wet. [They had just settled down and begun to make camp when...]--Col. Proudfit shouted 'Fall in' and we marched another 4 or 5 miles. Everything was very still, then we counter marched back to the place we had just left.

"The bummers had taken possession of the railroad that reached North Edisto on the 11th. We had just made camp on a plantation that afforded good bedding and had gotten to sleep when, again, Proudfit shouted, 'pack up.' Marched a short distance and went into camp again.

"The Twelfth was in the advance as we prepared to take Orangeburg, but most of the Rebels had gotten on a train and managed to escape, leaving about ninety of their comrades behind. The Rebs had set stores afire and there was a general conflagration when we arrived. We were put to work keeping order and fighting fires."

By the middle of February Sherman was knocking on the door of Columbia, the state's capitol, again the Rebs put up a spirited defense and again were put to flight. Sherman's capture of Columbia was a moral as well as a military victory for he had plunged his sword into the very heat of the secessionists. The Union military bands struck up "Hail Columbia" as they marched into the City. The occupation of Columbia, however, took and unexpected turn.

Hosea Rood: "We moved 30 miles north to Columbia, the capital of South Carolina, and on to dryer land. The 15th Corps had captured Columbia, but one of the bummers from the 17th Corps stole their flag and replaced it with one from the 17th Corps, so for a time we basked in the honor."

They camped northwest of the city. There was a strong wind blowing. No one is sure how the fire started, but there was soon a terrible conflagration. Sherman, his officers and all the men fought the blaze, helping the families evacuate their homes and save some of their possessions. They fought the fire all night, finally getting it under control at four in the morning. The soldiers then shared their rations with the burned out citizens. Several hundred buildings in the downtown area were destroyed.

By the end of February the armies were headed north again. The 17th Corps busy tearing up the tracks of the South Carolina Railroad as far as Winnsboro and Confederate General Beauregard rushing his troops to protect Charlotte, North Carolina. Sherman, however, wheeled his armies to the right and headed northeast towards Fayetteville, outsmarting Beauregard. Charleston fell without a fight. Sherman had cut off all supply lines and the Confederates had no choice but to abandon the city.

After marching through Winnsborough they reached the Wateree River where they were forced to march through a swamp in the pitch dark of night and did not cross the bridge across the river until daylight in a deluge of rain. They built a pontoon bridge over which six-mule teams pulling heavy wagons had to cross. It was as delicate a bit of teamstering as the boys had ever seen, but was accomplished without mishap. After the heavy rains the roads had to be corduroyed with fence posts and felled trees. Much of the work being performed by prisoners.

Changes had taken place in the Confederate army. General Joe Johnston was restored to command. Many southerners considered him equal to Lee, and Sherman had great respect for his ability. Johnston gathered together the armies of Beauregard, Hardee, Hampton and Hood and the garrisons from Charleston and Wilmington. Then hurried to cut off Sherman at a place called Cheraw, but had little time to throw up proper breastworks before the Yanks, led by the 17th Corps, were upon them. Cheraw was a depot filled with military supplies that the Rebs could not destroy before the Yanks drove them from the town. The Yanks took what they needed and destroyed the rest and then marched on towards Fayetteville.

Hosea Rood: "It was about the first day of March that we

went into camp near Cheraw. The weather was dark, cloudy and gloomy, and the roads were tramped and shaken into a jelly. We remained in camp there about three days; we were on short rations, as the country was wretchedly poor. Something occurred at this place that must have a paragraph by itself.

"The people along our route had begun to murder our foragers; that is, after having fairly captured them, they had cut their throats. Gen. Kilpatrick, on the 22nd of February, had reported to General Sherman that Wade Hampton's cavalry had murdered eighteen of his men, and left them in the road with labels upon them threatening a similar fate to all foragers. Sherman told Kilpatrick that his only alternative was to retaliate man for man at once.

"He also wrote, on February 24, to [Confederate] General Wade Hampton:

'It is officially reported to me that our foraging parties are murdered after being captured, and labeled 'death to all foragers,' one instance of a lieutenant and seven men near Chesterfield, and another of twenty near a ravine eighty rods from the main road, about three miles from Fosterville. I have ordered a similar number of prisoners in our hands to be disposed of in like manner.

'I hold about 1,000 prisoners captured in various ways, and can stand it about as long as you, but I hardly think these murders are committed with your knowledge, and would suggest that you give notice to the people at large that every life taken by them results in the death of one of your Confederates.

'Of course you cannot question my right to 'forage on the country.' It is a war right as old as history. The manner of exercising it varies with circumstances, and if the civil authorities will supply my requisitions, I will forbid all foraging. But I find no civil authorities who can respond to calls for forage and provisions, therefore must collect directly from the people. I have no doubt this is the occasion of much misbehavior on the part of our men, but I cannot permit an enemy to judge, and punish with wholesale murder.

'Personally, I regret the bitter feelings engendered by this struggle, but they are to be expected, and I simply allege that those who struck the first blow and made war inevitable, ought not in fairness to reproach us for the natural consequences. I merely assert our 'war right' to forage, and my resolve to protect my foragers life for life.'

Hosea Rood continues: "The above letter to Wade Hampton we afterwards read in a Rebel paper, and with it an answer from Hampton saying he would put to death two of the Union prisoners he held for every Rebel that Sherman should shoot in retaliation for the murdered men. All the same, General Sherman had his orders executed promptly--and that was the last of the matter. Wade Hampton backed down, and we had no more foragers murdered.

"One man of our own brigade was found murdered, a member of the 31st Illinois, and the members of his company were directed to attend to the execution of one of the Rebel prisoners held by our division. It was at our camp near Cheraw where this man was shot in retaliation. As I recall the matter, the prisoners were asked how many wished to be exchanged for the purpose of renewing their service against the Union cause, and also how many would prefer not to fight any more against the old flag. In answer to this question they separated into two groups. Among those who wished to return to their regiments, the lot was cast; it fell upon an old man who said he had, living near that place, a large family. It seemed sad to all of us that his life must be taken for such a purpose; but we did not know what else could be done. War is a stern business, anyhow, and it often calls for severe measures. I cannot undertake to say whether or not retaliation is the best thing to be done in such cases."

On the 11th of March they reached Fayettville. The Rebs foolishly tried to defend the city but were caught between two advancing columns of Sherman's army and soon fled. Fayetteville contained a huge arsenal, built by the Federal Government before the war, and put to good use by the Confederates, but as in Cheraw, it had to be completely destroyed.

Sherman sent to Wilmington, N.C., which had been evacuated by the Rebels, and asked that a boat be sent up the Cape Fear River with bread, coffee and sugar. Men without news or mail hailed the arrival of the steamer, but it brought oats, corn and hay for the horses instead of food or mail for the men. The steamer was loaded with captured cotton and sent back down the river.

Unlike South Carolina very little was burned in North Carolina. There was a vast difference in the way the army treated North Carolina.

General Joe Johnston still had 35,000 men at Raleigh. Lee reported that many men from his army were deserting. Hardee was fighting Slocum at Averysboro on the 16th, which largely involved regiments from Massachusetts attached to the 20th Corps and who lost many men. Hardee was defeated and forced to retreat to Smithfield, toward Raleigh.

Johnston's main strategy was to hit Sherman before he reached Goldsboro, at a place called "Bentonville." It was the fiercest fighting Sherman's men had encountered since Atlanta. Johnston faced Howard at Bentonville on the 19th in which the 15th Corps was hotly engaged. The Union loss at Bentonville was 1600 men, Johnston lost 3,000. The 17th Corps was also in the battle, but not where the severe fighting was. In all, it only delayed Sherman seventy hours. On the 22nd of March the advance of his army occupied Goldsboro. General Schofield, with 20,000 men from Gen. Thomas' western army had been brought east and transported by ship to Wilmington, N. C. They marched 100 miles inland to join Sherman's forces at Goldsboro. They arrived there on the 21st. Sherman arrived a couple of days later. There were nearly 100,000 men encamped.

Sherman's army had completed one of the longest and most important marches ever made by any organized army. 425 miles through hostile country, flooded with water and traversed with several large rivers. Many important cities were captured, railroads broken up, immense amounts of military equipment destroyed. Fifty days of midwinter marching with only 10 days of rest. The men were dirty, their uniforms ragged and many were without shoes. Yet, in spite of the hardships men and teams were in splendid condition, feeling they could not be beaten.

At Goldsboro they finally received a good supply of clothing and were given three weeks rest.

CHAPTER XIII
Conclusion

On the 28th of March Sherman met Grant and President Lincoln at City Point, near Richmond, Virginia. It was planned that Sherman would march on Richmond, but on April 2nd Lee abandoned Richmond and Grant went in pursuit.

Sherman's army left camp on April 10th toward Raleigh, 60 miles northwest. On the morning of April 13th they received the news that Lee had surrendered to Grant and his army paroled. The Rebs were going home. The Union soldiers were in high spirits. The bands played, the men sang and shouted. Sherman marched on through Raleigh in pursuit of Johnston who had pulled out and the Union army went into camp three miles from the town.

It was raining hard the next day as they were ordered to continue in pursuit of Johnston. They climbed a hill to an open field and found many regiments standing there in the rain.

Hosea Rood: "The troops to our left seemed crazy with joy and shouting. The cheering seemed to progress through one regiment after another with regularity, each cheering an announcement made to them. Finally, Col. Proudfit arrived and we crowded around him: 'Boys, Johnston has sent word that he would like to agree upon terms of surrender, and so we are halted. It is very likely that our chase after General Joe is at an end.' We, too, shouted and hurrahed. The rain ceased, the sky cleared to a brilliant blue as though in celebration of the end of the fighting. We set up camp on that field. It was there on April 17th we were told of the Assassination of Lincoln three days earlier. Our elation turned to shock and sadness.

"We had just been ordered again to march after Johnston when word of the final surrender came. The boys went wild with shouting and hijinks.

"On April 27th we marched back to Raleigh and on the 29th, three days after the surrender, we headed for Washington, D.C., by way of Richmond on what the boys termed the 'Foot and Walkers Railroad Line.' No pickets to put out. No enemy to worry about.

"General Blair, commander of the 17th Corps and General Logan commanding the 15th Corps had made a bet as to which corps could reach Petersburg, Virginia first. We were marched pretty hard, but didn't mind as long as we were going home. A cavalry colonel, on reaching Petersburg, telegraphed to Washington that the advance of the 17th Corps was there awaiting orders. Directions were sent back that the 17th should lead the advance of our army from there to Washington. When the main body of our Corps got to Petersburg we found the 15th all there; but the next morning they had, according to orders, to submit to our passing them and going on our way. Nathaniel Darrow has a somewhat different story to tell of this matter:

"We set out from Raleigh on Sunday evening, so as to have a fair start on the next day. In this way we got ahead of Logan, and put our Corps mark on the trees by the roadside. The following day we found marks of the 15th Corps on the trees as we advanced, and continued to find them till we came to a large river, I think the Roanoke, where our advance came to the bank and found Logan and his staff there claiming the right to cross first, as the advance of the 15th Corps was first there. Blair had to give way and go into camp two days to let Logan's corps cross; but Blair claimed that, as he did not anticipate this delay, we were likely to get out of rations. He, therefore, wanted to get a lot of wagons across, with a guard, to proceed to Petersburg for the purpose of getting a supply of provisions to bring back to us. he loaded us down with five days' rations, in order to empty the wagons, and had our best teams hitched to them. But Logan would not allow them to cross the river till his Corps was all over, and he even kept his rear from crossing till late at night, thinking that Blair would not then attempt to go over till morning.

"But Blair, with a part of a cavalry regiment as guard, and his picked teams hitched to the empty suppy wagons, crossed and drove sixty miles that same night, going by the whole of Logan's sleeping 15th Corps. Then there was a race between this supply train and Logan, with his staff, for Petersburg.

"Blair's train and cavalry so stopped up the road that Logan could not pass them. Then as they neared Petersburg, they even got to running their horses, but Blair came in ahead. He got permission from Washington to go through the city first, and we all felt highly elated over the strategy of our general. Of course, the 15th Corps had to go into camp till we passed them, and we were in no hurry; we were as slow about it as Logan had been to cross the Roanoke.

"To reward us for our victory we had all the whiskey dealt out to us we wanted, and then we were given time to sober off.

"When we marched past the 15th Corps, they were an angry lot of men. The conversation between them and us was more forcible than elegant. Indeed, it savored strongly of war. But it all ended in talk,--with a bit of crowing on our part. We marched up to near Richmond--22 miles distant--that day, May 8th, and went into camp, the 15th Corps, rather sullen, camping in our rear."

Hosea Rood: "General Halleck was in command at Richmond. His insult to General Sherman, with reference to the surrender of Johnston, had been forgotten by neither us nor our gallant commander. But now, as we had marched into his dominions, he desired to have us pass him in review in going through the city. This implied that he regarded Sherman as subordinate to his authority. Of course, Sherman resented any such action. He informed Halleck, by messenger, that if he could not pass through Richmond without being subject to his dictation he could go around it, and would do so. But Halleck took in his horns of authority, and for the very best of reasons-- he couldn't do any other way.

[Sherman had written terms of surrender which went considerably beyond what was necessary. Both he and Johnston agreed they did not have the authority to sign the document. Sherman gave his copy of the surrender terms to Grant who, in turn, showed it to Edward M. Stanton, the Secretary of War. Both men felt Sherman had included terms which were contrary to the plans Lincoln had for reconstruction and President Johnson and his cabinet rejected it. Grant returned to Sherman and diplomatically resolved the problem: Johnston was summond to a new conference and offered the same terms as were given to Lee. On April 26th, Sherman and Johnston signed the new document. Shortly after this, Stanton and General Halleck publically attacked Sherman, claiming he had willfully violated President Lincoln's orders. They stopped just short of calling him disloyal. It seemed to be an effort to drive Sherman out of public life altogether. Sherman was a hero to the people of the North and when they learned that Johnston had surrendered again, giving up 39,000 men and ending the war everywhere except the Gulf Coast, the attack had little effect. ed.]

Hosea Rood continues: "Because of this matter, we were hindered two or three days opposite Richmond, near the little town of Manchester. Our boys were so incensed that they sought in every possible way to show their indignation. They laughed at the white gloves and polished shoes of every soldier they saw belonging to the Army of the Potomac. And were a bit hard on the town as well."

They marched on to Fredericksburg, scene of the great Virginia battle ground and on the 16th passed by the battle ground of the Wilderness. On May 18th they camped near Washington, D.C. On the 23rd they moved camp to just below Long Bridge.

Hosea Rood: "This Grand Review was a fit closing scene to the great war just ending. On the 23rd of May '65, all of the Army of the Potomac that could be gotten together at Washington marched in review down Pennsylvania Avenue and passed the White House, which was the grand reviewing stand. Here upon a balcony sat President Andrew Johnson and the great generals of the war looking down upon the battle-scarred veterans of the Potomac as they marched by, proud in the thought that their work was at an end. All day long they swept by in one solid streetful of orderly moving, well disciplined soldiery.

"It would have been a great privilege for us to look upon that notable pagent, but we were in preparation for taking part in the no less interesting review of the following day. I suspect that even greater interest attached to our army than that of the Potomac. People everywhere had heard so much of 'Sherman's Bummers' and their doings that they regarded us as a fabulous lot of beings, allied perhaps to cyclops, or centaurs, or Mexican Greasers. In fact, we more than once heard ourselves mentioned in Virginia as 'Sherman's Greasers.' And so an immense mass of people crowded into Washington to see the 'menagerie' on street parade.

"When 'Ole Sol' peeped over the Maryland Hills at us on the 24th of May, he found us in a bustle of preparation. It was plain enough that something was to be done. We were rubbing the dust off our old shoes, shaking it out of our shabby coats and trousers, giving our rusty guns a rub and trying the effect of soap and hard water upon the tar, pitch, and lamp black that got stuck to us in the Carolinas.

"Just as we were getting into line, we were made happy by

a most agreeable surprise; for who should come into camp but our long-lost and deeply mourned, Captain John Gillespie. He was given a hearty greeting, but our joy in seeing him was not unmixed with sorrow. His pale face, that told plainly of much suffering, and his armless sleeve, caused no little sadness to come into our gladness. Our thoughts went back to the 21st of July, ten months before. We recalled his, 'Boys, you do me proud!' at the end of that terrible charge. His appearance among us seemed much like a resurrection from the dead.

"When all was in order, we moved up the road to the bridge, which is, I believe, a mile long, crossed over to the City and ascended the hill on which the Capitol stands; here we halted while all columns closed up. While waiting we gazed upon the great building and admired its wondrous beauty; we looked down the streets of the City, seeing here and there the spires and towers of its great churches and public buildings. We played all sorts of pranks and chased one another around. The people there abouts must have been surprised that the so-called 'Sherman's Greasers' did not steal something and set a few houses on fire.

"It was while waiting there that the heart of this writer of this sketch was made glad by his father coming to greet him. It was a happy meeting. His father and brother were members of the 37th Wisconsin, of the 9th Army Corps.

"Each regiment was formed by platoons, twelve men abreast. Each brigade preceeded by its commanding general and a brass band. Each regiment by its field officers and a martial band. It was a beautiful day. We moved around to the west side of the Capitol, along Pennsylvania Avenue to the White House, and then out to our camping ground about two miles north of the city.

"In this review there was no attempt at mere military display; the individuality of our army--if I may use the expression--was preserved. Those who watched the Potomac Army pass on the day previous, said that the men marched as if on a prize drill, erect, and as steadily as if moved by machinery; that our army, though in perfect order and straight lines, had the long, swinging step of one who has no short journey before him.

"It was an occasion worthy to be remembered. The day was beautiful. Thousands of people had gathered from all parts of the country to view the grand pagent, and see the men who had marched from Tennessee to Savannah, and from Savannah to Washington. Pennsylvania avenue was lined--*crowded*--on both sides with men, women and children; the windows were crowded, roofs covered and small boys perched in the trees. Never before was such a scene witnessed on the American continent. The President sat, surrounded by his cabinet, members of congress, foreign ministers, distinguished strangers with their wives and children, in front of the White House; all were interested spectators of what was passing before them.

"Suspended across the streets and over our heads, were all sorts of mottoes, banners and other devices to bid us welcome and do us honor; and, as we read them in passing, we felt proud that we were entitled to call ourselves 'Sherman's men.' At every step along the way handkerchiefs fluttered from fair hands, and cheers rang out from the thousands on either side of us. Besides this, it was a perfect carnival of music; patriotic airs from the bands in the procession echoed and re-echoed among the tall and stately buildings, while our drum corps rattled away at 'Yankee Doodle,' 'Dixie,' and 'The Girl I Left Behind Me.' In response to this halleluja chorus the dogs pertaining to our wagon trains barked, and the many roosters mounted on the wagon tops, or perched on the backs of our pack-mules, crowed lustily.

"One may well think of this as joyful occasion; for indeed it was. I wish I had the power to picture it to you more vividly, but it must have been *seen* rather than be *read* about, for full appreciation of it. Yet there were elements of sadness in it. Our bullet-riddled battle-flags, ragged and tattered with long exposure, told only too plainly of the perilous and severe service that had decimated our ranks. Those who looked on must have thought of these things, and I am sure that we boys whom God had spared to see that glorious day of triumph thought of our dead and wounded comrades and wished they could be with us.

"Aye, more,--wherever we turned our eyes that day, they were saddened by the heavy black drapings that told of Lincoln's death. Oh, that our beloved President--our 'Father Abraham' might have been spared to see his boys come marching home! That we might have looked upon his strong, manly, kindly face!

"The supreme moment of a 'review' in the army is that of passing the reviewing stand. Every soldier in a company has a pride in having that company pass the reviewing officer in the straightest line possible. It was hard to keep our faces straight to the front while our eye-balls strained in their sockets to see the President and the entourage surrounding him.

"We continued marching some two miles north of the City where both armies--east and west--camped in close proximity to each other. Some of our regiments did not get along very well with those of the Potomac Army alongside of which they were in camp. In some cases there were quite serious collisions. I suspect that our men were not very courteous in their manners, and that they were more than half to be blamed. Many of us found friends in the various Wisconsin regiments about us, and we enjoyed our visits with them. One day our Al Griffin had a visit with General Charles Griffin, a relative of his.

"It was on the 30th of May that General Sherman issued to his army his farewell address. It is so good that I shall copy it entire, for we shall all want to read it from time to time:

'Headquarters Military Division of the Mississippi,
In the field, Washington, D.C., May 30, 1865
'Special Field Orders, No. 76'

'The general commanding announces to the Armies of the Tennessee and Georgia, that the time has come for us to part. Our work is done, and armed enemies no longer defy us. Some of you will be detained in the service until further orders. And now, that we are about to separate, to mingle with the civil world, it becomes a pleasing duty to recall to mind the situation of national affairs when, but a little more than a year ago, we were gathered about the twining cliffs of Lookout Mountain, and all the future was wrapped in doubt and uncertainty. Three armies had come together from distant fields, with separate histories, yet bound by one common cause--the union of our country and the perpetuation of the government of our inheritance. There is no need to recall to your memories Tunnell Hill, with its Rock Face Mountain, and Buzzard Roost Gap, with the ugly forts of Dalton behind. We were in earnest, and paused not for danger and difficulty, but dashed through Snake Creek

Gap, and fell on Resaca, then on to Etowah to Dallas and Kennesaw; and the heats of summer found us on the banks of the Chattahoochee, far from home and dependent on a single line of road for supplies. Again we were not to be held back by any obstacle, and crossed over and fought four heavy battles for the possession of the citadel of Atlanta. That was the crisis of our history. A doubt still clouded our future, but we solved the problem and destroyed Atlanta, struck boldly across the state of Georgia, secured all the main arteries of life to our enemy, and Christmas found us at Savannah. Waiting there only long enough to fill our wagons, we again began a march which, for peril, labor and results, will compare with any ever made by an organized army. The floods of the Savannah, the swamps of the Cambahee and Edisto, the high hills and rocks of the Santee, the flat quagmires of the Pedee and Cape Fear rivers, were all passed in midwinter, with its floods and rains, in the face of an accumulating enemy; and after the battles of Averysborough and Bentonville, we once more came out of the wilderness to meet our friends at Goldsboro. Even than we paused only long enough to get new clothing, to reload our wagons, and again pushed on to Raleigh, and beyond, until we met our enemy suing for peace instead of war, and offering to submit to the injured laws of his and our country. As long as that enemy was defiant, nor mountains, nor rivers, nor swamps, nor hunger, nor cold had checked us; but when he who had fought us hard and persistently, offered submission, your general thought it wrong to pursue him further, and negotiations followed which resulted, as you all know, in his surrender. How far the operations of this army have contributed to the overthrow of the Confederacy, or the peace which now dawns on us, must be judged by others, not by us. But that you have done all that men could do, has been admitted by those in authority; and we have a right to join in the universal joy that fills our land because the war is over, and our government stands vindicated before the world by the joint action of the volunteer armies of the Unite States.

"To such as remain in the military service, your general need only remind you that successes in the past are due to hard work and discipline, and that the same work and discipline are equally important in the future. To such as go home, he will only say, that our favored country is so grand, so extensive, so diversified in climate, soil and productions, that every man may surely find a home and occupations suited to his tastes; and none should yield to the natural impatience sure to result from our past life of excitement and adventure. You will be invited to seek new adventure abroad; but do no yield to the temptation, for it will lead only to death and disappointment.

'Your general now bids you all farewell, with the full belief that, as in war you have been good soldiers, so in peace you will make good citizens; and if, unfortunately, new war should arise in our country, Sherman's army will be the first to buckle on the old armor and come forth to defend and maintain the Government of our inheritance and choice.

By order of
W. T. Sherman, Maj. General

Hosea Rood: General Sherman was in love with his army, and the army to a man fully believed and trusted in him. The most cordial relations always existed between him and his officers, and this 'good-bye' severed most tender ties. But, for all that, the old boys continued to cherish the same kindly feeling for the old general as long as he lived; and when he died, all who survived him were mourners."

From their camp two miles north of Washington on June 7th, they boarded a steamboat on the Ohio River. On the 12th they passed Cincinnati and soon thereafter went into camp at Louisville, Kentucky where they remained for some weeks. The camp commandant was General Logan whom the men knew and who was a favorite of theirs. General Sherman was also there for a last 'goodbye' to his troops.

The last of the Division to leave, which included the Twelfth Wisconsin, left camp on the 18th of July. They were transported to Chicago on open flat cars, dangerously crowded together and fearful of being knocked off by every jolt of the train. To add to their discomfort, it rained.

They arrived in Chicago on July 20th. Chicago was more hospitable. Again they were marched to the Soldier's Home and treated to a hot meal and waited upon by the many young women who volunteered there. Wisconsin was more generous to their soldiers in the matter of transportation and the men boarded passenger cars for the trip to Madison where they arrived on July 21st. They had already received their discharge so they soon after disbursed to their homes throughout the state.

In all, the Twelfth Wisconsin Infantry Volunteer Regiment had been transported by steamboat 3,159 miles; transported by railroad 2,506 miles; and marched 3,838 miles; and had lost 329 men, killed, died of wounds, disease or accidents.

ROSTER
TWELFTH WISCONSIN VOLUNTEER INFANTRY

FIELD AND STAFF

OFFICERS

Colonels

GEORGE E. BRYANT, Madison. Rank Sep. 27, '61. In comd. 3d Brig., 4th Div., 16th A.C., from Feb. 5, '63, to Jun. 10, '63; in comd. 1st Brig.., 3rd Div., 17th A.C., from Jul. 22, '64; M.O. Nov. 6, '64, term exp.
JAMES K. PROUDFIT, Madison. Rank Nov. 21,'64. Adjt., Sep. 27,'61; Lt. Col., Jul. 30, '63; A.A.A.G., Feb. 19, '63; Bvt. Brig. Gen. U.S.Vols., Mar.13'65; M.O.Jul 16, '65.

Lieutenant Colonels

DEWITT C. POOLE, Madison. RankSep. 25, '61. Res. Jul. 3, '63; Lieut. Col., V.R.C., Nov. 15, '63; M.O. Feb. 10, '66.
WILLIAM E. STRONG, Racine. Rank Nov. 21, '64. From Capt. Co. F. 2nd Wis. Inf; Maj., Sep. 7, '61; Asst. Insp. Gen., Dec. 13, '62; Bvt. Col., U.S. Vols., Sep. 1, '64; Brig. Gen. U.S. Vols., Mar. 21, '65; M.O. Sep. 1, '66.

Majors

JOHN M. PRICE, Barton. Nov. 21, '61. From Capt. Co. D; wnd. Dec. 19, '64, Savannah, Ga.; died Dec. 20, '64, wnds.
CARLTON B. WHEELOCK, Green Bay. Rank Jan. 6, '65. From Capt. Co.H; M.O. Jul 16, '65.

Surgeons

LUTHER H. CARY, Greenbush. Oct. 9, '61. Med. Insp. 16th A.C., May 10, '63; res. June. 22, '63.
EZRA M. ROGERS, Cascade. Oct. 10, '63. 2nd Asst. Surg., Aug. 13, '62; 1st Asst. Surg., Sep. 14, '62; M.O. Jul. 16, '65.

1st Asst. Surgeons

ELIJAH A. WOODWARD, Sun Prairie. Oct. 2, '61. Res. Apr. 16, '62.
AMAZIAH B. CARY, Fond du Lac. Apr. 29, '63. Died Sep. 14,'62, in Fond du Lac, Wis. disease.
SAMUEL L. MARSTON, Fond du Lac. Oct. 10, '63. 2nd Asst. Surg., Jul. 14, '63; M.O. Jul. 16, 65.

2nd Asst. Surgeons

F. ST. SURE LINDSFELDT, Sheboygan. Sep. 28, '61. Prom. Surg. 8th Wis. Battery, May 26, '62.

DEWITT BENNETT, Janesville. Sep. 17, '62. Res. Jan. 16, '63.
SHERWOOD E. SEELY, Richmond. Jul. 20, '64. From private Co. A; M.O. Jul. 16, '65.

Adjutant

LEVI M. BRESEE, Madison. Jul. 30, '63. From 2nd Lieut. Co. I; A.A.A.G., Jul. 1, '65; M.O. Jul. 16, '65.

Quartermasters

ANDREW SEXTON, Madison. Sep. 27, '61. A.A.Q.M., Mar. 5, '63; M.O. Nov. 26, '64, term exp.
FRANK B. BRYANT, Madison. Nov. 21, '64. From Q.M.Sergt; M.O. July 16, '63.

Chaplains

LEMUEL B. MASON, Madison. Nov. 1, '61. Res. Aug. 14, '63.
HENRY J. WALKER, Delona. Jul. 2, '64. From Co. A; M.O. Jul 16, '65.

NON-COMMISSIONED OFFICERS

Sergeant Majors

Charles Reynolds, Madison. Aptd. Sep. 27, '61. From Co. A; prom. 2nd Lieut. Co. A, Mar. 19, '62.
Henry Vilas, Madison. Aptd. May 1, '62. From Q.M. Sergt; prom. 2nd Lieut. Co. E 23rd Wis. Inf., Aug. 7, '62.
Harlan P. Bird, Menekaune. Aptd. Oct. 16, '62. From Co. F; prom 2nd Lieut. Co. G, Mar. 10, '63.
Norman S. Gillson, West Bend. Aptd. May 3, '63. From Co. D; disch. Oct. 13, '63, by order.
Augustus H. Johnson, Reedsburg. Aptd. Nov. 1, '63. From Co. B; Vet.; trans. to Co. A, Dec. 23, '64.
Robert R. Campbell, Green Bay. Aptd. Jan. 1, '65. From Co. H; M.O. Jul 16, '65.

Q. M. Sergeants

Henry Vilas, Madison. Aptd. Nov. 7, '61. Sergt. Major, May 1, '62.
Frank B. Bryand, Madison. Aptd. May 1, '62. From Co. C; Vet.; prom. Q.M., Nov. 21, '64.
Maurice A. Macauly, Lindina. Aptd. Jan. 1, '65. From Co. E; M.O. Jul. 16, '65.

Com. Sergeants

Levi M. Bresse, Madison. Aptd. Sep. 27, '61. Prom 2nd Lieut. Co. I, Mar. 19, '62.

William Stevens, Madison. Aptd. Jul. 1, '62. From Co. C; Vet.; prom. 1st Sergt. Co. C, Sep. 22, '64.
Francis Granger, Trenton. Aptd. Feb. 1, '65. From Co. D; M.O. Jul. 16, '65.

Hospital Stewards

Joseph W. Curtis, Madison. Aptd. Sep. 27, '61. Vet.; M.O. Nov. 23, '64, by order, for enl. as Hosp. Steward in U.S.A.
Bartlett Ashbaugh, Prescott. Aptd. Jan 1, '65. From Co. I; M.O. Jul. 16, '65.

Principal Musicians

Orrin C. Jillson, Delavan. Disch. Aug. 18, '62, by order.
Frederick E. Grimmer, Wauston. Disch. Aug. 18, '62, by order.
Robert M. Leighty, Viroqua. Aptd. Jan. 1, '64. From Co. C; M.O. Jul 16, '65.
Truman H. Hurlbut, Fairfield. Aptd. Jan. 1, '64. From Co. E; M.O. Jul. 16, '65.

Band

Bannan, James, Sturgeon Bay. Aptd. Oct. 14, '61. Trans to Co. H. Aug. 15, '62.
Barnes, William H., Elkhorn. M. O. Aug. 18, '62, by order.
Bartells, Frederick, Madison. Aptd. Nov. 15, '61. M.O. Aug. 18, '62, by order.
Bulow, Edward, Reedsburg. Aptd. Sep. 26, '61. Trans to Co. B. Aug. 15, '62.
Dipple Charles A, Fayette. M.O. Aug. 18, '62, by order
Dove, James, Elkhorn. Disch.
Gaylord, Josiah W., Elkhorn. M.O. Aug. 18, '62, by order.
Latham, Edward M., Elkhorn. M.O. Aug. 18, '62, by order.
Morehouse, Abram, Elkhorn. M.O. Aug. 18, '62, by order.
Potter, Parclete, Elkhorn. M.O. Aug. 18, '62, by order.
Potter, Monroe, Elkhorn.
Rice, Theodore F., Fitchburg. M.O. Aug. 18, '62, by order.
Robbins, Edwin B., Delavan. M.O. Aug. 18, '62, by order.
Shaver, Henry J., Elkhorn. M.O. Aug. 18, '62, by order.
Stansbury, Odgen, Elkhorn. Disch. Apr. 16,'62, disability.
Straight, Joel N., Woodland. Aptd. Oct. 17, '61. From Co. H; trans to Co. G. Aug. 18, '62.
Straight, David H., Pennington. M.O. Aug. 18, '62, by order.
Staight, Charles W., Manchester. M.O. Aug. 18, '62, by order.
Westcott, Willett R., Farmington. Aptd. Sep. 21, '61. From Co. D; trans to Co. D, Aug. 18, '62.
Young, Charles E., Prescott. Aptd. Sep. 21, '61. From Co. A; disch. Dec. 18, '61.

ROSTER OF COMPANY "A"

OFFICERS

Captains

NORMAN McLEOD; Prescott. Rank Oct. 9, '61. Res. Mar. 20, '62.
ORRIN F. MAXSON; Prescott. Rank Mar. 19. '62. 1st Lieut., Oct. 9, '61; res. Sept. 18, '64.
CHARLES REYNOLDS; Madison. Rank Oct. 7, '64. From Sergt. Maj.; 2nd Lieut., Mar. 19, '62; 1st Lieut., Apr. 7, '63; Actg. Adjt.; A.A.A.G. to Gen Ewing, since May 7, '65; M.O. Jul. 16, '65.

First Lieutenants

JAMES W. LUSK; Reedsburg. Rank Mar. 19, '62. From 2nd Lieut. Co. B; res. Apr. 7, '63.
WALLACE KELSEY; Owatonna. Rank Oct. 7, '64. Enl. Oct. 30, '61; Vet., Sergt., 1st Sergt.; 2nd Lieut., Jan. 21, '64; M.O. Jul. 16, '65.

Second Lieutenants

FRANCIS HOYT; Prescott. Rank Oct. 21, '61. Enl. Sep. 21, '61; prom. 1st Lieut. Co. I, Mar. 19, '62.
GORDON ALLEN; Sundersfield, MA. Rank Apr. 7, '63. Enl. Oct. 30, '61; Sergt., 1st Sergt.; died Aug. 4, '63.
ALVA McKEE; Brockford, MN. Rank Oct. 7, '64. Enl. Oct. 30, '61; Vet., Sergt., 1st Sergt; on Gen. Blair's Staff; M.O. Jul. 16, '65.

Enlisted Men

Aldrich, Lumbard B.; Prescott. Enl. Dec. 21, '63. M.O. Jul. 16, '65.
Allen, John E.; Hudson. Enl. Oct. 30, '61. Vet., Corp., Sergt.; M.O. Jul. 16, '65.
Anderson, Sven; Rush River. Enl. Oct. 13, '61. Disch. Dec. 16, '62, disability.
Anderson, Andrew; Rush River. Enl. Oct. 7, '61. Disch. Dec. 16, '62, disability.
Asbury, William H.; Victory. Enl Jan. 4, '64. From Co. A, 25th Wis. Inf.; M.O. Jul. 16, '65.
Ashbaugh, Bartlett; Prescott. Enl. Oct. 18, '61. Trans to Co. I, Dec. 31, '61.
Baker, Florence; Prescott. Enl. Sep. 29, '61. Trans to Co. G, Dec. 31, '61.
Balcom, James; Kinnickinnick. Enl. Oct. 11, '61. Trans to Co. I, May 1, '64.
Barlow, Henry; Prescott. Enl. Sep. 21, '61. Died Feb. 16, '64, St. Louis, Mo., disease.

Barrett, Francis M.; Prescott. Enl. Aug. 13, '63. Wnd. Atlanta; M.O. Jul. 16, '65.
Barrett, Albert J.; Prescott. Enl. Sep. 25, '61. From Co. G; Corp.; wnd. Atlanta; M.O. Jul. 16, '65.
Bartlett, Ezra J.; Prescott. Enl. Dec. 12, '63. M.O. Jul. 29, '65.
Beardsley, Alva S.; Perry. Enl. Feb. 6, '64. Wnd, Pocotaligo; M.O. Jul. 16, '65.
Beebe, Charles A.; New Richmond. Enl. Oct. 8, '61. Died Oct. 1, '63, Natchez, Miss.
Bennett, Cyrus C.; Centre Grove. Enl. Feb. 26, '61. From Co. A, 25th Wis. Inf.; M.O. Jul. 16, '65.
Benton, Ledyard E.; Springvale. Enl. Feb. 25, '64. M.O. Jul 16, '65.
Berry, Philip; Bergen. Enl. Jan. 4, '64. From Co. A. 25th Wis. Inf.; M.O. Jul. 16, '65.
Blaisdell, Nathaniel; Diamond Bluff. Enl. Sep. 25, '61. Trans to Co. I, May 1, '64; rejd. May 23, '64; M.O. Oct. 30, '64, term exp.
Blaisdel, Elijah; Diamond Bluff. Enl. Oct. 30, '61. Vet.; M.O. Jul. 16, '65.
Borner, John G.; Prescott. Enl. Sep. 25, '61. Disch. Dec. 21, '62, disability.
Boughton, Ezra; Prescott. Enl. Sep. 25, '61. Musician; died Jan. 24, '64, Natchez, Miss., disease.
Boughton, Hart; Prescott. Enl. Nov. 19, '61. Trans. to Co. G. Dec. 31, '61.
Bowen, George; Harrison. Enl. Oct. 18, '64. M.O. Jul. 16, '65.
Bowers, Henry; Marinette. Enl. Sep. 11, '62. From Co. H; killed in action, Jul 21, '64, Atlanta, Ga.
Brisbin, William O.; Muscatine, IA. Enl. Oct. 2, '61. Trans to Co. I, Dec. 31,'61.
Brooks, Nelson; Kinnickinnick. Enl. Oct. 30, '61. Vet., Corp.; M.O. Jul. 16, '65.
Buchanan, Franklin H.; Victor. Enl. Jan. 12, '64. From Co. A 25th Wis. Inf.; M.O. Jul 16, '65.
Burgeson, Abraham; Tuston. Enl. Oct. 12, '61. M.O. Jul. 16, '65.
Burnett, William A.; Clifton Mills. Enl. Oct. 30, '61. Vet., Corp.; M.O. Jul. 16, '65.
Canniff, Jeremiah; Prescott. Enl. Jan. 15, '61. Wnd. Atlanta; M.O. Jul. 16, '65.
Carr, Thomas; Bellville. Enl. Dec. 30, '61. Vet.; M.O. Jul. 16. '65.
Carr, John; La Crosse. Enl. Dec. 23, '63. M.O. Jul. 16, '65.
Caruthers, John; River Falls. Enl. Sep. 23, '61. Trans. to Co. I, May 1, '64; rej'd May 26, '64; Sergt.; M.O. Oct. 30, '64, term exp.
Chadwick, Albert; Star Praire. Enl. Feb. 25, '64. M.O. May 10, '65.
Chrisjohn, John; Oneida. Enl. Oct. 10, '64. M.O. Jul. 16, '65.
Cleveland, Edmund O.; Prescott. Enl. Oct. 30, '61. Vet.; M.O. Sep. 1, '65.
Colgan, James M.; River Falls. Enl. Sep. 23, '61. Died Camp Butler, Tenn., disease.
Comstock, Benjamin B.; Lawrens, NY. Enl. Sep. 21, '61. Did Jul 17, '62, Humboldt, Tenn., disease.

Connolly, William T.; River Falls. Enl. Sep. 23, '61. Died Mar. 19, '62, disease.
Copp, Joseph M.; Prescott. Enl. Sep. 21, '61. Corp.; pris. Atlanta; M.O. Jan. 16, '65, term exp.
Core, John; Madison. Enl. Feb. 27, '64. From Co. A, 25th Wis. Inf.; M.O. Jun. 6, '65.
Costello, Richard; Diamond Bluff. Enl. Oct. 30, '61. Vet., Corp.; M.O. Jul. 16, '65.
Crippin, John F.; Prescott. Enl. Oct. 30, '61. Vet., Corp., Sergt.; wnd. Atlanta; M.O. Jul. 16, '65.
Dale, Wilber P.; River Falls. Enl. Sep. 23, '61. Trans to Co. G. Dec. 31, '61; rej'd May 1, '62; trans to Co. I, Mar. 1, '64.
Darnall, Samuel; Forest. Enl. Feb. 2 '63. From Co. A, 25th Wis. Inf.; Corp.; M.O. Jun. 21, '65.
Davis, Isaac; Willow Springs. Enl. Oct. 12, '64. M.O. Jul. 16, '65.
Davis, Leander D.; Clifton. Enl. Dec. 21, '63. Died Mar. 13, '64. Memphis, Tenn., disease.
Dennison, William S.; Hastings, MN. Enl. Sep. 30, '61. Disch. May 18, '63, disability.
Denham, Morris; Pleasant Valley. Enl. Feb. 23, '64. Wnd. Atlanta; trans to V.R.C., Apr. 24, '65; M.O. Jul. 29, '65.
Deyarmond, Charles; River Falls. Enl. Sep. 23, '61. Died Mar. 7, '62, Leavenworth, Kan.
Dickinson, Samuel W.; River Falls. Enl. Oct. 13, '61. Disch. Jun. 7, '62.
Dresser, David L.; Kinnickinnick. Enl. Oct. 30, '61. Vet.; killed in action Jul. 21, '64, Atlanta, Ga.
Ducy, John; Moscow. Enl. Oct. 11, '64. Died Mar. 21, '65, in N.C., wnds. recd, at Bentonville.
Farnsworth, Erastus G.; River Falls. Enl. Dec. 22, '63. M.O. Jul. 16, '65.
Fisher, Charles; Clifton. Enl. Jan. 4, '64. M.O. Jul. 16, '65.
Fry, Isaiah; Ridgeway. Enl. Oct. 13, '64. M.O. Jul. 16, '65.
Gallagher, Edward; Elpaso. Enl. Jan. 12, '64. M.O. Jul. 16, '65.
Garland, Royal;Diamond Bluff. Enl. Dec. 18, '63. Trans to Co. C, May 24, '64.
Garit, Frederick; Martell. Enl. Nov. 7, '61. Vet.; M.O. Jul. 16, '65.
Gazelle, George; Castleton. Enl. Oct. 15, '64. M.O. Jul. 16, '65.
George, Jasper P.; Prescott. Enl. Dec. 28, '63. M.O. Jul. 16, '65.
Gibbs, James; River Falls. Enl. Oct. 13, '61. Died Oct. 1, '63, St. Louis, Mo.
Gibson, Arrington; River Falls. Enl. Sep. 23, '61. Sergt.; disch. Apr. 29, '62.
Gibson, Robert; River Falls. Enl. Oct. 30, '61. Vet., Corp., Sergt.; M.O. Jul. 16, '65.
Gielstad, Hans C.A.; Martell. Enl. Jan. 19, '64. Disch. Feb. 21, '65, disability.
Goodwin, George H. D.; River Falls. Enl. Sep. 30, '61. Disch. Jun. 7, '62.
Griffith, Zachariah; New Richmond. Enl. Oct. 3, '61. Disch. Jul.1, '62.
Hagar, John N.;Frontenac, MN. Enl. Oct. 30, '61. Vet.; M.O Jul. 16, '65.

Hammar, Nathan K.;Prescott. Enl. Oct. 30, '61. Vet.; M.O Jul. 16,'65.
Hanningson, Christian; Prescott. Enl. Aug. 19, '63. M.O. Jul. 16, '65.
Hawley, Miles L.;River Falls. Enl. Oct. 30, '61. Vet.; MO Jul. 16, '65.
Heimpel, Gottleib C.;New Richmond. Enl. Oct. 30, '61. Vet.; M.O. Jul. 16, '65.
Herriman, Peter H.; Hudson. Enl. Oct. 30, '61.
Hey, John T.; Rush River. Enl. Oct. 25, '61. Vet.; M.O. Jul. 29, '65.
Higbee, Chester G.;River Falls. Enl. Oct. 2, '61. 1st Sergt.; prom. 2nd Lieut. Co. B, Mar. 19, '62.
Hodges, William H.; Hudson. Enl. Oct. 30, '61. Vet.; killed in action, Jul. 21, '64, Atlanta, Ga.
Holman, James H.; Prescott. Enl. Oct. 30, '61. Vet.; wnd. Atlanta; died Sep. 17, '64, Marietta, Ga., wnds.
Holman, Hollis N.; Prescott. Enl. Sep. 23, '61. M.O. Oct 30, '64, term exp.
Hope, George W.; Diamond Bluff. Enl. Oct. 30, '61. Trans. to Co. I, May 1, '61; rejd. May 31, '64.
Howes, Walter M.; Prescott. Enl. Sep. 21, '61. Disch. Sep. 29, '62, disability.
Hudson, Josiah K.; Centerville. Enl. Oct. 22, '61. Trans. to Co. G, Dec. 31, '61.
Huddleston, Samuel; Prescott. Enl. Dec. 26, '63. Wnd. Atlanta; M.O. Jul. 16, '65.
Hull, William H.; Martell. Enl. Jan. 19, '64. M.O. Jul. 16, '65.
Hulverson, Tobion; Martell. Enl. Jan. 25, '64. Pris. Atlanta; wnd. Pocotaligo; M.O. May 23, '65.
Humphrey, Benjamin I.; New Richmond. Enl. Oct. 30, '61. Vet.; killed in action, Aug. 11, '64, Atlanta, Ga.
Hunter, John; Diamond Bluff. Enl. Dec. 18, '63. Wnd. Atlanta; disch. May 26, '65, disability.
Hunt, William G.; Prescott. Enl. Dec. 15, '63. M.O. Jul. 16, '65.
Huntington, Charles F.; New Richmond. Enl. Oct. 5, '61. Disch. Jul. 1, '62.
Hyatt, Bruner D.; Prescott. Enl. Oct. 3, '61. Disch. Jun. 7, '62, disability.
Hyatt, Sydney G.; Prescott. Enl. Dec. 28, '63. Trans to Co. C, May 24, '64.
Jay, William S.; Trimbelle. Enl. Oct. 11, '61. Trans. to V. R. C. Mar. 15, '64.
Jewell, Philip B.; Hudson. Enl. Oct. 30, '61. Vet.; trans. to V.R.C., Sep. 4, '64; disch. May 7, '65, disability.
Johnson, Augustus H.; Reedsburg. Enl Sep. 18, '61. From Sergt. Major; M.O. Jul. 22, '65.
Johnson, John J.; New Centerville. Enl. Nov. 7, '61. Died Jun. 22, '62, Columbus, Ky., disease.
Jones, John D.; Marinette. Enl Sep. 24, '62. From Co. H; deserted May 1, '64.
Kinney, Morgan D.; River Falls. Enl. Dec. 22, '63. Trans. to Co. C., May 24, '64.
Kitetinger, Thomas W.; Paris. Enl. Oct. 12, '64. M.O. Jul. 16, '65.
Kyle, James; Pleasant Valley. Enl. Feb. 22, '64. M.O. Jul. 16, '65.

Lafoe, Lewis; New Centerville. Enl. Nov. 7,'61. Vet.; M.O. Jul. 16, '65.
Law, Harvey, Jr.; New Richmond. Enl Oct. 30, '61. Vet.; M.O. Jul. 16, '65.
Lease, John N.: Point Douglas, MN. Enl. Oct. 30, '61. Vet.; M.O. Jul. 16, '65.
Lee, Archibald; Viroqua. Enl. Oct. 3, '61. From Co. A, 25th Wis. Inf.; M.O. Jul. 16, '65.
Lester, Erastus S.; Clifton. Enl. Dec. 21, '63. Wnd, Atlanta; M.O. Jul. 16, '65.
Letson, Albert H.; New Centreville. Enl. Oct. 8, '61. Trans. to Co. G, Dec. 31, '61.
Levings, Edward D.; River Falls. Enl. Oct. 30, '61. Vet.; M.O. Jul. 16, '65.
Levings, Homer W.; River Falls. Enl. Oct. 30, '61. Vet.; M.O. Jul. 16, '65.
Libbey, Warren; Hammond. Enl. Sep. 23, '61. Trans. to Co. I, May 1, '64; rejd. May 23, '64; Sergt.; M.O. Oct 30, '64, term exp.
Loring, Horace G.; River Falls. Enl. Sep 23, '61. Died Oct. 14, '63, St. Louis, Mo.
Meacham, Cornelius E.; Prescott. Enl. Sep. 21,'61. Corp.; M.O. Oct. 30, '64, term exp.
Merriman, James M.; Clifton. Enl. Dec. 21, '63. M.O. Jul. 16, '65
McConnell, John A.; Prescott. Enl. Jan. 4, '74. M.O. Jul. 16, '65
McClurg, Robert J.; Bergen. Enl. Jan. 12, '64. From Co. A, 25th Wis. Inf.; M.O. Jul. 16, '65.
McCrillis, John H.; Sterling. Enl. Feb. 29, '64. From Co. A, 25th Wis. Inf.; M.O. May 10, '65.
McCann, Christopher.; Beetown. Enl. Oct. 19, '64. Pris. Nov. 20, '64, in Ga.
McCallum, John; Prescott. Enl. Aug. 19, '63. M.O. Jul. 16, '65.
McCormick, Patrick; New Richmond. Enl. Oct. 30, '61. Vet., Corp.; M.O. Jul. 16, '65.
McGeorge, James; Prescott. Enl. Oct. 28, '61. Corp.; died Oct. 12, '63, Natches, Miss.
McIntyre, Dougald; Cottage Grove, MN. Enl. Sep. 21, '61. Died Aug. 25, '63, Natches, Miss., disease.
McLaughlin, David W.; Perry. Enl. Feb. 6,'64. M.O. Jul 16, '65.
McLeod, Eugene V.; Prescott. Enl. Sep. 21,'61. Disch. Apr. 23, '62.
McMillan, John; Prescott. Enl. Sep. 21, '61. Trans. to Co. I, Mar. 1.'64.
McPilson, David; Trenton. Enl. Feb. 29, '61. Trans to Co. C, May 24, '64.
Miley, James; Prescott. Enl. Oct. 23, '61. Killed in action, Jun. 21, '63, Vicksburg, Miss.
Miller, Charles F.; Clifton. Enl. Dec. 21, '63. M.O. Jul. 16, '65.
Miller, Alonzo; Prescott. Enl. Dec. 28, '63. M.O. Jul. 16, '65.
Miles, George F.; Prescott. Enl. Dec. 26,'64. Wnd. Atlanta; M.O. Jun. 12, '65.
Miner, William E.; New Centreville. Enl. Oct.30, '61. Vet.; M.O. Jul. 16, '65.

Moulton, William E.;Calais, ME. Enl. Oct. 3, '61. Disch.Jun.7, '62.
Nelson, Peter; Martell. Enl. Oct. 28, '61. Died Jan. 27, '63, Bolivar, Tenn., Disease.
Nichols, James G.; Hastings, MN. Enl. Sep. 21, '61. Died Aug. 28, '63, on Hosp. Boat, disease.
Northrop, David B.; Hudson. Enl. Oct. 3, '61. Died Jul. 26, '63, St. Louis, Mo., disease.
Oleson, Julius O.; Prescott. Enl. Oct. 30, '61. Vet.; killed in action Jul. 21, '64? unofficially reported pris.
Oleson, Ole O.; New Centreville. Enl. Oct. 13, '61. Trans to Co. G, Dec. 31, '61.
Olin, Anthony N.; River Falls. Enl. Oct. 30, '61. Vet.;M. O. Jul. 16, '65.
Otis, John A.; Trimbelle. Enl. Dec. 18, '63. Died Jun. 11, '64, Rome, Ga., disease.
Ottman, Andrew F.; Trimbelle. Enl. Oct. 30, '61. Vet.; Corp.; wnd, Atlanta; trans. to VRC Apr. 24, '65; M.O. Jul. 28, '65.
Parker, William; Ridgewood. Enl. Oct. 11, '64. M.O. Jul. 16, '65.
Patterson, Jacob B.; River Falls. Enl. Sep. 18, '61. Died Apr. 1,'62, Weston, Mo.
Pierce, Elgreen C.; Parks Cor's,ILL. Enl. Oct. 30, '61. Vet., Sergt.; pris. Dec. 25, '62;M.O. Jul 16, '65.
Prebble, Jeremiah; Troy. Enl. Jan. 4, '64. M.O. Jul. 16, '65.
Prescott, George W.; New Centerville. Enl. Oct. 19, '61. Died Nov. 8,'62, Bolivar, Tenn., disease.
Pulham, William; Victory. Enl. Jan. 4, '64. From Co. A, 25th Wis. Inf.; M. O. Jul. 16, '65.
Pulver, John W.; Springville. Enl. Jan. 4, '64. From Co. A. 25th Wis. Inf.; M.O. Jul. 16, '65.
Pumplin, William L. H.; Trenton. Enl. Sep. 27, '61. Died Jul 6, '63, Vicksburg, Miss, disease.
Quirk, John; Prescott. Enl. Sep. 21,'61. Died Aug. 11, '63, St. Louis, Mo.
Reynolds,Lewis; River Falls. Enl. Sep.23, '61. Disch. Apr. 29, '62.
Roberts, Henry T.; Victory. Enl. Jan. 5,'64. From Co. A, 25th Wis. Inf.; M.O. Jul. 16, '65.
Roberts, Samuel C.; New Richmond. Enl. Oct. 30, '61. Vet., Corp,; pris. Atlanta; M.O. Jul. 16, '65.
Rockstad, John C.; Martell. Enl. Oct. 7, '61. Trans to Co. G. Dec. 31, '61.
Rockstad, Ole C.; Martell. Enl. Oct. 7,'61. Trans to Co. G. Dec.31,'61.
Roesch, Herman; Waterloo. Enl. Oct. 15, '64. M.O. Jul. 16, '65.
Rogers, Josiah B.; Clifton. Enl. Jan. 4, '64. Wnd. Kennesaw; died Jul. 14, '65, Westchester, Pa.
Russell, Solomon M.; Richmond. Enl. Oct. 5, '61. Died Jun. 26, '63. Vicksburg, Miss., disease.
Rider, Haskell; ntonagan. Enl Oct. 22, '61. Trans to Co. I Mar. 1,'64.
Sanford, Albert; Dryden, NY. Enl. Oct. 30. '61. Vet.; M.O. Jul. 16,'65.
Schuyler, Thomas; Grand Chute. Enl. Oct. 5, '64. Died Jun. 26, '65, St. Louis, Mo. disease.
Seely, Sherwood E.; New Richmond. Oct. 30, '61. Prom. 2nd Asst. Surg., Jul. 20, '61.

Severance, Joseph; River Falls. Enl. Dec. 29, '63. M.O. Jun. 17, '65.
Shasby, John; New Centerville. Enl. Oct. 7, '61. Trans. to Co. I, Dec. 31, '61.
Smith, Thomas; New Richmond. Enl. Oct. 5, '61. Died Jan. 16, '62, Madison, Wis.
Smith, Andrew J.: Pleasant Valley. Enl. Feb. 23, '64. M.O. Jul.16,'65.
Sorkness, Ebert G.; Martell. Enl. Jan. 19, '64. M.O. Jul. 16, '65.
Strong, Ezra B.; Somersett, MI. Enl. Oct. 2, '61. Prom 2nd Lieut. Co. F, 30th Wis. Inf., Aug. 5, '62.
Styles, Leonard C.; River Falls. Enl. Oct. 4, '61. Trans. to Co. I, Mar. 1, '64.
Synes, Michael E.; Martell. Enl. Jan. 19, '64. M.O. Jul. 16, '65.
Taylor, James H.; Delavan. Enl. Dec. 30,'63. Died Feb. 19, '64, Camp Randall, Wis., disease.
Ticknor, George W.; Prescott. Enl. Dec. 21, '63. M.O. Jul. 16, '65.
Ticknor, Charles H.;Prescott. Enl. Sep. 21, '61. Trans to Co. I, Mar. 1, '64.
Tomlinson, John; Diamond Bluff. Enl. Dec. 18, '63. M.O. Jul. 16, '65.
Triggs, Robert, Jr.; Kinnickinnick. Enl. Oct. 30, '61. Vet.; killed in action Jul. 21, '64, Atlanta, Ga.
Tripp, Samuel; Troy. Enl. Jan. 4, '64. Trans. to Co. C, May 24, '64.
Tubbs, Edwin C.; River Falls. Enl. Sep. 28,'61. Died Dec. 7, '61, Madison, Wis.
Tubman, Edward; Hammondtown. Enl. Oct. 30, '61. Vet.; wnd. Atlanta, M.O. Jul. 16, '65.
Van Warner, Francis; New Centerville. Enl. Oct. 30, '61. Vet.,Corp., Sergt.; M.O. Aug. 4, '65.
Walker, Henry J.; Delona. Enl. ? '61. Vet., Musician; prom. Chaplain Jul. 2, '64.
Waltz, Andrew J.; Cedar Rapids. Enl. Oct. 30, '61. Vet.; M.O. Jul. 16,'65.
Ward, James; Ironton. Enl. Dec. 24, '62. M.O. Jul. 16, '65.
Warner, Elisha H.; Hockley. Enl. Mar. 7, '64. From Co. A, 25th Wis. Inf.; M.O. Jun. 24, '65.
Weed, Roswell A; Clifton. Enl. Jan. 2, '64. M.O. Jul. 16, '65.
Welles, John; River Falls. Enl. Sep.30,'61. Trans to Co. I Dec. 31, '65
Weston, Horace E.; River Falls. Enl. Dec. 24, '63. M.O. Jul. 16, '65.
Wheeler, Paul H.; Hartland. Enl. Feb. 13, '64. M.O. Jul. 16, '65.
Whipple, John N.; Prescott. Enl. Sep. 23, '61. Trans. to Co. I, '64; rej. May 31, '64; Corp.; M.O. Oct. 30, '64, term exp.
Whitlock, Richard A.; Martell. Enl. Jan. 26, '64. M.O. Jul. 16, '65.
Widlin, Halvor S.; Martell. Enl. Jan. 19, '64. M.O. Jul. 16, '65.
Williams, Ira A.; River Falls. Enl. Sep. 23, '61. M.O. Oct. 30, '64. term exp.
Williams, Linneas M.; Malone. Enl. Dec. 22, '63. M.O. Jul. 16, '65.
Williams, Clark M.; River Falls. Enl. Dec. 18, '63. M.O. Jul. 16, '65.
Wilson, Robert; Prescott. Enl. Oct. 21, '61. Died Aug. 29, '63, Natchez, Miss.
Wiley, Pratt J.: Diamond Bluff. Enl. Dec. 18, '63. Trans. to Co. C. May 24, '64.
Wiley, Wesley; River Falls. Enl. Oct 8,'61. Trans. Co. G., Dec. 31, '61.
Womack, James H.; New Diggings. Enl. Oct. 13,'64. M.O. Jul. 16, '65.

Womack, William; Mineral Point. Enl. Oct. 12, '64. M.O. Jul. 16, '65.
Wonsetler, Abner; Youngstown, OH. Enl. Sep 23, '61. Disch. Dec. 16, '62, disability.
Wright, Charles W.; Prescott. Enl. Dec. 12, '63. Disch. Jun. 8, '65.
Young, Charles E.; Prescott. Enl. Sep. 21, '61. Trans to Band.
Young, Joseph; Prescott. Enl. Dec. 18, '63. M.O. May 16, '65.
Young, John F.; Prescott. Enl. Sep. 21, '61. Trans. to V.R.C., Mar. 9, '64; M. O. Oct. 29, '64, term exp.

ROSTER OF COMPANY "B"

OFFICERS

Captains

GILES STEVENS; Reedsburg. Rank, Sep. 30, '61. Wnd. Atlanta; M.O. Oct. 30, '64, term exp.
JONATHAN W. ROOT; Logansville. Rank, Jan. 6, '65. Enl. Sep. 7, '61; Vet., Corp, Sergt.; wnd. Atlanta; M.O. Jul. 16, '65.

First Lieutenants

BENJAMIN F. BLACKMAN; Ironton. Rank, Sep. 30, '61. M.O. Oct. 30, '64, term exp.
HARRISON P. BALLARD; LaValle. Rank Nov. 21, '64. Enl. Sep. 6, '61; Vet., Corp., Sergt.; pris. Atlanta; M.O. Jul 16, '65.

Second Lieutenants

JAMES W. LUSK; Reedsburg. Rank Sep. 30, '61. Prom 1st Lieut. Co. A, Mar. 19, '62.
CHESTER G. HIGBEE; Hudson. Rank Mar. 19, '62. From 1st Sergt. Co. A; Capt., Nov. 21,'64, not mustered; M.O. Dec. 20, '64, term exp.

Enlisted men

Allbee, Daniel N.; Mount Hope. Enl. Oct. 4, '64. From Co. C, 25th Wis. Inf.; M.O. Jul. 16, '65.
Allen, James F.; Amherst. Enl Oct. 11,'64. Died Dec. 15, '64, Savannah, Ga., disease.
Armstrong, George G.; Greenfield. Enl. Sep. 17, '61.Vet.; M.O. Jul. 16, '65.
Auble, Jacob; Freedom. Enl. Oct. 28, '61. Vet.; M.O. Jul. 16, '65.
Bailey, George W.; LaValle. Enl. Sep. 18, '61. M.O. Oct. 31, '64, term exp.
Baldridge, Stephen C.; Ironton. Enl. Jul. 15,'62. M.O. May 31, '65.
Barnett, Samuel C.; Ironton. Enl. Sep. 14, '61. Vet.; pris.; M.O. Jul. 16, '65.
Barnhardt, John; Ridgeway. Enl. Feb. 4, '64. M.O. Jul. 16, '65.
Bates, John T.: Milwaukee. Enl. Oct. 5, '64. M.O. Jul. 16, '65.

Beaty, Franklin N.: Platteville. Enl. Feb. 27, '61. From Co. C. 25th
Wis. Inf.; M.O. Jul. 16, '65.
Bell, Mark C.; Oregon. Enl. Jan 15, '64. M.O. Jul. 16, '65.
Bell, George W.; Wonewoc. Enl. Sep. 18, '61. Vet., Corp.; wnd.
Atlanta; died Aug. 4, '64, Marietta, Ga., wnds.
Bemis, Levi J.; Reedsburg. Enl. Sep.18, '61. Vet., Corp.; M.O. Jul.
16, '65.
Benson, Almeron; Ironton. Enl. Sep. 6, '61. Drummer; disch. Aug. 29,
'62, disability.
Bitney, Charles; Washington. Enl. Oct. 30, '61. Disch. Dec. 17, '61,
civil authority.
Bitney, Lewis; Washington. Enl. Oct. 16, '61. Vet., Corp.; M.O. Jul.
16, '65.
Blakeslee, Ephraim; LaValle. Enl. Sep. 6, '61. 1st Sergt.; prom 2nd
Lieut, Co. H, May 11, '62.
Bodine, William; Platteville. Enl. Feb. 7, '65. From Co. C, 25th Wis.
Inf.; M.O. Jul. 16, '65.
Bowen, Peter P.; Platteville. Enl. Mar. 30, '61. From Co. C, 25th
Wis. Inf.; M.O. Aug. 12, '65.
Buchat, Constant; Ironton. Enl. Sep. 6, '61. Disch. Mar. 31, '62,
disability.
Bulow, Edward; Reedsburg. Enl. Sep. 26,'61. From Regtl. Band; Vet.;
M.O. Jul. 16,'65.
Bundy, William; Marston. Enl. Sep. 17, '61. Vet.; M.O. Jul. 16, '65.
Campbell, Charles L.: Winfield. Enl Sep. 16, '61. Died Mar. 1, '62,
Hospital.
Camp, Nathaniel; Ironton. Enl. Oct. 28, '61. Vet.; wnd. Jun. 15, '64,
Kenesaw; died Jun. 24, '64, wnds.
Carr, Lucius G.: Ironton. Enl. Sep. 6, '61. Vet.; M.O. Jul. 16, '65.
Carnes, Clifford; Wonewoc. Enl. Sep. 18, '61. Vet.; wnd. Atlanta;
pris. Pocotaligo; M.O. May 12, '65.
Christopherson, Rand; Greenwood. Enl. Sep. 21, '64. Drafted; M.O.
May 31,'65.
Chubb, Ira F.; New Orleans, LA. Sep. 30, '61. Corp.; disch. Jan 1, '62.
Clark, Stephen; Boscobel. Enl. Feb. 27, '64. From Co. C, 25th Wis.
Inf.; M.O. Jul. 16, '65.
Clayton, James; Ridgeway. Enl. Jan. 23, '64. M.O. Jul. 16, '65.
Coleman, John; Seven Mile Cr'k. Enl. Sep. 19, '64. Drafted; M.O.
Aug. 24, '65.
Colgan, Francis; LaValle. Enl. Oct.16, '61. Disch. Jan. 11, '63.
Conklin, Malachi; Ironton. Enl. Sep. 14, '61. Died Aug. 29, '63,
Vicksburg, Miss., disease.
Cornwalt, Luther B.; Winfield. Enl. Sep. 10, '61. Vet.; killed in
action, Jul. 21, '64, Atlanta, Ga.
Cover, John C.; Boscobel. Enl. Dec. 6, '63. From Co. C, 25th Wis.
Inf.; see Co. C. 25th Inf.
Cowles, Elba; Centralia. Enl. Oct. 5, '64. Trans to V.R.C., Apr. 22,
'65; disch. Jun. 29, '65, disability.
Croft, Lewis H.; Mt. Ida. Enl. Oct. 21, '64. From Co. C. 25th Wis.
Inf.; M.O. Jul. 16, '65.
Croft, Charles; Mt. Ida. Enl. Dec. 1, '63. From Co. C, 25th Wis. Inf.;
M.O. Jul. 16, '65.

Cronan, Timothy; Madison. Enl. Oct. 1, '62. M.O. Jul. 16, '65.
Crouch, Horace; Middleton. Enl. Jan. 15, '64. M.O. May 20, '65.
Curly, Matt; Milwaukee. Enl. Oct. 7, '64. M.O. Jul. 16, '65.
Curtis, Lewis; Winfield. Enl. Sep. 12, '61. Corp.; wnd. Vicksburg;
    M.O. Oct. 31, '64, term exp.
Curtis, Dennis; Winfield. Enl. Sep. 12, '61. Vet., Corp.; M.O. Jul.
    16, '65.
Curtis, Horace; Winfield. Enl. Sep. 12, '61. Died Jun. 29, '63,
    Vicksburg, Miss., disease.
Curtis, George; Winfield. Enl. Sep. 12,'61. Died Dec. 11, '62, Holly
    Springs, Miss., disease.
Dano, Frank E.; Elgerton. Enl. Sep. 4, '61. Vet. M.O. Jul. 16, '65.
Darrow, Albert; Winfield. Enl. Oct. 21, '61. Vet. M.O. Jul. 16, '65.
Davis, Edward; Seven Mile Cr'k. Enl. Sep. 16, '61. M.O. Oct. 31, '64,
    term exp.
Davis, Stephen J.;Woodland. Enl. Sep. 30, '61. Vet., Corp., Sergt.;
    wnd. Atlanta; 2nd Lieut., Jan. 6, '65, not mustered;
    M.O. Jul. 16, '65.
Dearholt, Henry; Westfield. Enl. Sep. 7, '61. Died May 6, '62, Fort
    Riley, Kan.
Dickens, George W.; Marston. Enl. Oct. 18, '61. Trans to V.R.C.;
    M.O. Oct. 27, '64, term exp.
Dickens, Le Roy D.; Reedsburg. Enl. Sep. 27, '61. Vet.; M. O. May
    15, '65.
Dickens, John W.; Reedsburg. Enl. Sep. 6, '61. Vet., M.O. Jul. 16, '65
Dodge, Darius; Hillsboro. Enl. Oct. 14, '61. Disch. Mar. 19, '64.
    disability.
Dorward, alexander W.; Caledonia. Enl. Oct. 17, '64. M.O. Aug. 8. '65
Dowden, Andrew; Ironton. Enl. Dec. 18, '63. Wnd. Jul. 22, '64,
    Atlanta; died Jul. 24, '64, wnds.
Dowden, David; Ironton. Enl. Nov. 21, '63. M.O. Jul. 16, '65.
Dougal, John; Loganville. Enl. Oct. 14, '61. Vet.; M.O. Jul. 16, '65.
Doug, John; Ironton. Enl. Oct. 17, '62. Musician; trans. to Co. D,
    May 1, '64.
Doug, James; Ironton. Enl. Sep. 6, '61. Wnd. Atlanta; M.O. Oct. 31,
    '64, term exp.
Draper, James; Wonewoc. Enl Sep. 18, '61. Deserted May 20, '62.
Dudleston, Hamilton; Ironton. Enl. Sep. 11, '62. Died Feb. 7, '63,
    Collierville, Tenn., disease.
Dunn, Duane; Milwaukee. Enl. Oct. 12, '64. M.O. Jun. 9, '65.
Elliott, Jacob W.; Harmony. Enl. Dec. 30, '63. Killed in action, Jul.
    28, '64, Atlanta, Ga.
Featherstone, Thomas; Harmony. Enl. Dec. 31, '63. Wnd. Atlanta;
    M.O. May 31, '65.
Feight, George; Ironton. Enl. Sep. 11, '62. Wnd. Atlanta; M.O. May
    31, '65.
Fellor, Eustis; Freedom. Enl. Oct. 4, '61. M.O. Jul. 27, '63.
Fessy, John; Winfield. Enl. Sep. 30, '61. Disch. Aug. 29,'62, disability
Fields, Harrison O.; Bear Creek. Enl. Nov. 9, '61. Wnd. Kenesaw;
    M.O. Jan. 10, '65, term exp.
Ford, Amos; Middleton. Enl. Jan. 19, '64. Killed in action Jul. 21, '64,
    Atlanta, Ga.

Ford, George; Harmony. Enl. Dec. 26, '63. Killed in action Jul. 21, '64, Atlanta, Ga.
Fosdick, Frank; Westfield. Enl Oct. 16,'61. M.O. Oct. 31, '64, term exp
Froats, William; Wyocena. Enl. Oct. 14, '64. M.O. Jul. 16, '65.
Fuller, Henry; Westfield. Enl. Sep. 27, '61. Vet., Corp.; M.O. Jul. 16, '65.
Giles, Frederick; Westfield. Enl. Sep. 7, '61. Vet. Corp.; M.O. Jul. 16, '65.
Goodell, John A.; Dexter. Enl. Oct. 11, '64. M.O. Jul. 16, '65.
Gorman, Eugene; Dunkirk. Enl. Jan. 2, '64. Wnd. Atlanta; trans. to V.R.C., Apr. 24, '65; M.O. Jul. 19, '65.
Griffis, John H.; Mt. Ida. Enl. Oct. 6, '64. From Co. C, 25th Wis. Inf. M.O. Jul. 16, '65.
Groat, Frederick J.; Ironton. Enl. Sep. 6, '61. Vet., Sergt.; M.O. Jul.16,'65.
Gulbranson, Ole; Perry. Enl. Oct. 8, '61. M.O. Jun. 17, '65.
Guillford, Charles W.; Westfield. Enl. Sep. 7, '61. Vet.; wnd. Atlanta; M.O. Jul. 16, '65.
Hagaman, Jebial D.; LaValle. Enl. Sep. 6, '61. Died Aug. 21, '63, Natchez, Miss., disease.
Hagaman, Evart H.; Mauston. Enl. Nov. ? '61. Vet.; killed in action, Jul. 22, '64, Atlanta, Ga.
Hawkins, Hawkins; Ironton. Enl. Sep. 6, '61. Vet., Corp., Sergt., 1st Sergt., wnd. Jul. 5,'64, and Jul. 21,'64; M.O. Jul.16,'65
Henry, Frank W.; Reedsburg. Enl. Sep. 26, '61. Vet., Sergt.; pris. Apr. 18, '63, Hernando; killed in action, Jul. 22, '64, Atlanta, Ga.
Higbee, Albert E.; Madison. Enl. Aug. 19,'62. Corp.; M.O. May 31,'65
Hindorf, Anton; Racine. Enl. Oct.17, '64. M.O. Jul. 16, '65.
Hobart, Alvin; Franklin. Enl. Nov. 20, '61. Died Mar. 7, '62, Weston, Mo.
Hobart, Benjamin F.; Winfield. Enl. Dec. 23, '61. Trans. to V.R.C. Nov. 9, '63.
Hobart, Anderson; Winfield. Enl. Dec. 23, '61. Died Jun. 17, '63, Memphis, Tenn., disease.
Horebeck, Joseph; Middleton. Enl. Jan. 15, '64. M.O. Jul. 16, '65.
Hoyt, Ralph; Hillsboro. Enl. Sep.17,'61. Vet.;wnd. Jul 5,'64 and Jul. 21,'64, Atlanta; died Aug. 19, '64. Rome, Ga., wnds.
Hutchinson, Joseph: Lancaster. Enl. Feb. 1,'64. From Co. C, 25th Wis. Inf.; M.O. Jul. 16, '65.
Inman, George; Ironton. Enl. Jan. 27, '64. M.O. Jul. 16, '65.
Inman, John; Ridgway. Enl. Jan. 20,'64. M.O. Jul. 16, '65.
Inman, William H. H.; Washington. Enl. Sep. 7, '61. Sergt.; wnd. Atlanta; M.O. Oct. 31, '64, term exp.
Iverson, Gunder; Deerfield. Enl. Sep. 30, '64. M.O. May 31, '65.
Jackson, William H.; Westfield. Enl. Oct. 14, '61. Vet.; M.O. Jul 16, '65.
Johnson, Augustus H.; Reedsburg. Enl. Sep. 18, '61. Prom. Sergt. Maj., Nov. 1, '63; rej. Co. Dec. 23, '64; M.O. Jul. 22, '65.
Jones, Charles O.; Madison. Enl. Jan. 4, '64. From Co. C, 25th Wis. Inf.; M.O. Jul. 16, '65.

Juby, John; LaValle. Enl. Oct. 14, '61.
Kays, Levitt W.; Platteville. Enl. Feb. 29, '64. From Co. C, 25th Wis. Inf.; M.O. Jul. 16, '65.
Keltey, Layfayette; Winfield. Enl. Jan. 25, '64. Wnd. Atlanta; M.O. Jul 16, '65.
Kerstetter, John; Ironton. Enl. Sep. 11, '62. M.O. May 31, '65.
Kivel, John; Winfield. Enl. Oct. 3, '61. Vet.; wnd. Jul 5, '64, Nickajack; disch. May 26 '65, wnds.
Kinnaman, John L.; Ironton. Enl. Sep. 25, '61. Disch. Nov. 30, '63, disability.
Kyle, John; LaValle. Enl. Sep. 25,'61. Disch. Nov. 30,'63. disability
Lane, Daniel; Ironton. Enl. Sep. 11, '62. Died Feb. 10, '63. Camp Butler, Tenn., disease.
Lane, Pailo; Reedsburg. Enl. Sep. 26, '61. Disch. Jan. 30, '63, disability.
Lind, Peter; Hillsboro. Enl. Sep. 28, '61. Vet.; M.O. Jul. 16, '65.
Lind, Henry, Harmony. Enl. Jan. 5, '64. M.O. Jul. 16, '65.
Long, Mark B.; Ironton. Enl. Sep. 6, '61. Died Nov. 23, '64, Chattanooga; left leg amp.
Lowery, Johnston; Potosi. Enl. Nov. 17, '63. From Co. C. 25th Wis. Inf.; M.O. Jul. 16, '65.
Mason, James B.; Mineral Point. Enl. Jan. 2, '64. Died Apr. 13, '61, Cairo, Ill., disease.
Mason, Elwood; LaValle. Enl Sep. 27,'61. Vet., Corp.; wnd. Atlanta; M.O. Jul. 16, '65.
Mead, George S.; Westfield. Enl. Oct. 18, '61. Disch. May 1, '62.
Mead, James S.; Westfield. Enl. Feb. 3, '64. Died Oct. 1, '64, Atlanta, Ga.
Mellon, Archibald, Ironton. Enl. Sep. 14, '61. Corp.; disch. Jun. 21, '62, disability.
Miller, John S.; Ridgeway. Enl. Jan. 19, '64. Disch. Jan. 31, '65, Madison, disability.
Miller, Joel; Stark. Enl. Oct. 8, '64. M.O. Jul. 16, '65.
Miller, Adam H.; Lancaster. Enl. Dec. 3, '63. From Co. C, 25th Wis. Inf.; M.O. Jul. 16, '65.
Miles, James; Reedsburg. Enl. Oct. 16, '61. Vet.; wnd, Atlanta; disch. Mar. 28, '65, wnds., left arm amp.
Miles, Spencer S.; Reedsburg. Enl. Sep. 23, '61. Vet., Sergt., 1st Sergt.; wnd, Atlanda; died Aug. 10, '64, Marietta, Ga. wnds.
Morrill, Oel; Winewoc. Enl. Sep. 27, '61. Vet., Corp.; wnd. Atlanta; M.O. Jul. 16, '65.
Murray, Martin; LaValle. Enl. Nov. 21, '63. M.O. Jul. 16, '65.
Myer, Herman; Liberty. Enl. Oct. 12, '64. M.O. Jul. 16, '65.
Oliver, John; LaValle. Enl. Oct. 14, '61. Vet.; M.O. Jul. 16, '65.
Osborne, Watson C.; Ironton. Enl. Sep. 14, '61. Died Aug. 21, '63, Natchez, Miss., disease.
Palmer, Henry C.; LaValle. Enl. Oct. 14, '61. Wnd. Kenesaw and Atlanta; M.O. Oct. 31, '64, term exp.
Palmer, James; Milwaukee. Enl. Oct. 5, '64. Died Feb. 10, '65, Chattanooga, Tenn., disease.

Pearson, Charles; Ironton. Enl. Sep. 27, '61. Wnd. Atlanta; M.O. Oct. 31, '64, term exp.
Perkins, George; Westfield. Enl. Sep. 27, '61. Disch. Aug. 13, '62, disability.
Platta, John; Sharon. Enl. Oct. 13, '64. M.O. Jul. 16, '65.
Pollock, James T.; Reedsburg. Enl. Sep. 16, '61. Died Nov. 30, '62, Bolivar, Tenn., disease.
Pond, Ellis; Reedsburg. Enl. Sep. 12, '61. Vet., Corp.; M.O. Jul. 16, '65.
Premo, Henry; Ironton. Enl. Nov. 29, '61. Vet.; M.O. Jul. 16, '65.
Premo, Franklin A.; Ironton. Enl. Dec. 18, '63. M.O. Jul. 16, '65.
Rathbun, Baldwin; Reedsburg. Enl. Dec. 9, '61. Disch Jun. 13, '65, disability.
Reifenrath, Charles; Reedsburg. Enl. Sep. 2, '61. Vet.; wnd. Jun. 23, '64, Kenesaw; died Jun. 27, '64, wnds.
Robinson, Elias A.; Ironton. Enl. Sep. 16,'61. Vet.; wnd. Atlanta; M.O. Jul. 16, '65.
Robinson, Joseph; Franklin. Enl. Sep. 5, '61. Disch. Oct. 22, '64, disability.
Rogers, William H.H.; Boscobel. Enl. Dec. 11, '61. M.O. Jul. 16, '65.
Rogers, Seth; Wonewoc. Enl. Sep. 18, '61. Disch. Sep. 10, '62, disability.
Rose, William W.; Enl. Feb. 18, '64. From Co. C, 25th Wis. Inf.; M.O. Jul. 16, 65.
Rice, Robert; Barton. Enl. Oct. 5, '64. M.O. Jul. 16, '65.
Richards, William; Ironton. Enl. Sep. 27, '61. Vet., Corp.; wnd Jul. 22, '64, Atlanta; died Jul. 26, '64 in Field Hosp., wnds.
Richards, Sylvanus; Westfield. Enl. Oct. 30, '61. Pris. Atlanta; M.O. Oct. 31, '64, term exp.
Sainsbury, Joseph; Dunkirk. Enl. Nov. 18, '63. M.O. Jul. 16, '65.
Sainsbury, James; Winfield. Enl. Sep. 27, '61. M. O. Oct. 31, '64, term exp.
Samon, James; Ironton. Enl. Sep. 17, '61. Wnd. Vicksburg; died Jul. 3, '63, on Hosp. Str. "Crescent City," wnds.
Sanborn, Wilbur F.; Melton. Enl Sep. 24, '61. Vet., Corp.; M.O. Jul. 16, '65.
Sanborn, John; Marston. Enl. Oct. 14, '61. Vet., Corp., Sergt.; M.O. Jul. 16, '65.
Sweitzer, Henry J.; Racine. Enl. Oct. 19, '64. M.O. Jul. 16, '65.
Scoon, Alfred F.; Middleton. Enl. Jan. 15, '64. Trans. to V.R.C., Nov. 25, '64; M.O. Jul. 31, '65.
Sebastian, Bernard; Caledonia. Enl. Oct. 17, '64. M.O. Jul. 16, '65.
Seeley, Morris E.; Reedsburg. Enl. Sep. 12, '61. Vet., Corp.; M.O. Jul. 16, '65.
Seeley, Levi; Marston. Enl. Sep. 2, '61. Vet., Corp., Sergt.; wnd. Kenesaw and Atlanta; M.O. Jul. 16, '65.
Seldon, Albert; Middleton. Enl. Jan. 19, '64. Wnd. Atlanta; disch. May 25, '65, wnds.
Seldon, John; Westfield. Enl. Jan. 4, '62. M.O. Jan. 11, '65, term exp
Sergeant, Henry; Westfield. Enl. Sep. 7, '61. Vet.; M.O. Jul 16, '65.
Settle, Thomas; Westfield. Enl. Jan. 4, '62. Died Mar. 7, '62.

Seymour, Elijah; Delona. Enl. Sep. 14, '61. Died Mar. 5, '63, Jackson, Tenn.
Shreves, Edson; Reedsburg. Dec. 16,'61. Disch. Aug. 18,'64, disability
Sinclair, George A.; Harmony. Enl. Dec. 26, '63. Trans to V.R.C. Aug. 2, '64.
Smith, John; Casco. Enl. Jun. 29,'64. M.O. Jul. 16, '65.
Spicer, david G.; Reedsburg. Enl. Sep. 18, '61. Vet., pris. Feb. 19, '65, Columbia, S.C.; M.O. Jun. 21, '65.
Sprague, Albert J.; Ironton. Enl. Aug. 20, '62. M.O. May 31, '65.
Starks, Edgar; Amherst. Enl. Oct. 11, '64. M.O. Jul. 16, '65.
Stettleburg, James H.; Ironton. Enl. Nov. 21, '63. Wnd. Atlanta; M.O. Jul. 16, '65.
Strong, Victor E.; Lancaster. Enl. Feb. 12, '63. From Co. C, 25th Wis. Inf.; M.O. Jul. 16, '65.
Stroud, Alfred; Spring Prairie. Enl. Mar. 3, '64. M.O. Jul. 16, '65.
Taber, Oscar G.; Woodland, Enl. Oct. 16, '61. Vet.; M.O. Jul. 16, '65.
Talbot, Daniel L.; Bear Creek. Enl. Nov. 11, '61. Deserted Dec. 13,'61
Taylor, Mortimer G.; LaValle. Enl. Sep. 6, '61. Corp.; disch. Feb. 9,'63, by order.
Tenant, William; Mt. Ida. Enl. Oct. 19, '64. From Co. C, 25th Wis. Inf.; M.O. Jul. 16, '65.
Thompson, Austin; Hillsboro. Enl. Oct. 28, '61. Vet.; M.O. Jul 16, '65
Townsend, Lewis; Sandusky. Enl. Oct. 16, '61. Vet.; wnd. Atlanta; M.O. Jul. 16, '65.
Tuckwood, Thomas; Mt. Ida. Enl. Jan. 1, '63. From Co. C, 25th Wis. Inf.; M.O. Jul. 16, '65.
Velvick, John M.; New Buffalo. Enl. Dec. 31, '63. Died Feb. 15, '64, Madison, Wis., Pest Hosp.
Wickersham, John E.; Ironton. Enl. Sep. 27, '61. Vet.; killed in action, Jul. 21, '64, Atlanta, Ga.
Woods, Fernando C.; Ironton. Enl. Sep. 2, '61. Died Jul 18, '63 steamer "Nashville" disease.
Worden, Warren D.; Lancaster. Enl. Mar. 23, '64. From Co. C, 25th Wis. Inf.; absent wnd. M.O. of Regt.

ROSTER OF COMPANY "C"

OFFICERS

Captains

CHARLES F. LOEBER; Dodgeville. Rank Sep. 19, '61. Enl. Aug. 9, '61; res. Apr. 29, '62.
FRANCIS WILSON; Arena. Rank Apr. 29, '62. Enl. Sep. 9, '61; 1st Lieut., Sep. 19, '61; wnd. Atlanta; M.O. Jan. 16, '65, term exp.
DANIEL G. JONES; Ridgeway. Rank Jan. 6, '65. Enl. Sep. 13, '61; Sergt., 1st Sergt.; 2nd Lieut., Jul. 30, '63; M. O. Jul. 16, '65.

First Lieutenanta

MICHAEL J. CANTWELL; Madison. Rank Apr. 29, '62. Enl. Nov. 1, '61; 2nd Lieut., Nov. 1, '61; Act. Q.M. since Nov. 28, '63; M.O. Jan. 16, '65, term exp.
WILLIAM C. STEVENS; Madison. Rank. Jan. 13, '65. Enl. Nov. 14, '61; Com. Sergt., Jul. 1, '62; rejoined Sep. 22, '64; 1st Sergt.; A.D.C. in 1st Brig., 3rd Div., 17th A.C.; M.O. Jul. 16, '65.

Second Lieutenants

EDWARD L. WHITNEY; Adrian, MI. Rank Qpr. 29, '62. Enl. Nov. 5, '61; 1st Sergt.; A.A.C.S. onGen. McKean's Staff; res. Jul. '63.
JAMES SEXTON; Marion. Rank Jan. 13, '65. Enl. Nov. 15, '61; Vet., Corp., Sergt.; M.O. Jul. 16, '65.

Enlisted Men

Anthony, S lah; Wyoming. Enl. Sep. 5, '61. Vet.; M.O. Jul. 16, '65.
Anunson, Ole; Perry. Enl. Oct. 11, '61. M.O. Jul. 16, '65.
Bailey, Thomas; Dodgeville. Sep. 25,'61. Vet., Corp.; M.O. Jul. 16,'65
Baker, Gilbert; Linden. Enl. Sep. 7, '61. Vet., Corp.; wnd and pris. Atlanta; died while pris., wnds.
Bartells, Frederick; Madison. Enl. Nov. 15, '61. Trans. to Band.
Baxter, Charles; Linden. Enl. Sep. 7, '61. Vet.; M.O. Jul. 16, '65.
Beisswanger, Gottlieb; Blue Mounds. Enl. Sep. 8, '61. Vet.; M.O. Jul. 16, '65.
Berkin, William; Blue Mounds. Enl. Sep. 30, '61. Vet.; M.O. Jul. 16, '65.
Billington, Alonzo; Eldorado. Enl. Oct. 5, '64. From Co. K, 25th Wis. Inf.; M.O. Jul. 16, '65.
Bishop, Willet H.; Ridgeway. Enl. Oct. 11, '64. M.O. Jul. 16, '65.
Blodgett, Albert J.; Dodgeville. Enl. Aug. 29, '61. Vet., Corp.; det. A.G.O. Washington, D.C.; M.O. Aug. 4, '65.
Blodgett, Andrew; Ridgeway. Enl. Dec. 10, '64. M.O. Jul. 16, '65.
Bresee, William G.; Columbus. Enl. Nov. 26, '61. Vet.; disch. Feb. 4, '65, to ac. prom. in 58th U.S.C.T.
Briggs, George; York. Enl. Oct. 10, '64. M.O. Jul. 16, '65.
Briggs, Deighton; Adams. Enl. Oct. 11, '64. M.O. Jul. 16, '65.
Bryant, Frank B.; Madison. Enl. Nov. 1,'61. Prom. Q.M. Sergt., May 1, '62.
Bulow, Charles; Milwaukee. Enl. Apr. 30, '64. Musician; M.O. Jul. 16, '65.
Butterfield, Benjamin S.; Wyoming. Enl. Dec. 13, '61. M.O. Dec. 25, '64, term exp.
Chapman, Alfred L.; Wyocena. Enl. Oct. 17, '64. M.O. May 30, '65.
Chapman, Austin J.; Spring Lake. Enl. Nov. 15, '61. Vet., Corp.; M.O. Jul. 16, '65.
Chestleson, Sever; Perry. Enl. Jan. 8, '62. Vet.; M.O. Jul. 16, '65

Chestleson, Asleg; Ridgeway. Enl. Sep. 30, '61. Died Jul. 30, '63, Vicksburg, Miss., disease.
Chestleson, Targe; Ridgeway. Enl. Sep. 30, '61. Died Jul. 27, '63, St. Louis, Mo., disease.
Christench, Charles F.; Janesville. Enl. Dec. 30, '63. M.O. Jul. 16,'65
Clemens, Peter; Dodgeville. Enl. Sep. 14, '61. Vet.; wnd, Atlanta; M.O. Jul. 16, '65.
Colding, Christian H.; Madison. Enl. Oct. 20, '61. Vet.; died Dec. 9, '64, Nashville, Tenn.
Conrad, John; Eldorado. Enl. Mar. 29, '64. From Co. K, 25th Wis. Inf..; M.O. Jul. 16, '65.
Crellin, John; Dodgeville. Enl. Nov. 21, '61. Vet., M.O. Jul. 16, '65.
Crook, John; Dodgeville. Enl. Sep. 16, '61. Vet., Corp; M.O. Jul. 16, '65.
Davidson, James E.; Blue Mounds. Enl. Sep. 1, '61. Corp., Sergt.; M.O. Oct. 17, '64, term exp.
Dixon, Theron W.; Milwaukee. Enl. Oct. 11, '64. M.O. Jul. 16, '65.
Duheme, Elzeord; New Denmark. Enl. Apr. 26, '64. Wnd. Atlanta; M.O. Jul. 16, '65.
Dunstan, Thomas; Ridgeway. Enl. Sep. 11, '61. Vet., Corp., Sergt.; M.O. Jul. 16, '65.
Dwyre, Thomas P.; Highland. Enl. Sep. 6, '61. Vet.; M.O. Jul. 16, '65.
Eberlein, Frederick; Ridgeway. Enl. Sep. 16, '61. Vet.; wnd..; trans. to V.R.C., Apr. 24, '65.
Eddy, Thomas R.; Dodgeville. Enl. Sep. 6, '61. Died Jul. 15, '63, on Hosp. Boat "City of Memphis," disease.
Egan, John; Empire. Enl. Feb. 29, '64. M.O. Jul. 16, '65.
Elder, Charles H.; Nepuskin. Enl. Mar. 9, '64. M.O. Jul. 16, '65.
Ellingson, Thomas; Dodgeville. Enl. Sep. 6, '61. Disch.
Erickson, Sylvester; Dodgeville. Enl. Sep. 6, '61. Vet., Corp., Sergt.; M.O. Jul. 16, '65.
Erickson, Peter; Dodgeville. Enl. Sep. 12, '61. Vet.; M.O. Jul. 16, '65.
Evans, Hector; Ridgeway. Enl. Sep. 25, '61. M.O. Oct. 17, '64, term exp.
Fellor, Peter; Greenfield. Enl. Oct. 6, '64. M.O. Jul. 16, '65.
Fenster, Frank; Perry. Enl. Mar. 31, '64. M.O. Jul. 16, '65.
Fenster, Charles; Ridgeway. Enl. Mar. 21, '64. M.O. Jul. 16, '65.
Fish, Charles; Mineral Point. Enl. Jan. 29, '64. Died Aug. 7, '64, Rome, Ga, disease.
Fuller, George W.; Moscow. Enl. Sep. 7, '61. Vet.; M.O. Jul. 16, '65.
Gardner, William; Chippewa Falls. Enl. Oct. 8, '64; M.O. Jul. 16, '65.
Garland, Royal. Diamond Bluff. Enl. Dec. 18, '63. From Co. A; M.O. Jul. 16, '65.
Garthwait, George; Milton. Enl. Dec. 5, '63. From Co. K, 25th Wis. Inf.; M.O. Jul. 16, '65.
Geer, Elmore; Wyoming. Enl. Sep. 19, '61. Pris. Nov. 29,'62, Holly Springs; died May 7, '64, in Wis., disease.
Gerard, George; Monroe. Enl. Oct. 13, '64. M.O. Jul. 16, '65.
Glanville, James H.; Dodgeville. Enl. Sep. 19, '61. Vet.; M.O. Jul. 16, '65.
Goldsworthy, Thomas; Linden. Enl. Oct. 7, '61. Vet.; wnd. and pris. Atlanta; M.O. Jul. 16, '65.

Guyer, Edward; Beetown. Enl. Oct. 21, '61. Vet.; M.O. Jul. 16, '65.
Halstinson, Gilbert; Vermont, WI. Enl. Oct. 13, '64; M.O. Jul 16, '65.
Hannan, Patrick; Madison. Enl. Dec. 8, '61. Vet.; M.O. Jul. 16, '65.
Harmony, Noah; Blue Mounds. Enl. Sep. 16, '61; Vet., M.O. Jul. 16, '65.
Harmony, William; Vermont, WI. Enl. Sep. 23, '61. Deserted, Jan. 5, '62.
Hart, Cornelius; Blue Mounds. Enl. Sep. 21, '61. Vet.; M.O. Jul. 16, '65.
Henkle, John; Blue Mounds. Enl. Oct. 3, '61. Vet., Corp.; wnd. and pris. Atlanta; died Jul. or Aug. '64 in Rebel Prison.
Henry, Charles H.; Vienna. Enl. Jan. 23, '64; From Co. K, 25th Wis. Inf., M.O. Jul. 16, '65.
Higgins, Richard; Wyoming. Enl. Oct. 31, '61. Vet.; M.O. Jul. 16, '65.
Hocking, Samuel; Linden. Enl. Oct. 7, '61. Vet.; wnd.; disch. May 13, '65, wnds.
Hover, Ole H.; Dodgeville. Enl. Sep. 15, '61. Disch. Jul. 10, '62, disability.
Hudson, John, Jr.; Pleasant Valley. Enl. Feb. 24, '64. Killed in action Jul. 21, '64, Atlanta, Ga.
Hyatt, Sydney G.; Prescott. Enl. Dec. 28, '63. From Co. A; M.O. Jul. 16, '65.
Johnson, Cornelius J.; Dodgeville. Enl. Sep. 19, '61. Died Dec. 22, '62, Oxford, Miss., disease.
Jegium, Kittle J.; Perry. Enl. Oct. 13, '64; M.O. Jul. 16, '65.
Johnson, John; Pleasant Valley. Enl. Feb. 24, '64. M.O. Jul. 16, '65.
Johnson, Knudt; Perry. Enl. Sep. 30, '61. Vet., Corp.; M.O. Jul. 16, '65.
Jones, William H.; Delona. Sep. 30, '61. Disch. Apr. 9, '64. disability.
Jones, Washington; Clyde. Sep. 30,'61. Vet., Corp.; M.O. Jul 16, '65.
Jones, Henry; Wyoming. Enl. Oct. 24, '61. Wnd.; M.O. Oct. 17, '64, term exp.
Jones, Henry E.; Dodgeville. Enl. Sep. 3, '61. Vet., Sergt., 1st Sergt.; M.O. Jul. 16, '65.
Keedling, Frederick; White Creek. Enl. Jan. 16, '64. From Co. K, 25th Wis. Inf; M.O. Jul. 16, '65.
Kinney, Morgan D.; River Falls. Enl. Dec. 22, '63. From Co. A; wnd. '64; pris. Mar. 11,'65. Lafayette,N.C.; M.O.May 17, '65.
Knudson, Hans; Dodgeville. Enl. Sep. 12, '61. Vet.; wnd. Atlanta; M.O. Jul. 16, '65.
Krug, William; Blue Mounds. Sep. 8, '61. Vet.; killed in action, Jul. 13, '64, Chattahoochie, Ga.
Laird, Jacob; Moscow. Enl. Sep. 7, '61. Vet., Corp.; wnd, Atlanta; M.O. Jul. 16, '65.
Langua, Eazel; New Denmark. Enl. Apr. 23, '61. Deserted Aug. 1, '61.
Lattimer, William; Vermont, WI. Enl. Sep. 18, '61. Discharged.
Lean, William H.; Arena. Enl. Sep. 22, '61. M.O. Oct. 17,'64, term exp.
Leighty, Robert M.; Viroqua. Enl. Oct. 9, '61. From Co. I; Vet.; prom. Principal Musician, Jan. 1, '64.
Lemair, Stephen E.; Fond du Lac. Enl. Jul. 1, '62. M.O. May 31, '63.

Lent, Simeon F.; Oakland. Enl. Dec. 27, '62. From Co. K, 25th Wis. Inf..; M.O. Jul. 16, '65.
Leonard, William M.; Madison. Enl. Nov. 8, '61. Vet.; M.O. Jul. 16, '65.
Levake, John M.; Wyoming. Enl. Oct. 11, '61. Vet., Corp., Sergt.; M.O. Jul. 16, '65.
Level, Jonas; Ridgeway. Enl. Sep. 14, '61. Died Nov. 13, '62, La Grange, Miss.
Lloyd, Thompson P.; Cataract. Enl. Oct. 18, '61. Corp.; died Sep. 13, '62, Humboldt, Tenn., disease.
Mattison, Evan; Dodgeville. Enl. Sep. 11, '61. Deserted Jan. 5, '62.
McCleary, Archibald; Salem. Enl. Feb. 25, '64. M.O. Jul. 16, '65.
Merchant, Thomas; Eldorado. Enl. Oct. 5, '64. From Co. K, 25th Wis. Inf.; M.O. Aug. 16, '65.
Morris, William; Wyoming. Enl. Dec. 12, '61. Died Jun. 2, '63 on Hosp. boat "Nashville," disease.
Mills, John A.; Macomb. Enl. Nov. 7, '63. From Co. K, 25th Wis. Inf.; M.O. Jul. 16, '65.
Mills, Carver G.; Fon du Lac. Enl. Feb. 15,'64. M.O. Jul. 16, '65.
Minsart, Ignace M.; Morrison. Mar. 12, '64. Wnd.; M.O. Aug. 1. '65.
Mitta, William; Ridgeway. Enl. Oct. 11, '64. M.O. Jul. 16, '65.
Nicholson, Sivert; Ridgeway. Enl. Feb. 10, '64. M.O. Jul. 16, '63.
Oleson, Martin; Perry. Enl. Sep. 30, '61. Wnd. Atlanta; trans. to V.R.C., Apr. 21, '65.
Oleson, Ole; Madison. Enl. Nov. 11,'61. Vet., Corp.;wnd. Atlanta; M.O. Jul. 16, '65.
Oleson, Hans; Ridgeway. Enl. Sep. 30,'61. Vet., Corp., Sergt.; M.O. Jul. 16, '65.
Orcutt, Cyrus; Dodgeville. Enl. Sep. 18, '61. Died Jan. 9, '64, Vicksburg, Miss., disease.
Ottman, George F.; Walworth. Enl. Jan. 4, '64. M.O. May 31, '65.
Parker, Levi M.; Walworth. Enl. Jan. 4, '61. Died Jun. 7, '64, Pulaski, Tenn., disease.
Paul, Edward; Wyoming. Enl. Aug. 29, '61. Corp., Sergt.; died Jul 15, '63 on Hosp. Boat, disease.
Paul, Lewis; Wyoming. Enl. Dec. 7, '61. wnd. Atlanta; M.O. Jul 16, 65.
Paulson, Erik; Wyoming. Enl. Aug. 29, '61. Vet.; wnd. and pris. Kenesaw; M.O. May 30, '65.
Pillson, David M.C.; Trenton. Enl. Feb. 29, '61. From Co.A; M.O. Jul. 16, '65.
Pine, William B.; Ridgeway. Sep. 7, '61. Vet.; wnd. Atlanta; M.O. Jul. 16, '65.
Pitts, John R.; Linden. Enl. Sep. 19, '61. Corp.; M.O. Jul. 16, '65.
Powers, Benjamin; Moscow. Enl. Sep. 7, '61. Corp.; died Jan. 19, '61,Memphis, Tenn., disease.
Probst, Christopher; West Bend. Oct. 13, '61. From Co. D; disch. Apr. 10, '62.
Pyncheon, William W.; Marion. Nov. 15, '61. Disch. Dec. 16, '62, disability.
Rallston, Stanley; Pleasant Valley. Enl. Feb. 23, '61. Killed in action, Jul. 21, '64, Atlanta, Ga.

Reed, William S.; Wyoming. Enl. Sep. 16, '61. Vet.; M.O. Jul. 16, '65.
Reese, Timothy; Ridgeway. Oct. 11, '64. M.O. Jul. 16, '65.
Reid, Otis; Blue Mounds. Enl. Sep. 1, '61, Died Apr. 23, '62, Fort Riley, Kans.
Regan, Patrick; Madison. Enl. Mar. 13, '62. Vet.; M.O. Jul. 16, '65.
Rein, John; Blue Mounds. Enl. Jan. 6, '62. From Co. K; Vet.; M.O. Jul. 16, '65.
Rich, Henry; Blue Mounds. Enl. Sep. 1,'61. Died Apr. 20, '62, Fort Riley, Kans.
Richmond, Lewis; Sheboygan. Enl. Mar. 23, '64.; M.O. Jul. 27, '65.
Roberts, Cyrus; Linden. Enl. Sep. 22, '61. Vet.; M.O. Jul. 16, '65.
Roberts, Thomas L.; Dodgeville. Enl. Aug. 24, '61. Vet., Musician; M.O. Jul. 16, '65.
Roedon, Miner; Wyoming. Enl. Sep. 12, '61. Vet.; wnd. Atlanta; M.O. Jul. 16, '65.
Roedon, Plimpton; Wyoming. Enl. Aug. 30, '61. Vet.; killed in action, Jul. 21, '64, Atlanta, Ga.
Rossback, John C.; Vermont, WI. Enl. Sep. 15, '61. Vet.; M.O. Jul. 16, '65.
Rowe, John H. D.; Dodgeville. Enl. Aug. 24, '61. Sergt.; died Nov. 17, '62, LaGrange, Tenn.
Schilling, John G.; Madison. Enl. Nov. 9, '61. Disch. Mar. 10, '63, disability.
Skinner, Charles C.; Blue Mounds. Enl. Nov. 18, '61. Vet., Corp.; M.O. Jul. 25, '65.
Slater, James; Moscow. Enl. Sep. 12, '61. Vet., Corp.; wnd.; M.O. Jul. 16, '65.
Stark, Henry; West Bend. Enl. Oct. 6, '61. From Co. D; died Feb. 6, '62, Camp Randall, Wis.
Stevens, Oliver; Dodgeville. Enl. Sep. 5, '61. Vet.; M.O. Jul. 16, '65.
Stroud, Alfred; Spring Prairie. Enl. Mar. 3, '64. Trans. to Co. B, Aug. 1, '64.
Swanson, Andrew; Wyoming. Enl. Sep. 5, '61. Killed in action Jul. 21, '64, Atlanta, Ga.
Talle, Peter P.; Dodgeville. Enl. Aug. 26, '61. Vet.; M.O. Jul. 16, '65.
Taylor, Henry H.; West Bend. Enl. Sep. 11, '61. Vet.; trans to Co. D, Mar. 1, '64.
Telford, James; Milwaukee. Enl. Oct. 10, '64. M.O. Jul. 16, '65.
Temby, Peter; Dodgeville. Enl. Mar. 30, '64. Died Nov. 26, '64, at Ocona River, on march from Atlanta to Savannah, Ga., disease.
Thomas, John W.; Ridgeway. Enl. Oct. 12, '64. M.O. Jul. 16, '65.
Thomas, William C.; Ridgeway. Enl. Oct. 11, '64. M.O. Jul. 16, '65.
Tipton, John; Rome. Enl. Oct. 3, '64. From Co. K. 25th Wis. Inf.; M.O. Aug. 12, '65.
Trelour, James; Elk Grove. Enl. Sep. 3, '61. Vet.; M.O. Jul. 16, '65.
Tripp, Samuel; Troy. Enl. Mar. 3, '64. From Co. A; deserted Aug. 1, '64.
Van Gorder, Herman W.; Ridgeway. Enl. Sep. 16, '61. Vet.; died Jul. 20, '65, Ridgeway, Wis.
Walrath, Hamilton; Cottage Grove. Enl. Jan. 4, '64. From Co. K. 25th Wis. Inf.; M.O. Jul. 16, '65.

Williams, David; Dodgeville. Enl. Sep. 18, '61. Vet., Corp.; M.O. Jul. 16, '65.
Williams, John; Ridgeway. Enl. Sep. 7, '61. Deserted Jan. 5,'62.
Williams, Howell; Ridgeway. Enl. Sep. 7, '61. M.O. Oct. 17, '64, term exp.
Wilson, Thomas; Vermont, WI. Enl. Sep. 9, '61. Corp., Sergt.; wnd. Aug. 11, '64, Atlanta; M.O. Nov. 22, '64.
Wilson, Joseph; Arena. Enl. Oct. 29, '61. Vet.; M.O. Jul. 16, '65.
Williamson, William; Dodgeville. Enl. Sep. 4, '61. Sergt., 1st Sergt.; prom. 2nd Lieut. Co. C, 31st Wis. Inf., Sep. 16, '62.
Williamson, Samuel; Dodgeville. Enl. Oct. 2, '62. Disch. Apr. 25, '63, disability.
Wiley, Pratt J.; Diamond Bluff. Enl. Dec. 18, '63. From Co. A; M.O. May 15, '65.
Wood, Enoch P.; Wyoming. Enl. Aug. 26, '61. Vet., Corp., Sergt.; wnd. Jul. 21, '64, Atlanta; died Jul. 23, '64, wnds.
Wood, David C.; Wyoming. Enl. Sep. 18, '61. Corp.; died Jul. 5, '63, Vicksburg, Miss., disease.

ROSTER OF COMPANY "D"

OFFICERS

Captains

JOHN M. PRICE; Barton. Rank Oct. 11, '61. Enl. Sep. 17, '61; A.A.I.G., 3rd Brig. 4th Div. 17th A.C. Gen McPherson; A.A.I.G. 1st Brig. 4th Div. 17th A.C.; wnd. Atlanta; prom. Major Nov. 21, '64.
WILLIAM NUNGESSER; Barton. Rank Jan. 6, '65. Enl. Oct. 4, '61; Vet., Sergt., 1st Sergt.; 1st Lieut., Oct. 7, '64; M.O. Jul. 16, '65.

First Lieutenants

THOMAS FARMER; West Bend. Rank Oct. 11, '61. Enl. Sep. 17, '61; res. May 23, '62.
WILLIAM J. NORTON; West Bend. Rank Apr. 29, '62. Enl. Sep. 17, '61; 2nd Lieut. Oct. 11, '61; det. in mounted Inf.; Actg. Regtl. Q.M.; dismissed Apr. 21, '64; re-enl., see below.
DANIEL J. SULLIVAN; Trenton. Rank Jan. 6, '65. Enl. Sep. 17, '61; Vet., Corp., Sergt.; and Lieut. Oct. 19, '64; wnd Atlanta; A.D.C. in 1st Brig. 3rd Div. 17th A.C.; M.O. Jul. 16, '65.

Second Lieutenants

HARLOW M. WALLER; Barton. Rank Apr. 29, '62. Enl. Sep. 17, '61; 1st Sergt.; res. Sep. 17, '64.
GEORGE T. WESCOTT; Farmington. Rank Jan. 6, '65. Enl. Sep. 17, '61; Vet., Corp., Sergt., 1st Sergt.; M.O. Jul. 16, '65.

Enlisted Men

Albright, Samuel; Scott. Enl. Feb. 19, '64. M.O. Jul. 16, '65.
Ayers, Albert; Pole Grove. Enl. Dec. 23, '61. From Co. D, 25th Wis. Inf.; M.O. Jul. 16, '65.
Ball, James L.; Scott. Enl. Sep. 28, '61. M.O. Oct. 31, '64, term exp.
Bailey, Charles H.; Vienna. Enl. Jan. 21, '64. Died Mar. 24, '64, Memphis, Tenn., disease.
Ball, William L.; Barton. Enl. Oct. 8, '61. Disch.Apr. 30,'62. disability
Barchlay, Marcus; Rochester. Enl. Oct. 14, '64. Pris.; died Dec. 1, '64, Burton, Ga.
Bass, Charles H.; Tomah. Enl. Feb. 29, '64. From Co. D, 25th Wis. Inf.; M.O. Jul. 16, '65.
Bentley, George; Barton. Enl. Oct. 8, '61. Vet.; M.O. Jul. 16. '65.
Birdsell, John; Sparta. Enl. Feb. 15,'63. From Co. D, 25th Wis. Inf.; absent sick at M.O. of Regt.
Bowen, George J.; Scott. Enl. Oct. 3, '61. Vet.; M.O. Jul. 16, '65.
Bowen, David C.; Kewaskum. Enl. Feb. 29, '64. Wnd. Savannah, Ga; M.O. Jul. 16, '65.
Bracken, Owen; Farmington. Enl. Sep. 29, '64. M.O. May 31, '65.
Brady, Luke; Milwaukee. Enl. Oct. 5, '64. M.O. Jul. 16, '65.
Brattan, Edward F.; Tomah. Enl. Dec. 17, '63. From Co. D, 25th Wis. Inf.; M.O. Jul. 16, '65.
Broughton, Timothy B.; Tomah. Enl. Dec. 15, '63. From Co. D, 25th Wis. Inf.; M.O. Jul. 16, '65.
Bullard, Andrew J.; Farmington. Enl. Sep. 17, '61. Corp.; disch. Jun. 11, '62; re-enl. Oct. 3, '62; M.O. Jul. 16, '65.
Bunce, Ebenezer S.; Scott. Enl. Sep. 18, '61. Disch. Jun. 7, '62, disability.
Bunn, Leroy; Bangor. Enl. Feb. 29,'64. From Co. D, 25th Wis. Inf.; M.O. Jul. 16, '65.
Callaghan, Eugene; Farmington. Enl. Sep 23, '61. Vet.,Corp., Sergt.; wnd. Atlanta; M.O. Jul. 16, '65.
Cameron, Malcom; Trenton. Enl. Sep. 23, '61. Vet., Corp.; M.O. Jul. 16, '65.
Ceh or Zeh, Christian; Granville. Enl. Oct. 12, '64. Died Nov. 26, '64, Toombsburg, Ga., disease.
Clark, Selden; Kewaskum. Enl. Oct. 3, '62. Prom. 2nd Lieut, 64th U.S.C.T., Jun. 30, '64.
Cleveland, Daniel F.; Tomah. Enl. Jan. 4, '64. From Co. D, 25th Wis. Inf.; M.O. Jul. 26, '65.
Cole, John M.; West Bend. Enl. Sep. 17, '61. Vet., Corp.; M.O. Jul. 31, '65.
Cossentine, John T.; Auburn. Enl. Oct. 6, '61. Vet., Corp.; M.O. Jul. 16, '65.
Cowan, Hugh; Farmington. Enl Oct. 18, '61. Died Nov. 28, '63, Racine, Wis., disease.
Cumbershaw, Nicholas B.; Barton. Enl. Feb. 22, '64. M.O. Jul. 16, 65
Darling, Solon; West Bend. Enl. Sep. 30,'61. Vet.,M.O. Jul. 16, '65.
Darwin, Samuel N.; Sparta. Enl. Jan. 8, '64. From Co. D, 25th Wis. Inf.; absent sick at M.O. of Regt.
Deasel, August; Waukesha. Enl. Oct. 18, '64. M.O. Jul. 16, '65.

Devlin, Patrick; Kewaskum. Enl. Oct. 17, '61. M.O. Oct. 31, '64, term exp.
Doug, John; Ironton. Enl Oct. 17, '62. From Co. B, May 5, '64; Musician; M.O. Jul. 16, '65.
Dwire, Patrick; Scott. Enl. Feb. 22, '64. Corp.; M.O. Jul. 16, '65.
Dutcher, Nathaniel; Barton. Enl. Oct. 10, '61. Died Sep. 27, '63, Natchez, Miss., disease.
Eberhardt, Christian; West Bend. Enl. Oct. 4, '61. Corp.; M.O. Oct. 31, '64, term exp.
Ebert, William; Scott. Enl. Feb. 22, '64. Wnd. Atlanta; disch. Jan. 9, '65, wnds.
Fairbanks, Byron; Trenton. Enl. Oct. 4, '61. Vet., Musician; wnd. Atlanta; M.O. Jul. 16, '65.
Fairman, Peter D.; Polk. Enl. Oct. 8, '61. Vet.; M.O. Jul. 16, '65.
Fitzner, Ernst H.T.; West Bend. Enl. Oct. 21, '61. Vet.; M.O. Jul. 16, '65.
Frisby, Edwin. E.; Trenton. Enl. Sep. 17, '61. Vet., Corp.; killed in action Jul. 21, '64, Atlanta, Ga.
Fryer, Alexander; Deerfield. Enl. sep. 30, '64. M.O. May 31, '65.
Gilson, Pembroke E.; Trenton. Enl. Sep. 17, '61. Vet.; wnd. Atlanta; M.O. Jul. 16, '65.
Gilson, Norman S.; West Bend. Enl. Sep. 17, '61. Sergt.; prom. Sergt. Major, May 3, '63.
Goldner, Henry; Scott. Enl. Feb. 19, '64. Wnd. died Aug. 19, '64, Atlanta, Ga. wnds.
Gordon, Mark H.; Auburn. Enl Oct. 7, '61. Vet.; M.O. Jul. 16, '65.
Granger, Francis; Trenton. Enl. Sep. 21, '61. Vet., Corp.; prom. Com. Sergt., Feb. 1, '65.
Green, James H.; Trenton. Enl. Sep. 17, '61. Died Aut. 7, '63, St. Louis, Mo., disease.
Gunter, Sebastian; Chippewa Falls. Enl. Oct. 13, '64. M.O. Jul. 16,'65.
Hagerty, Hiram B.; Pine Hill. Enl. Dec. 16, '63. From Co. D. 25th Wis. Inf.; M.O. Jul. 16, '65.
Hallows, Frank D.; Trenton. Enl. Oct. 29, '61. Disch. Apr. 29, '62, disability.
Hawzer, Franz; Milwaukee. Enl. Oct. 7, '64. M.O. Jul. 16, '65.
Harris, Nicholas; Farmington. Enl. Sep. 17, '61. Vet.; wnd and pris. Atlanta; died Nov. 26, '64, Andersonville, Ga.
Harris, James; Farmington. Sep. 17, '61. Vet., Corp., Sergt.; M.O. Jul. 16, '65.
Hard, Francis C.; Kewaskum. Enl. Oct. 6, '61. Trans. to Co. I, Dec. 31, '61.
Hardike, Leopold; Carlton. Enl. Oct. 15, '64. M.O. Jul. 16, '65.
Haskins, Nathaniel, Sparta. Enl. Dec. 15, '63. From Co. D. 15th Wis. Inf.; M.O. Jul. 16, '65.
Hazen, Andrew; Montreal, WI. Enl. Oct. 10, '64. M.O. Jul. 16, '65.
Hertzog, Frederick; Granville. Enl. Oct. 14, '64. M.O. Jul. 16, '65.
Hockman, William; Farmington. Enl. Sep. 17, '61. Vet.; killed in action Jul. 21, '64., Atlanta, Ga.
Hogle, George J.; East Troy. Enl. Oct. 4, '64. M.O. Jul. 16, '65.
Hollister, Arthur A.; Fountain. Enl. Sep. 28, '64. M.O. May 31, '65.

Holt, George R; Farmington. Enl. Sep. 17, '61. Corp.; wnd. Atlanta; M.O. Jan. 12, '65, term exp.
Holt, John M.; Farmington. Enl. Sep. 17, '61. Vet.; wnd. Atlanta; died Oct. 11, '64, Rome, Ga., wnds.
Huntington, William; Barton. Enl. Feb. 17, '64. M.O. Jul. 16, '65.
Huxley, Richard; Ridgeway. Enl. Feb. 14, '63. From Co. D, 25th Wis. Inf. ; absent sick at M.O. of Regt.
Jacket, Victor; Benton. Enl. Oct. 12, '64. M.O. Jul. 16, '65.
Jackson, James A.; Farmington. Enl. Sep. 18, '61. Vet.; M.O. Jul. 16, '65.
Jenks, Henry; Milwaukee. Oct. 7, '64. M.O. Jul. 16, '65.
Jenkins, Allen; Trenton. Enl. Sep. 17, '61. Disch. Feb. 23, '63. disability.
Jones, John B.; West Bend. Enl. Sep. 17, '61. Vet., Sergt.; 2nd Lieut., Oct 7, '64, declined; prom. 2nd Lieut. Co. G, 44th Wis. Inf., Sep. 13, '64.
King, George W.; Davis Corners. Enl. Dec. 12, '63. From Co. D, 25th Wis. Inf.; M.O. Jul. 16, '65.
Kingsland, William; Kewaskum. Enl. Oct. 3, '62. M.O. Jul. 16, '65.
Kringie, Herman; Waukesha. Enl. Oct. 11, '64. M.O. Jul. 16, '65.
Kurtz, Phillip; Joined Co. Nov. 8, '64; M.O. Jul. 16, '65.
Lampert, Mathias, 1st; West Bend. Enl. Oct. 4, '61. M.O. Oct. 31, '64, term exp.
Lampert, Mathias, 2d; West Bend. Enl. Oct. 6, '61. Killed in action, Jul. 21, '64, Atlanta, Ga.
Lampert, John; West Bend. Enl. Oct. 4, '61. Killed in action, Jul. 21, '64, Atlanta, Ga.
Lamb, William H.; Tomah. Enl. Mar. 1, '64. From Co. D, 25th Wis. Inf.; M.O. Jul. 16, '65.
Landgraf, Andrew; Scott. Enl. Feb. 19, '64. M.O. Jul. 16, '65.
Lessenden, George C.; Farmington. Enl. Oct. 21, '61. Trans to V.R.C., Nov. 9, '63; M.O. Nov. 3, '64, (?) term exp.
Lester, David; Kenosh. Enl. Oct. 5, '64. M.O. Jul. 16, '65.
Lieb, John; Lake. Enl. Oct. 13, '64. M.O. Jul. 16, '65.
Longhurst, George W.; Auburn. Enl. Nov. 29, '61. Vet., Corp.; M.O. Jul. 16, '65.
Lord, Edward K.; Farmington. Feb. 29, '64. Corp.; M.O. Jul. 16, '65.
Lynch, Peter; Farmington. Enl. Sep. 30, '61. Vet.; M.O. Jul. 16, '65.
Maas, John P.; Milwaukee. Enl. Oct. 11, '64. M.O. Jul. l6, '65.
Martin, Henry; Tennessee. Enl. Oct. 16, '62. Died Jul. 19, '63, on Str. "Crescent City," disease.
Marsden, Benjamin F.; Galena. Enl. Feb. 6, '64. Wnd. Atlanta; disch. Jan. 4, '65, wnds.
Matcheit, James; Sparta. Enl. Mar. 15, '64. From Co. D, 25th Wis. Inf.; M.O. Jul. 16, '65.
Melter, Frederick; Scott. Enl. Oct. 13, '61. Died Mar. 23, '62, Quincy, Ill.
McClement, John; Farmington. Enl. Sep. 19, '61. Vet.; died Nov. 9, '64, Chattanooga, Tenn., disease.
McCarty, William; Farmington. Enl. Sep. 17, '61. Vet., Corp.; M.O. Jul. 16, '65.

McDonald, William W. Trenton. Enl. Oct. 8, '61. Died Dec. 15, '62, Holly Springs, Miss., disease.
McDonald, Thomas; Trenton. Enl. Oct. 30, '61. Wnd. Feb. 12, '64 foraging; M.O. Nov. 15, '64, term exp.
McHenry, James; Trenton. Enl. Sep. 26, '61. Vet.; M.O. Jul. 16, '65.
McHugh, Peter; Kewaskum. Enl. Oct. 21, '61. Vet.; trans. to Co. I, Jan. 19, '62; re-joined Jan. 1, '64; trans to V.R.C., Nov. 8, '64.
McLaughlin, John; Trenton. Enl. Oct. 31, '61. Died Jul. 18, '62. Union City, Tenn., disease.
Miller, Henry; Wayne. Enl. Oct. 22, '61. M.O. Oct. 31, '64, term exp.
Miller, Jacob; Farmington. Enl. Feb. 19, '64. M.O. Jul. 16, '65.
Miller, Nelson; Auburn. Enl. Feb. 17, '64. Died May 6, '63, Newbern, N.C., disease.
Munger, Israel; Barton. Enl. Sep. 24, '61. Trans. to Co. I, Dec. 31, '61.
Meyers, William W.; Linden. Enl. Feb. 18, '64. Pris. Feb. 12, '64, Decatur, Ala.; wnd Atlanta; M.O. Jul. 16, '65.
Meyers, William G., Farmington. Enl. Sep. 17, '61. Vet.; pris. Feb. 12, '64, Decatur; M.O. Jul. 16, '65.
Nash, Edwin M.; Hortonville. Enl. Oct. 9, '61. Vet.; M.O. Jul 16, '65.
Neimeir, August; Jackson. Enl. Oct. 8, '61. M.O. Oct. 31, '64, term exp.
Newcomb, Henry C.; Trenton. Enl. Sep. 21, '61. Corp., Sergt.; M.O. Oct. 31, '64, term exp.
Norton, William J.; West Bend. Feb. 14, '63. M.O. Jul. 16, '65.
Norton, Vinal W.; Auburn. Enl. Oct. 10, '61. Vet., Corp., Sergt, 1st Sergt.; M.O. Jul. 16, '65.
Nowork, Wenzel; Highland. Enl. Oct. 1, '64. M.O. Jul. 16, '65.
Obirst, Adam; Milwaukee. Enl. Oct. 15, '61. M.O. Jul. 16, '65.
Oliver, William; Scott. Enl. Oct. 2, '61. Died Dec. 26, '61, Madison, Wis.
Peat, Thomas; Trenton. Enl. Sep. 17, '61. Vet. Corp., Sergt.; M.O. Jul. 16, '65.
Peterson, Christopher; Tomah. Enl. Jan. 8, '64. From Co. D, 25th Wis. Inf.; absent sick at M.O. of Regt.
Peters, Nicholas; Charleston. Enl. Oct. 11, '64. M.O. Jul. 16, '65.
Phelps, Truman O.; Barton. Enl. Nov. 29, '61, Vet.; M.O. Jul. 16, '65.
Parshall, Wm. H.H.; Sparta. Enl. Dec. 16, '63. From Co. D. 25 Wis. Inf.; Corp.; M.O. Jul. 16, '65.
Pizak, Mathias; Carlton. Enl. Oct. 12, '64. M.O. Jul. 16, '65.
Porter, William H.; Trenton. Enl. Sep. 17, '61. Trans. to Co. I, Dec. 31, '61; re-joined Jan. 18, '62; Vet.; M.O. Jul. 16, '65.
Pride, Albert; Dover. Enl. Oct. 4, '64. M.O. Jul. 16, '65.
Probst, Christopher; Farmington. Enl. Oct. 13, '61. Trans to Co. C, Dec. 31, 61.
Purcell, Walter W.; Tomah. Dec. 28, '63. From Co. D, 25th Wis. Inf..; M.O. Jul. 16, '65.
Putnam, Charles H.; Sparta. Enl. Dec. 24, '63. From Co. D. 25th Wis. Inf.; M.O. Jul. 16, '65.
Quackenbush, Ernest; Pine Hill. Enl. Dec. 21, '63. From Co. D, 25th Wis. Inf.; M.O. Jul. 16, '65.

Rakskopf, George; Polk. Enl. Oct. 7, '61. M.O. Oct. 31, '64, term exp.
Rand, Philander; Osceola. Enl. Oct. 22, '61. Vet.; M.O. Jul. 16, '65.
Randall, James H.; Barton. Enl. Oct. 29, '61. Vet.; M.O. Jul. 16, '65.
Randall, George A.; Barton. Enl. Dec. 30, '62. M.O. Jul. 16, '65.
Richardson, Perry; Glendale. Enl. Jan. 7, '63. From Co. D. 25th Wis. Inf.; M.O. Jul. 16, '65.
Robbins, Aaron; Trenton. Enl. Sep. 17, '61. Died Feb. 13, '63, LaGrange, Miss., disease.
Roohr, Henry F.L.; Kewaskum. Enl. Oct. 8, '61. Died Jul 21, '63, Vicksburg, Miss., disease.
Ross, George E.; Farmington. Enl. Aug. 15, '62. M.O. Jun. 16, '65.
Rugg, Alfred H.; Bloomfield. Enl Mar. 29, '64. From Co. D, 25th Wis. Inf.; M.O. Jul. 16, '65.
Rusco, Oscar A.; Barton. Enl. Sep. 17, '61. Corp., Sergt.; M.O. Oct. 31, '64, term exp.
Schwendener, Christian; Wayne. Enl. Oct. 22, '61. M.O. Oct. 31, '64, term exp.
Schwendener, John S.; Wayne. Enl. Oct. 22, '61. M.O. Oct. 31, '64, term exp.
Scott, Benjamin; Kewaskum. Enl. Sep. 17, '61. Vet.; M.O. Jul 25, '65
Scott, Leonard; Sparta. Enl. Jan. 4, '64. From Co. D. 25th Wis. Inf.; M.O. Jun. 12, '65.
Scott, Moses; Auburn. Enl. Feb. 17, '64. Wnd. Kenesaw; M.O. Jul. 16, '65.
Seuberlich, Joseph; La Crosse. Enl. Oct. 5, '64. M.O. Jul. 16, '65.
Shaw, Joseph; Richford. Enl. Dec. 28, '63. From Co. D, 25th Wis. Inf.; M.O. Jul. 16, '65.
Singer, John; Wayne. Enl. Oct. 21, '61. Vet., Corp.; M.O. Jul 16, '65.
Sischo, Herman A.; Auburn. Enl. Feb. 17, '64. M.O. Jul. 16, '65.
Siver, William J.; Milwaukee. Enl. Oct. 4, '64. M.O. Jul. 16, '65.
Smith, Christopher D.; West Bend. Enl. Sep. 17, '61. Vet., wnd. Jul 21, '64, Atlanta; died Jul 23, '64, wnds.
Smith, Franklin L.; Farmington. Enl. Sep. 24, '61. Vet.; M.O. Aug. 8, '65.
Smith, Emery P.; Trenton. Enl. Sep. 17, '61. Vet., Corp.; killed in action, Jul. 21, '64, Atlanta, Ga.
Smith, Augustus; Polk. Enl. Sep. 17, '61. Vet.; M.O. Jul. 16, '65.
Smith, Charles C.; Trenton. Enl. Oct. 10, '61. Vet.; M.O. Jul. 16, '65.
Smith, Jacob; Kewaskum. Enl. Oct. 11, '61. M.O. Oct. 31, '64, term exp.
Smith, Elias; Polk. Enl. Mar. 16, '64. M.O. Jul. 16, '65.
Southwick, William P.; Kewaskum. Enl. Oct. 6, '61, Died Nov. 8, '62, LaGrange, Tenn., disease.
Spielman, John; Wayne. Enl. Oct. 21, '61. Disch. Apr. 21, '62, disability.
Stahl, Charles; Milwaukee. Enl. Oct. 8, '64. M.O. Jul. 16, '65.
Stannard, Henry R; West Bend. Enl. Oct. 10, '61. Musician; died Aug. 22, '63, St. Louis, Mo.
Stannard, Wellington C.; West Bend. Enl. Sep. 23, '61. Vet.; killed Jul. 21, '64, Atlanta, Ga.
Stacks, Joseph H.; Polk. Enl. Oct. 2, '61. Vet.; trans. to V.R.C. Jun. 30, '64.

Stacks, Daniel D.; Polk. Enl. Oct. 9, '61. Vet.; trans to Co. I, Dec. 31, '61; rejd. Jan. 1, '64; M.O. Jul. 16, '65.
Stark, Henry; Barton. Enl. Oct. 6, '61. Trans to Co. C, Dec. 31, '61.
Starkey, Joseph B.; Barton. Enl. sep. 17, '61. Vet.; wnd. Atlanta; disch. Apr. 9, '65, wnds.
Stilwell, Paine; Winon, MN. Enl. Dec. 15, '62. From Co. D, 25th Wis. Inf.; M.O. Jul. 26, '65.
Stitzer, Augustus; Burr Oak. Enl. Feb. 29, '64. From Co. D, 25th Wis. Inf.; M.O. Jul. 16, '65.
St. John, Lewis D.; Polk. Enl. Mar. 16, '64. Died May 10, '65, Washington, D.C., disease.
Stroop, Peter; Kewaskum. Enl. Oct. 16, '61. Vet., Corp.; M.O. Jul. 16, '65.
Strong, Henry F.; Trenton. Enl. Oct. 3, '61. Trans to Co. I, Dec. 31, '61.
Senn, Andrew; West Bend. Enl. Oct. 22, '61. M.O. Oct. 31, '64, term exp.
Taylor, Henry H.; Barton. Enl. Sep. 17, '61. Vet.; trans. to Co. C, Dec. 31, '61; rejd. Mar. 1, '64; M.O. Jul. 29, '65
Tobacco, Frank; Kewaskum; Enl. Oct. 6, '61. M.O. Oct. 31, '64, term exp.
Trowbridge, George M.; Tomah. Enl. Jan. 4, '64. From Co. D, 25th Wis. Inf.; M.O. Jul. 16, '65.
Turner, Caleb W.; Kewaskum. Sep. 30, '61. Disch. Mar. 27, '62, disability.
Tuthill, John; Sparta. Enl. Dec. 16, '63. From Co. D, 25th Wis. Inf.; M.O. Jul. 16, '65.
VanKirk, Jeremiah; Sparta. Enl. Dec. 15, '63. From Co. D, 25th Wis. Inf.; M.O. Jul. 16, '65.
Varny, Samuel A.; Farmington. Enl. Oct. 8, '62. M.O. Jul. 16, '65.
Vaughn, Harrison H.; Tomah. Enl. Dec. 28, '63. From Co. D, 25th Wis. Inf.; M.O. Jul. 16, '65.
Vunk, Edward; Polk. Enl. Aug. 26, '62. Wnd. Jan. 28, '63; disch. May 18, '63, wnds.
Waldo, Charles D.; West Bend. Enl. Sep. 17, '61. Sergt., 1st Sergt.; disch. Sep. 17, '64.
Walter, David M.; Trenton. Enl. Sep. 17, '61. Vet.; wnd. and pris. Atlanta; died Sep. 20, '64, Andersonville, Ga.
Warren, Horace H.; Trenton. Enl. Oct. 30, '62. Absent on detch. ser. at M.O. of Regt.
Webber, Nicholas; Troy. Enl. Oct. 14, '64. Died Apr 1, '65, Goldsboro, N.C., disease.
Westcott, Ananias; Farmington. Enl. Oct. 22, '61. Disch. Mar. 27, '62 disability.
Westcott, Garner; Oak Creek. Enl. Oct. 15, '64. M.O. Jul. 16, '65.
Westcott, Willet R.; Farmington. Enl. Sep. 21, '61. Vet.; Musician; trans. to Band, Jul. 1, '62; rej. Aug. 18, '62; disch. May 14, '64, disability.
Westcott, Erskine; Farmington. Enl. Sep. 23, '61. Musician; disch. Mar. 26, '63, disability.
Whalen, Moses; Scott. Enl. Feb. 19, '64. Wnd. and pris. Atlanta; died Nov. 21, '64, Andersonville, Ga.

Wheeler, Jason M.; Auburn. Enl. Feb. 17, '64. Wnd. Atlanta; M.O. Jul. 16, '65.
Wheeler, Franklin B.; Auburn. Enl. Oct. 2, '61. Sergt.; died Mar. 13, '63, Memphis, Tenn., disease.
Willis, James R.; Farmington. Enl. Oct. 30, '61. Vet.; M.O. Oct. 31. '64, term exp.
Wills, James E.; Farmington. Enl. Sep. 17, '61. Vet.; M.O. Jul. 16, '65
Winney, Charles W.; Kewaskum. Enl. Oct. 21, '61. Vet., Corp.; M.O. Jul. 16, '65.
Wipe, Henry; Barton. Enl. Sep. 23, '61. Died Mar. 14, '62, disease.
Wolf, Frank; Wayne. Enl. Oct. 21, '61. Vet., Corp., Sergt.; M.O. Jul. 16, '65.
Worden, Ira J.; Kewaskum. Enl. Oct. 6, '61. Vet.; M.O. Jul. 16, '65.
Wright, John R.; Kewaskum, Enl. Oct. 6, '61. Wagoner; disch. Jun. 7, '62, disability.

ROSTER OF COMPANY "E"

OFFICERS

Captains

ABRAHAM VANDERPOEL; Newport. Rank Oct. 3, '61. Enl. Sep. 4, '61; res. May 3, '62.
JOHN GILLISPIE; Dellona. Rank. May 11, '62. Enl. Sep. 7,'61; 1st Lieut., Oct. 3, '61; wnd. and pris. Jul. 21, '64. Atlanta; M.O. Jun. 7, '65, term exp.

First Lieutenants

LEWIS T. LINNELL; Dellona. Rank, May 11, '62. Enl. Sep. 7, '61; 2nd Lieut., Oct. 3, '61; Actg Adgt; Actg. Adjt., 3rd Iowa Vet. Vols; Actg Ord. Officer, Gen. Howard's Staff; M.O. Dec. 26, '64., term exp.
ALPHEUS E. KINNEY; Fairfield. Rank Feb. 11, '65. Enl. Sep. 11, '61; Vet., Sergt., 1st Sergt.; 2nd Lieut., Nov. 21, '64; Capt., Jul. 5, '65, not mustered; M.O. Jul 16, '65.

Second Lieutenants

JAMES H. THAYER; Newport. Rank May 11, '62. Enl. Sep. 7, '61; 1st Sergt.; wnd. Aug. 14, '64, Atlanta; died Oct. 7, '64, near Atlanta, wnds.
MICHAEL GRIFFIN; Newport. Rank Feb. 11, '65. Enl. Sep. 11, '61. Vet., Sergt., 1st Sergt.; wnd, Atlanta; 1st Lieut., Jul. 5, '65, not mustered; M.O. Jul. 16, '65.

Enlisted Men

Adams, George E.; Delton. Enl. Dec. 15, '63. M.O. Jun. 7, '65.
Allen, Silas W.; Bad Axe. Enl. Feb. 28, '64. M.O. Jul. 16, '65.
Allen, Abner B.; Bad Axe. Enl. Feb. 27, '64. Wnd. Jun. 18, '64,
    Atlanta Campaign; M.O. Jun. 23, '65.
Amundson, Amund; Coon. Enl. Oct. 13, '64. Died Feb. 1, '65,
    Savannah, Ga., disease.
Anderson, August; Coon. Enl. Oct. 13,'64. M.O. Jul. 16, '65.
Artus Frederick; La Crosse. Enl. Dec. 23, '63. From Co. F, 25th Wis.
    Inf.; Corp.; M.O. Jul. 16, '65.
Attleson, Neilse; Deerfield. Enl. Oct. 5, '61. M.O. Jul. 3, '63.
Bailey, George W.; Newport. Enl. Sep. 16, '61. Vet.; died May 20, '65,
    Kilbourn City, Wis., disease.
Banker, Henry; Clinton. Enl. Sep. 22, '64. Drafted; M.O. May 31, '65
Barton, Ethelbert W. ; Linden. Enl. Feb. 5, '64. Died May 29, '65,
    Washington, D.C., disease.
Beardsley, Hiram S.; Dell Prairie. Enl. Oct. 24, '61. Corp.; M.O.
    Nov. 4, '64, term exp.
Bell, Walter D.; La Crosse. Enl. Dec. 18,'63. From Co. F, 25th Wis.
    Inf.; M.O. Jul. 16, '65.
Bender, Batheson; Sharon. Enl. Sep. 22, '64. M.O. May 31,'65.
Bennett, Edmund F.; Newport. Enl. Oct. 23, '61. M.O. Nov. 4, '64,
    term exp.
Bennett, David E.; La Crosse. Enl. Dec. 19, '64. From Co. F, 25th
    Wis. Inf.; M.O. Jul. 16, '65.
Bennett, Henry H.; Kilbourn. Enl. Sep. 8, '61. Accidentally wnd.
    Apr. '64, Paducah, Ky.; M.O. Nov. 5, '64, term exp.
Berry, Charles H.; La Crosse. Enl. Jan. 5, '64. From Co. F, 25th Wis.
    Inf.; M.O. May 13, '65.
Benson, Benjamin; La Crosse. Enl. Jan. 14, '64. From Co. F, 25th
    Wis. Inf.; M.O. Jun. 30, '65.
Bliss, Albert; Bad Axe. Enl. Mar. 12, '64. M.O. Jul. '16, '65.
Bohn, Frederick; Racine. Enl. Oct. 14, '64. M.O. Jul. 16, '65.
Bond, Robert; Dellona. Enl. Aug. 30, '62. M.O. May 31, '65.
Boartlman, George; La Crosse. Enl. Dec. 26, '63. From Co. F, 25th
    Wis. Inf.; M.O. Jul. 16, '65.
Boughton, Clement A.; Delton. Enl. Sep. 217, '61. Vet.; actg. Sergt.
    Maj.; wnd. Jul. 21, '64, Atlanta, Ga.; died Jul. 23, '64,
    wnds.
Bowman, James J.; Madison. Enl. Nov. 1, '61. Vet.; M.O. Jul. 16, '65.
Bowman, William H.; Kingston. Enl. Oct. 1, '61. Vet.; M.O.
    Jul 16, '65.
Boyd, Joshua L.; Greenville. Enl. Oct. 11, '64. Died Apr. 9, '65,
    David's Island, N.Y., disease.
Briggs, Charles S.; Newport. Enl. Sep. 11, '61. Vet.; M.O. Jul. 16, '65
Briggs, William S.; Newport. Enl. Sep. 20, '61. Vet.; M.O. Jul. 16, '65
Bromley, John; Delton. Enl. Oct. 16, '61. Disch. Jun. 21, '64,
    disability.
Brown, Francis H. ; Delton. Enl. Oct. 25, '61. Disch. Apr. 18, '62,
    disability.

Bullis, John W.; Delton. Enl. Oct. 23, '61. Disch. May 1, '62, disability.
Bunce, Chauncey; Sparta. Enl. Jan. 5, '64. From Co. F, 25th Wis. Inf.; M.O. Jul. 16, '65.
Burhaus, Samuel D.; Delton. Enl. Aug. 14, '62. Accidently wnd. Feb. 11, '63; M.O. May 31, '65.
Camp, James. Dellona. Enl. Sep. 22, '61. Vet.; wnd. Atlanta; disch. Sep. 20, '65, wnds.
Campbell, Samuel; Delton. Enl. Oct. 11, '61. On Det. Ser. at M.O. of Regt.
Campbell, Erastus; Ridgeville. Enl. Dec. 22, '63. From Co. F. 25th Wis. Inf.; M.O. Jul. 16, '65.
Canfield, Fletcher; Newport. Enl. Oct. 18, '61. Vet.; M.O. Jul. 16, '65
Champlin, Wilmot; Melrose. Enl. Jan 21, '64. From Co. F, 25th Wis. Inf.; M.O. Jul. 16, '65.
Clary, Carver; Jefferson. Enl. Sep. 19, '64. Drafted; M.O. May 31, '65
Clement, James H.; New Buffalo. Enl. Dec. 15, '63. Died Aug. 6, '64, 3rd Div. Hosp., disease.
Clement, James M.; Delton. Enl. Sep. 7, '61. Vet.; wnd. Atlanta; disch. Nov. 10, '65, wnds.
Clement, Lorenzo; Delton. Enl. Sep. 7, '61. Vet.; M.O. Jul. 16, '65.
Colbourn, William; Rochester. Enl. Oct. 12, '64. M.O. Jul. 16, '65.
Coleman, Arthur P.; Delton. Enl. Feb. 28, '64. M.O. Jul. 16, '65.
Coleman, Charles; Fairfield. Enl. Sep. 11, '61. Vet.; M.O. Jul. 16, '65.
Cole, Eddy; Lindina. Enl. lOct. 17, '61. Vet., Corp., Sergt.; M.O. Jul. 16, '65.
Cope, James A.; Linden. Enl. Aug. 30, '62. M.O. May 31, '65.
Cornish, James G.; Fairfield. Enl. Sep. 11, '61. Vet.; M.O. Jul. 16, '65
Cosper, Erastus; Delona. Enl. Sep. 22, '61. Disch. Nov. 15, '61.
Cotton, William S.H.; Mauston. Enl. Sep. 19, '61. Wnd, Atlanta; M.O. Nov. 4, '64, term exp.
Craker, Judson; Newport. Enl. Oct. 3, '61. Vet.; M.O. Jul. 16, '65.
Darrow, Nathaniel; Reedsburg. Enl. Dec. 17, '63. M.O. Jul. 16, '65.
Davis, Henry C.; Pine Hill. Enl. Mar. 10, '65. From Co. F, 25th Wis. Inf.; M.O. Jul. 16, '65.
Denning, William B.; St. Louis. Enl. Jan. 5, '64. From Co. F, 25th Wis. Inf.; M.O. Jul. 16, '65.
Dunham, William H.; Newport. Enl. Sep. 12, '61. M.O. Nov. 4, '64, term exp.
Dyer, Henry H.; Delton. Enl. Sep. 21, '61., Corp., Sergt.; 2nd Lieut. Jul. 5, '65, not mustered; M.O. Jul. 16, '65.
Easterbrook, LeRoy; Eau Galle. Enl. Jan. 2, '64; From Co. F, 25th Wis. Inf.; Corp.; M.O. Jul 16, '65.
Edmonds, Joseph C.; Dell Prairie. Enl. Sep. 13, '61. Died Aug. 30, '63, Natchez, Miss., disease.
Edwards, James A.; Linden. Enl. Oct. 7, '61. Disch. Jun. 11, '62, disability.
Eighmy, Benson L.; Delton. Enl. Oct. 16, '61. M.O. Nov. 4, '64, term exp.
Eighmy, Obadiah W.; Delton. Enl. Sep. 21, '61. Vet.; M.O. Jul 16, '65
Fairchild, Stephen D.; Sterling. Enl. Sep. 21, '64. Drafted; M.O. May 31, '65.

Fields, Charles W.; Lindina. Enl. Sep. 28, '61. Vet., Corp.; killed in
action, Jul. 21, '64, Atlanta, Ga.
Fisher, William H.; Newport. Enl. Oct. 18, '61. Died Sep. 14, '62,
Humboldt, Tenn., disease.
Fluno, Henry A.; Lindina. Enl. Sep. 23, '61. Vet.; wnd. Jul. 5, '64,
Chattahoochee; died Jul. 6, '64, 4th Div. Hosp., wnds.
Fosbinder, Charles W.; Linden. Enl. Sep. 23, '61. Corp.; wnd. Apr. 9,
'63, Coldwater, Miss.; trans to V.R.C., Apr. 10, '64;
M.O. Sep. 21, '64, term exp.
Freeman, Joel M.; New Buffalo. Enl. Dec. 15, '63. Died Jul. 9, '64,
Rome, Ga., disease.
Freer, George W.; Delton. Enl. Sep. 17, '61. Vet., Corp.; M.O.
Jul. 16, '65.
Freer, Justus; Delton. Enl. Sep. 22, '61. Vet.; M.O. Jul. 16, '65.
Gaddis, John; Dellona. Enl. Oct. 25, '61. Corp.; disch., Nov. 5, '64,
disability.
Gastmyer, Christian; Dellona. Enl. Oct. 25, '64. Drafted; M.O. May
31, '65.
Getts, John; La Crosse. Enl. Dec. 30, '63. From Co. F, 25th Wis. Inf.;
M.O. Aug. 10, '65.
Gillispie, Daniel; Dellona. Enl. Jan. 15, '64. M.O. Jul. 16, '65.
Gloyd, Charles L.; New Buffalo. Enl. Dec. 17, '63. Died Jun. 25, '64,
Big Shanty, Ga., disease.
Gloyd, Charles E.; Delton. Enl. Oct. 19, '61. Disch. Jan. 2, '62,
disability.
Gloyd, Alfred E.; Delton. Enl. Sep. 20, '61. Disch. Apr. 18, '62,
disability.
Goodrich, George; La Crosse. Enl. Dec. 15, '63. From Co. F, 25th Wis.
Inf.; M.O. Jul. 16, '65.
Green, Reuben W.; Reedsburg. Enl. Sep. 2, '61. Musician; disch. Dec.
11, '63, to accept prom. in 6th Miss. U.S.C.T.
Griffin, John; Linden. Enl. Oct. 1, '61. Vet., Corp.; M.O. Jul. 16, '65.
Griffin, Alvaro N.; Linden. Enl. Oct. 23, '61. Vet.; M.O.Jul. 16, '65.
Gutic, James M.; Kilbourn. Enl. Sep. 19, '61. Vet., Corp.; Musician;
M.O. Jul. 16, '65.
Hall, George C.; Granger, MN. Enl. Feb. 25, '64. From Co. F, 25th
Wis. Inf.; M.O. Jul. 16, '65.
Hamlin, Oscar E.; Amherst. Enl. Mar. 10, '64. From Co. F, 25th Wis.
Inf.; M.O. May 30, '65.
Harbaugh, Wesley; Linden. Enl. Oct. 8, '61. Died Nov. 19, '63,
Memphis, Tenn., disease.
Harrison, Nathan D.; New Buffalo. Enl. Aug. 14,'62. M.O. May 31,'65
Harrison, William H.; New Buffalo. Enl. Aug. 14, '62. Corp.; M.O.
May 31, '65.
Hawes, Joseph; Kilbourn. Enl. Sep. 14, '61. Vet.; M.O. Jul. 16, '65.
Headstream, Charles; Mauston. Enl. Sep. 28, '61. Absent sick at
M.O. of Regt.
Helneck, christopher; Greenfield. Enl. Dec. 23, '63. From Co. F, 25th
Wis. Inf.; M.O. Jul. 16, '65.
Heiser, Charles; La Crosse. Enl. Dec. 24, '63. From Co. F, 25th Wis.
Inf.; absent sick at M.O. of Regt.

Hendrickson, Ole; La Crosse. Enl. Jan. 4, '64. From Co. F, 25th Wis. Inf.; M.O. May 13, '65.
Henry, Isaac; Dellona. Enl. Oct. 1, '61. Vet., Corp., Sergt.; M.O. Jul. 16, '65.
Hildreth, Milton M.; Fairfield. Enl. Sep. 17, '61. Vet., Corp.; M.O. Jul. 16, '65.
Horsington, James E.; Baraboo. Enl. Dec. 28, '63. M.O. Jul. 16, '65.
Hubbell, John G.; Dell Prairie. Enl. Sep. 7, '61. Corp.; disch. Sep. 9, '62.
Humphrey, Aaron M.; Delton. Enl. Oct. 21,'61. Vet.; M.O. Jul 16, '65
Hutchinson, Almond T.; Dell Prairie. Enl. Sep. 14, '61. Vet.; accidentally wnd. Nov. 8, '64; disch. Jun. 18, '65. disability.
Hurlbut, Truman H.; Fairfield. Enl. Sep. 11, '61. Vet., Musician; prom. Prin. Musician, Jan. 1, '64.
Ingalls, John; New Buffalo. Enl. Dec. 17, '63. M.O. Jul. 16, '65.
Jameson, Amos J. ; Dellona. Enl. Sep. 21, '61. Disch. Apr. 24, '62, disability.
Johnston, Enos; Arlington. Enl. Oct. 25, '61. Died Aug. 217, '62, Humboldt, Tenn.
Johnson, Rufus; Summit. Enl. Sep. 28, '61. Vet.; M.O. Jul. 16, '65.
Jones, Lorenzo; Union. Enl. Feb. 22, '64. From Co. F, 25th Wis. Inf.; M.O. Jul. 16, '65.
Kauffman, Benjamin; Hillsboro. Enl. Jan. 5, '64. From Co. F, 25th Wis. Inf.; M.O. Jul. 16, '65.
Knapp, Isaac I.; Manitowoc, Enl. Aug. 18, '64. M.O. Jul. 116, '65.
Knapp, Abraham; Freedom. Enl. Sep. 30, '61. Vet.; pris while with Div. Train; died Nov. 8, '64, Millen Ga., disease.
Knapp, James C.; Freedom. Enl. Sep. 30, '61. Disch. Aug. 3, '62, Humboldt, Tenn.
Knapp, Ithamar; Freedom. Enl. Oct. 26, '61. M.O. Nov. 4, '64, term exp.
Knower, Samuel E.; Sterling. Enl. Sep. 21, '64. Drafted; M.O. Jul. 1, '65.
Lamere, Edward; Somerset. Enl. Jan. 2, '64. From Co. F, 25th Wis. Inf.; M.O. Jun. 21, '65.
Lane, Caleb C.; La Crosse. Enl. Dec. 31, '63. From Co. F, 25th Wis. Inf.; M.O. Jun. 30, '65.
Larson, Christopher; Franklin. Enl. Oct. 13, '64. M.O. Jul. 5, '65; died Jul. 15, '65, Louisville, Ky.
Larson, Reinert; Coon. Enl. Sep. 14, '64. M.O. May 31, '65.
Laskey, Thomas; La Crosse. Enl. Mar. 7, '64. From Co. F, 25th Wis. Inf.; M.O. Jul. 16, '65.
Latsch, John; Fountain City. Enl. Feb. 27, '64. From Co. F, 25th Wis. Inf.; M.O. Jul. 16, '65.
Lawsha, Jacob; New Buffalo. Enl. Feb. 26, '64. M.O. Jul. 16, '65.
Lawsha, George; Delton. Enl. Sep. 20, '61. Vet., Corp.; M.O. Jul. 16, '65.
Lewis, Timothy A.; La Crosse. Enl. Jan. 4, '64. From Co. F, 25th Wis. Inf.; M.O. May 10, '65.
Livingston, James; Roaring Creek. Enl. Dec. 26, '63. From Co. F, 25th Wis. Inf.; M.O. Jul. 16, '65.

Lowman, John I.; Kilbourn. Enl. Sep. 19, '61. Corp.; died Jun. 27, '62, Troy, Tenn., disease.
Macauley, Maurice A.; Lindina. Enl. Sep. 28, '61. Vet., Corp.; prom. Q.M. Sergt., Jan. 1, '65.
Malloy, Michael; Canada. Enl. Mar. 11, '64. From Co. F, 25th Wis. Inf.; M.O. Jul. 16, '65.
Marlow, Benjamin; Caledonia, MN. Enl. Mar. 7, '64. From Co. F, 25th Wis. Inf.; Corp.; M.O. Jun. 27, '65.
Marston, Henry; Fairfield. Enl. Sep. 19, '61. Vet.; M.O. Jul 16, '65.
Marshall, George W.; Delton. Enl. Sep. 21, '61. Died Sep. 22, '63, Vicksburg, Miss., disease.
Mathews, James; Summit. Enl. Sep. 28, '61. Vet.; wnd. Atlanta; M.O. Jul. 16, '65.
McVey, James; Newport. Enl. Sep. 7, '61. Corp.; M.O. Nov. 4, '64, term exp.
Meims, Elwood; Greenfield. Enl. Oct. 17, '64. M.O. Jul. 16, '65.
Montanye, George C.; Newport. Enl. Mar. 30, '64. Died Jun. 25, '64, Big Shanty Station, Ga., disease.
Montanye, John C.; Delton. Enl. Sep. 7, '61. Trans. to V.R.C., Apr. 22, '64.
Mosier, William L.; Lindina. Enl. Oct. 23, '61. Vet., Corp.; M.O. Jul. 16, '65.
Mott, Oscar; ? Enl. Jan. 5, '64. From Co. F, 25th Wis. Inf.; M.O. Jul. 16, '65.
Moulton, Johnson; Newport. Enl. Sep. 12, '61. Sergt., 1st Sergt.; disch. May 4, '64, disability.
Nelson, Gilbert; Coon. Enl. Oct. 12, '64. M.O. Jul. 8, '65.
Newland, George; Summit. Enl. Oct. 14, '61. Vet.; M.O. Jul. 16, '65.
Oleson, Ole; ? Enl. Oct. 12, '64. M.O. Jul. 16, '65.
Oleson, Soren; Coon. Enl. Oct. 13, '64. M.O. Jul. 16, '65.
Ostrander, Horace; Viola. Enl. Sep. 23, '61. From Co. I, Jan. 1, '64; Vet.; died Feb. 25, '64, Hebron, Miss., disease.
Phillips, Jason T.; Jefferson. Enl. Oct. 11, '64. M.O. Jul. 16, '65.
Price, James; Tennessee. Enl. Aug. 27, '62. M.O. May 22, '65.
Rice, Nelson W.; La Crosse. Enl. Jan. 2, '61. From Co. F, 25th Wis. Inf.; M.O. May 27, '65.
Richardson, Chauncey R.; Delton. Enl. Sep. 12, '61. Sergt.; disch. Mar. 18, '63, disability.
Robinson, Edwin; Dell Prairie. Enl. Sep. 12, '61. M.O. Nov. 4, '64, term exp.
Rockwell, Henry; Dell Prairie. Enl. Sep. 7, '61. Died Feb. 23, '63, LaGrange, Tenn., disease.
Rolison, William; Dell Prairie. Enl. Oct. 30, '61. Disch. Oct. 26, '62, disability.
Rood, Hosea W.; Vienna. Enl. Oct. 6, '61. Vet., Corp.; wnd, Atlanta; M.O. Jul. 16, '65.
Runger, John D.; Jefferson. Enl. Oct. 1, '64. M.O. Jul. 16, '65.
Shaffner, Jacob; Fountain City. Enl. Feb. 27, '64. From Co. F, 25th Wis. Inf.; M.O. Jul. 16, '65.
Schroeder, Henry; La Crosse. Enl. Feb. 27, '64. From Co. F, 25th Wis. Inf., M.O. Jul. 16, '65.

Severson, James; La Crosse. Enl. Jan. 4, '64. From Co. F, 25th Wis. Inf.; M.O. Jul. 16, '65.
Sexton, James; Dell Prairie. Enl. Sep. 16, '61. M.O. Nov. 4, '64, term exp.
Sexton, Aikin J.; Dell Prairie. Enl. Oct. 11, '61. M.O. Nov. 4, '64, term exp.
Sharpe, Leonard; Delton. Enl. Dec. 30, '64. M.O. Jul. 16, '65.
Slater, James; Newport. Enl. Sep. 12, '61. Disch. Jan. 1, '62, disability.
Smith, Laredo S.; New Haven. Enl. Oct. 7, '61. Died Apr. 17, '62, Lawrence, Kans., disease.
Smith, Henry; ? Enl. Jan. 5, '64. From Co. F, 25th Wis. Inf.; Corp.; M.O. Jun. 22, '65.
Smith, John; Willow Springs. Enl. Oct. 12, '64. M.O. Jul. 16, '65.
Solomon, James N.; Dell Prairie. Enl. Sep. 7, '61. Disch. Nov. 17, '62, disability.
Squires, Stephen; Delton. Enl. Nov. 20, '61. From Co. I; M.O. Aug. 1, '65, term exp.
Squires, William H.; Waterloo. Enl. Oct. 11, '61. Trans. to V. R. C. Jan. 7, '64.
Squires, Harlan A.; Madison. Enl. Nov. 5, '61. Died Jun. 28, '63, Vicksburg, Miss., disease.
Squires, Thomas B.; Waterloo. Enl. Oct. 11, '61. Vet.; Musician; M.O. Jul. 16, '65.
Starks, Alfred; Delona. Enl. Oct. 19, '61. Vet., Corp., Sergt.; M.O. Jul. 16, '65.
Stevens, Elias, L.; Linden. Enl. Aug. 30, '62. M.O. May 31, '65.
Stowell, William; Seven Mile Creek. Enl. Oct. 1, '61. Vet.; wnd, Jul. 21, '64, Atlanta; died Jul. 22, '65, wnds.
Stowell, Ahira; Dellona. Enl. Sep. 7, '61. Vet.; M.O. Jul. 16, '65.
Stults, John; Seven Mile Creek. Enl. Oct. 1, '61. Vet., Corp.; killed in action, Jul. 21, '64, Atlanta, Ga.
Stutson, Henry W.; Dellona. Enl. Sep. 7, '61. Vet., Corp., Sergt.; wnd Atlanta; disch. Jun. 16, '65, wnds.
Swain, Samuel G.; Newport. Enl. Sep. 30, '61. Vet., Corp.; disch. Nov. 13, '64, to accept prom. in 6th Miss. C.T.
Tiffany, Leander; Dellona. Enl. Oct. 1, '61. Vet., Corp.; M.O. Jul. 16, '65.
Titus, Daniel A.; Richford. Enl. Nov. 1, '61. Vet.; Killed in action, Jul. 28, '64, Atlanta, Ga.
Travis, James; New Amsterdam. Enl. Dec. 23, '63. From Co. F, 25th Wis. Inf.; M.O. Jul. 16, '65.
Tucker, Joshua L.; Dellona. Enl. Jan. 15, '64. M.O. Jul. 16, '65.
Truel, Ferdinand; Linden. Enl. Aug. 30, '62. M.O. May 31, '65.
Truel, Edwin M.; Linden. Enl. Aug. 309, '62. Wnd. Atlanta; Bvt. 1st Lieut., Jul. 21,'64; awarded metal of honor by Res. of Congress for gallantry in action, Jul. 21, '64, Atlanta; M.O. May 31, '65.
Uebersetzig, Arnold; La Crosse. Enl. Feb. 27, '64. From Co. F, 25th Wis. Inf.; M.O. Jun. 30, '65.
Vanderpoel, Clarence C.; Newport. Enl. Sep. 10, '61. Disch. Jul. 20, '63, disability.

Vanhoosen, William; Orange. Enl. Sep. 16, '61. M.O. Nov. 4, '64. term exp.
Vaughn, Henry D.; Dellona. Enl. Jan. 15, '64. Wnd. Kenesaw; M.O. Jul. 16, '65.
Vincent, William A.; Dellona. Enl. Oct. 1,'61. Vet.; M.O. Jul. 16, '65.
Waddell, Joseph M.; Freedom. Enl. Sep. 23, '61. Wagoner; disch. May 15, '62, disability.
Walke, Henry; Dellona. Enl. Jan. 15, '64. M.O. Jul. 16, '65.
Ward, Charles M.; Newport. Enl. Sep. 11, '61. Disch. Jul. 5, '62. disability.
Watson, William L.; Kilbourn. Enl. Sep. 8, '61. Disch. Aug. 17, '62, disability.
Wharry, Oran M.; Dellona. Enl. Oct. 1, '62. M.O. May 31, '65.
Wharry, William O.; Delton. Enl. Sep. 30, '61. Vet.; M.O. Jul. 16, '65.
Wheeler, Aaron M.; Dell Prairie. Enl. Jan. 14, '61. Vet.; M.O. Jul. 16, '65
Whitbeck, George; La Crosse. Enl. Dec. 28, '63. From Co. F, 25th Wis. Inf.; M.O. Jul. 16, '65.
Wilson, Warren; Lincoln. Enl. Oct. 15, '61. Trans. to V.R.C., Fall of '63; M.O. Oct. 15, '64, term exp.
Woodworth, Leonard P.; Newport. Enl. Sep. 21, '61. Vet.; disch. Dec. 19, '64, to accept prom. in 64th U.S.C.T.
Wright, Orson, Jr.; Lindina. Enl. Sep. 28, '61. Wnd, Sep. 2, '64, Lovejoy's Station, Ga.; M.O. Nov. 4, '64, term exp.
Young, Christopher; Franklin. Enl. Oct. 17, '64. M.O. Jul. 13, '65.

ROSTER OF COMPANY "F"

OFFICERS

Captains

GEORGE C. NORTON; Racine. Rank Oct. 22, '61. Enl. Oct. 8, '61; A.A.I.G., Army Tennessee, from Aug. 1, '63, to M.O. Nov. 5, '64, term exp.
FREDERICK J. BARTELS; Peshtigo. Rank Nov. 21, '64. Enl. Oct. 15, '61; Vet., Sergt., 1st Sergt.; 2nd Lieut., Oct. 25, '64; M.O. Jul. 16, '65.

First Lieutenants

LEVI ODELL; Menekaunee. Rank. Oct. 22, '61. Enl. Oct. 14, '61; Comdg. Co. from Dec. 31, '63, to Jul 17, '64; M.O. Nov. 17, '64, term exp.
JAMES W. LOUGHRY; Marinette. Rank Jan. 6, '65. Enl. Oct. 14,'61; Vet., Sergt., 1st. Sergt.; 2nd Lieut., Nov. 21, '64; M.O. Jul. 16, '65.

Second Lieutenants

HENRY TOURTILLOTTE; Oconto. Rank, Oct. 22, '61. Enl. Sep. 27, '61; res. May 5, '62.
DAVID JONES; Oconto. Rank, May 11, '62. Enl. Sep. 27, '61; 1st Sergt.; res. Oct. 1, '64.

Enlisted Men

Abrey, James; Oconto. Enl. Feb. 15, '64. M.O. Jul. 16, '65.
Adams, Charles W.; Union. Enl. Sep. 21, '64. Drafted; M.O. Aug. 8, '65.
Allquers, Alpheus; Marinette. Enl. Sep. 16, '62. Trans. to Co. H, Oct. 16, '62.
Ames, Hiram; Pensaukee. Enl. Dec. 28, '63. Died Oct. 17, '64, near Villanow, Ga., disease.
Anderson, Gunder C.; Manitowoc. Enl. Oct. 7, '61. Vet.; M.O. Jul. 16, '65.
Arsnow, Reuben; Menekaunee. Enl. Nov. 23, '61. Vet.; wnd. Atlanta; trans. to V.R.C., Apr. 24, '64; M.O. Jul. 29, '65.
Baldrick, Louis; Oconto. Enl. Oct. 15, '61. Vet.; M.O. Jul. 16, '65.
Bartels, John; Peshtigo. Enl. Oct. 15, '61. Vet.; absent at M.O. of Regt.
Barker, Benjamin B.; Pensaukee. Enl. Feb. 15, '64. M.O. Jul 16, '65.
Barber, Jesse O.; Oconto. Enl. Sep. 27, '61. Sergt.; disch. Oct. 17, 63, to accept prom. 2nd Lieut. 6th Miss. C.T.
Barrington, Richard; Oconto. Enl. Oct. 15, '61. Vet.; M.O. Jul 11, '65
Barnum, John W.; Durand. Enl. Dec. 5, '62. From Co. G, 25th Wis. Inf.; M.O. Jul. 16, '65.
Bartels, Henry; Peshtigo. Enl. Oct. 15, '61. Wnd. Sep. 3, '64, Jonesboro; died Sep. 5, '64, Atlanta, Ga. wnds.
Bearss, Sylvester; Durand. Enl. Jan. 4, '64. From Co. G, 25th Wis. Inf.; M.O. Jul. 16, '65.
Beaver, John; Reed's Landing. Oct. 6, '61. M.O. Jul. 16, '65.
Beanshaw, Felix; Depere. Enl. Oct. 7, '61. Vet.; M.O. Jul. 16, '65.
Beckwith, Reuben F.; Oconto. Enl. Sep. 27, '61. Vet.; prom. 1st Lieut. Co. G, 38th Wis. Inf., May 10, '64.
Bell, Archibald; Maxville. Enl. Jan. 23, '64. From Go. G, 25th Wis. Inf.; M.O. Jun. 21, '65.
Bennett, Ferdinand; Menekaunee. Enl. Oct. 14, '61. Vet., Corp.; wnd. Jul. 21, '64, Atlanta; died Jul. 28, '64, 3d Div. Hosp., wnds.
Benjamin, William; Pensaukee. Enl. Oct. 31, '61. Deserted May 27, '62.
Benware, Sever; Menekaunee. Enl. May 10, '64. M.O. Jul. 16, '65.
Berry, John A.; Oconto. Enl. Sep. 27, '61. Disch. Mar. 17, '63, disability.
Bird, Harlan P.; Menekaunee. Enl. Oct. 14, '61. Prom. Sergt. Maj., Oct. 16, '62.
Bishop, Joseph; Angelo. Enl. Jan. 2, '64. From Co. G, 25th Wis. Inf.; M.O. Jul. 16, '65.

Bishop, Amos; Angelo. Enl. Jan. 2, '64. From Co. G, 25th Wis. Inf.; M.O. May 15, '65.
Black, Mathew; Oconto. Enl. Oct. 17, '61. Disch. Mar. 17, '63, disability.
Bowers, Henry; Marinette. Enl. Sep. 11, '62. Trans. to Co. A, Oct. 16, '62.
Brady, Franklin; Marinette. Enl. Oct. 14, '61. Vet.; M.O. Jul. 16, '65.
Brien, Louis; Menekaunee. Enl. Nov. 27, '61. Vet.; M.O. Jul. 16, '65.
Brinker, John; Plover. Enl. Oct. 13, '64. M.O. Jul. 16, '65.
Brooks, Gardner R.; Peshtigo. Enl. Oct. 22, '61. Vet., Corp., Sergt., 1st Sergt.; 2nd Lieut., Jul. 25,'65, not mustered; M.O. Jul. 16, '65.
Brophy, John. Oconto. Enl. Oct. 17, '61. Vet., Corp.; M.O. Jul 16, '65
Brunette, David; Appleton. Enl. Oct. 15, '61. Vet.; wnd. Jul. 21, '64. Ackworth Station; disch. Jun. 11, '65, wnds.
Brunette, John; Appleton. Enl. Oct. 15, '61. Vet.; M.O. Jul. 11, '65.
Brunette, Louis; Peshtigo. Enl. Oct. 15, '61. M.O. Nov. 5, '64, term exp.
Bruette, Antoine; Peshtigo. Enl. Oct. 14, '61. Vet.; M.O. Jul. 16, '65.
Bruette, Phillip; Peshtigo. Enl. Apr. 14, '64. M.O. Jul. 16, '65.
Bruette, George; Peshtigo. Enl. Oct. 15, '61. Vet.; killed in action, Jul. 21, '64, Atlanta, Ga.
Buck, Amos F.; Oconto. Enl. Feb. 6, '64. M.O. Jul. 16, '65.
Bundy, Daniel; Menekaunee. Nov. 23, '61. Vet.; M.O. Jul. 16, '65.
Bundy, James C.; Pensaukee. Enl. Oct. 9, '61. Vet.; wnd.; M.O. Jul. 16, '65.
Bunkey, Lewis W.; Franklin. Enl. Sep. 28, '61. Vet., Corp., Sergt.; disch. Apr. 30, '64.
Byers, Frederick; Oconto. Enl. Oct. 9, '61. Vet., Corp., Sergt.; wnd. Jun. 16, '64, Atlanta; M.O. Jul. 16, '65.
Campbell, William A.; Maxville. Enl. Dec. 25, '62. From Co. G, 25th Wis. Inf.; M.O. Jul. 16, '65.
Campbell, John; Menekaunee. Enl. Oct. 14, '61. Disch. Mar. 17, '63, disability.
Campion, Edward. Menekaunee. Enl. Oct. 15, '61. Deserted Nov. 26, '61.
Carney, Jeremiah; Appleton. Oct. 14, '61. Vet.; wnd. Aug. 12,'64, Atlanta; disch. Jun. 14, '65. wnds.
Cassady, Terrence; Menekaunee. Enl. Oct. 4, '61. Musician; M.O. Nov. 5, '64, term exp.
Colson, Alvin S.; Pensaukee. Dec. 28, '63. Pris. Wartrace, S.C.; M.O. May 11, '65.
Connard, John B.; Bay Settlement. Enl. Oct. 15, '61. Vet.; M.O. Jul. 24, '65.
Connelly, Patrick. Stiles. Enl. Apr. 29,'64. Disch. Feb. 7, '65. disability.
Cook, Gabriel; Marinette. Enl. May 10, '64. Wnd. Kenesaw; M.O. Jul. 16, '65.
Corbin, George; Oconto. Enl. Oct. 7, '61. M.O. Nov. 5, '64. term exp.
Council, William A.; Phillips, AK. Enl. Jan. 11, '64. From Co. G, 25th Wis. Inf.; M.O. Jul. 16, '65.

Covarts, Franklin; Peshtigo. Enl. Oct. 15, '61. Vet.; killed in action, Jun. 15, '64, Kenesaw, Ga.
Cowles, Anzi W., Jr.; Durand. Enl. Dec. 17, '63. From Co. G, 25th Wis. Inf.; M.O. Jun. 10, '65.
Cowles, William P.; Durand. Enl. Dec. 11, '63. From Co. G, 25th Wis. Inf.; M.O. Jul. 16, '65.
Crawford, Joseph C.; Oconto. Enl. Oct. 17, '61. M.O. Nov. 5, '64, term exp.
Cusick, Milan C.; Pensaukee. Enl. Feb. 22, '64. Wnd. Kenesaw; died Oct. 8, '64, Rome, Ga.
DeGraff, Allen H.A.; Maxville. Enl. Jan. 23, '64. From Co. 1G, 25th Wis. Inf.; M.O. Jul. 16, '65.
Deheck, John; Marinette. Enl. Sep. 16, '62. Trans. to Co. H, Oct. 16, '62.
Delano, Moses; Peshtigo. Enl. Oct. 22, '61. Died Apr. 16, '62. Ft. Leavenworth, Kan.
Delano, Mortimer C.; Pensaukee. Enl. Oct. 9, '61. Corp.; disch. Jun. 12, '62, disability; re-enl. Dec. 29, '63; M.O. Jul. 16, '65.
Delano, William W.; Pensaukee. Enl. Oct. 9, '61. Disch. Nov. 14, '62, disability.
Dish, Joseph; Chicago, IL. Enl. Jan. 18, '62. Vet.; wnd. Kenesaw; trans. to V.R.C., Apr. 24, '65; M.O. Jul. 29, '65.
Dress, Joseph T.; Peshtigo. Enl. Apr. 14, '64. M.O. Jul. 16, '65.
Duame, Acedor; Menekaunee. Enl. Sep. 8, '62. Died Sep. 10, '63, Natchez, Miss., disease.
Dwyre, Thomas; Menekaunee. Enl. Oct. 14, '61. Disch. Apr. 29, '62, disability.
Dyer, John W.; Menekaunee. Enl. Oct 14, '61. Vet.; M.O. Jun 16, '65
Dyer, Samuel J.; Oconto. Enl. Sep. 28, '61. Died Oct. 13, '63, Keokuk, Ia., disease.
Eagan, Michael H.; Meeme. Enl. Oct. 14, '61. M.O. Nov. 5, '64, term exp.
Easton, Andrew J.; Menekaunee. Enl. Oct. 14, '61. Trans to V.R.C., Nov. 9, '63
Engfert, John; Milwaukee. Enl. Oct. 4, '64. M.O. Jul. 16, '65.
Erwin, Moses; Durand. Enl. Jan. 2, '64. From Co. G, 25th Wis. Inf.; trans. to V.R.C., Apr. 24, '65.
Fallows, William; Madison. Enl. Sep. 27, '62. Corp.; trans to Co. H, Oct. 16, '62.
Foster, William L.; Oshkosh. Enl. Sep. 27, '61. Corp.; died Jan. 15, '63, La Grange, Tenn.
Francis, Russell; Sylvan. Enl. Nov. 23, '61. From Co. I; Musician; M.O. Nov. 5, '64, term exp.
Garland, James; Oconto. Enl. Feb. 19, '64. Died Apr. 4, '64, Memphis, Tenn.
Goddard, John H.; Pensaukee. Enl. Dec. 24, '63. M.O. Jul. 16, '65.
Goddard, John; Pensaukee. Enl. Oct. 16, '61. M.O. Nov. 5, '64, term exp.
Green, James B.; Maxville. Enl. Jan. 23, '64. From Co. G, 25th Wis. Inf.; M.O. Jul. 16, '65.

Green, George W.; Marinette. Enl. Jun. 4, '64. Trans to V.R.C. Apr. 21, '65.
Grover, Samuel; Kewaunee. Enl. Sep. 28, '61. Corp.; disch. Jun. 12, '62, disability.
Haggett, Reuben; Pensaukee. Enl. Dec. 28, '63. Wnd. Atlanta; died Oct. 15, '64. Rome, Ga., wnds.
Hale, William E.; Pensaukee. Enl. Dec. 28, '63. Killed in action, Jul. 21, '64, Atlanta, Ga.
Hannan, Patrick; Durand. Enl. Jan. 2, '64. From Co. G, 25th Wis. Inf.; M.O. Jul. 16, '65.
Hannan, Jean J.; Green Bay. Enl. Oct. 12, '64. Absent at M.O. of Regt.
Harting, Charles; Milwaukee. Enl. Oct. 5, '64. M.O. May 31, '65.
Hayes, Philander; Peshtigo. Enl. Oct. 15,'61. Died Aug. 13, '63. Vicksburg, Miss., disease.
Hayward, James A.; Milwaukee. Enl. Oct. 14, '64. Disch. Apr. 6,'65.
Heldenworth, Christian; Peshtigo. Enl. Oct. 15, '61. Vet.; wnd. Atlanta; M.O. Jul. 16, '65.
Heldenworth, David; Peshtigo. Enl. Oct. 15, '61. Vet., Corp.; M.O. Jul. 16. '65.
High, Lyman T.; Big Suamico. Enl. Sep. 27, '61. Corp.; disch, Jun. 14, '62, disability.
Hollister, Silas S.; Mauston. Enl. Oct. 4,'64. M.O. Jul. 16, '65.
Howe, Anson; Green Bay. Enl. Oct. 18, '64. M.O. Jun. 17, '65.
Hurley, Edmund J.; Fort Howard. Enl. Dec. 28, '63. M.O. Jul. 13, '65.
Hurst, James W.; Peoria, KS. Enl. Mar. 26, '62. Wnd. Atlanta; M.O. May 22, '65, term exp.
Ireland, Truman L.; Menekaunee. Enl. Oct. 14, '61. Disch. Oct. 19, '62, disability.
Irwin, Moses; (see Moses Erwin)
Jaques, Peter; Oconto. Enl. Oct. 15, '61. Vet.; M.O. Jul. 16, '65.
Jessey, Joseph; Oconto. Enl. Oct. 17,'61. Vet. Corp.; pris. Atlanta; M.O. Jul. 16, '65.
Jones, Willis P.; Humboldt, TN. Enl. Aug. 4, '62. Wnd. Atlanta; disch. May 31,'65, wnds.
Jones, Joseph V.; Burnside. Enl. Feb. 1, '64. From Co. G, 25th Wis. Inf.; M.O. Jul. 16, '65.
Jones, John D.; Marinette. Enl. Sep. 24, '62. Trans. to Co. H, Oct. 16, '62.
Kanaley, John; Waukesha. Enl. Oct. 15, '61. Died Jan. 19, '62, Madison, Wis., disease.
Kezar, Luther, Jr.; Burnside. Enl. Feb. 1,'64. From Co. G, 25th Wis. Inf.; M.O. Jul. 16, '65.
Kile, Werner; Fort Howard. Enl. Oct. 28, '62. M.O. Jul. 16, '65.
Kingsland, John P.; Madison; Jan. 23, '64. From Co. G, 25th Wis. Inf.; M.O. Jul. 16, '65.
Klemer, August; Fond du Lac. Enl. Sep. 29, '64. M.O. May 31, '65.
Koch, Anthony; Milwaukee. Enl. Oct. 5, '64. M.O. Jul. 16, '65.
Kramreiter, Frederick; Watertown. Enl. Oct. 5, '64. M.O. Jul. 16, '65.
Lathrop, Elias; Peshtigo. Enl. Oct. 15, '61. Died Aug. 1, '63, on Hosp. Boat, Miss. River, disease.

Lavallette, Matthias; Menekaunee. Enl. May 10, '64. M.O.
Jul. 16, '65.
Lawe, Joseph; Appleton. Enl. Oct. 17, '61. Vet., Corp.; M.O.
Jul. 16, '65.
Leach, Hiram; Peshtigo. Enl. Oct. 15, '61. Trans. to Co. F, Aug. 31,
'63; rejd. Sep. 8, '63; died Aug. 16, '63. St. Louis, Mo.
Leake, Edward; Fort Howard. Enl. Oct. 14, '61. Wnd. Kenesaw; M.O.
Nov. 5, '64, term exp.
Lee, Isaac; Milwaukee. Enl. Oct. 10, '64. Absent at M.O. of Regt.
Leeson, James; Bay Settlement. Enl. Oct. 15, '61. Vet., M.O.
Jul. 16, '65.
Leeson, William N.; Oconto. Enl. Oct. 17, '61. Vet., Corp., Sergt.;
M.O. Jul. 16, '65.
Leiser, William J.; Fon du Lac. Enl. Sep. 27, '64. M.O. May 31, '65.
Leonard, Henry L.; Peshtigo. Enl. Oct. 15, '61. Wnd. Atlanta; M.O.
Dec. 28, '61, term exp.
Lempke, Ferdinand; Highland. Enl. Oct. 4, '64. M.O. Jul. 16, '65.
Leverenz, Leo; Milwaukee. Enl. Oct. 6, '64. M.O. Jul. 16, '65.
Libbey, Isaac S.; Pensaukee. Enl. Oct. 16, '61. Vet., Sergt., 1st
Sergt.; killed in action, Jul. 21, '64. Atlanta, Ga.
Libbey, Peter. Oconto. Enl. Oct. 15, '61. Vet.; M.O. Jul. 16, '65.
Letterman, Joseph; Fond du Lac. Enl. Oct. 5, '64. Absent at M.O. of
Regt.
Loughrey, Alexander; Marinette. Enl. Sep. 26, '62. M.O. Jul. 16, '65.
Luck, William; Oconto. Enl. Sep. 28, '61. Vet.; wnd. Atlanta; M.O.
Jul. 16, '65.
Luhn, John M.; Peshtigo. Enl. Oct. 17, '61. Vet., Corp., Sergt.; M.O.
Jul. 16, '65.
Lyon, Albert A.; Menekaunee. Enl. Sep. 10, '62. Wnd. Kenesaw; died
Jul. 10, '64, Rome, Ga.
Mahony, Dennis; Peshtigo. Enl. Oct. 15, '61. Corp.; disch. May 27,
'64, disability.
Maxfield, James L; Peshtigo. Enl. Oct. 22, '61. Trans. to Co. H,
Nov. 5, '61.
McCollum, Alexander; Menekaunee. Enl. Sep. 10, '62. Died Aug. 4,
'63, Vicksburg, Miss., disease.
Midane, Dennis; Appleton. Enl. Oct. 7, '64. M.O. Jul. 16, '65.
Mitchell, James; Marinette. Enl. Sep. 16, '62. Trans to Co. H,
Oct. 16, '62.
Mooney, Michael J.; Menekaunee. Enl. Nov. 27, '61. Disch. Nov. 11,
'62, disability.
Morris, Charles W.; Green Bay. Enl. Aug. 3, '64. M.O. Jul. 16, '65.
Morris, Joseph I.; Fort Howard. Enl. Oct. 8, '61. Vet., Corp.; M.O.
Jul. 16, '65.
Murray, William; Oconto. Enl. Nov. 27, '61. Killed in action, Jul. 21,
'64, Atlanta, Ga.
Nason, Daniel P.; Menekaunee. Enl. Sep. 10, '62. Wnd. Atlanta;
M.O. Jul. 16, '65.
Norton, Charles; Oconto. Enl. Oct. 9, '61. Drowned May 8, '64,
Cairo, Ill.
Olive, Maxime; Peshtigo. Enl. Oct. 15, '61. From Co. H; Vet.; M.O.
Jul. 16, '65.

Olive, Franklin; Peshtigo. Enl. Oct. 7, '61. Vet.; M.O. Jul. 16, '65.
Partlow, Hollis; Pensaukee. Enl. Dec. 14, '63. M.O. Jul. 16, '65.
Pease, George T.; Marinette. Enl. Sep. 16, '62. Corp., Sergt.; M.O. Jul. 16, '65.
Penree, William; Peshtigo. Enl. Oct. 15, '61. M.O. Nov. 26, '64, term exp.
Penree, Alfred; Peshtigo. Enl. Oct. 15, '61. Vet.;M.O. Jul. 16, '65.
Penree, Leonard W.; Peshtigo. Enl. Oct. 15, '61. Died Sep. 9, '64, Natchez, Miss., disease.
Pentany, John; Oconto. Enl. Oct. 17, '61. Disch. Mar. 21, '63, disability.
Place, Doctor S.; Peshtigo. Enl. Oct. 15, '61. Disch. Nov. 20, '61. (Minor)
Pleasure, Octave; Menekaunee. Enl. Oct. 14, '61. Vet.; wnd. Jonesboro; died Sep. 29, '64, Marietta, Ga., wnds.
Plush, David; Peshtigo. Enl. Apr. 14, '64. Wnd. and Pris. Atlanta; died Aug. 28, '64, Atlanta, Ga.
Pricket, Paul; Appleton. Enl. Oct. 19, '61. Vet.; M.O. Jul. 16, '65.
Primrose, Jacob; Oconto. Enl. Sep. 27, '61. M.O. Nov. 5, '64, term exp.
Pulford, Ezekiel; Oconto. Enl. Oct. 9, '61. Disch. Jul 25, '62, disability.
Pung, John; Marinette. Enl. Sep. 16, '62. Trans to Co. H, Oct. 16, '65.
Reed, George W.; Menekaunee. Oct. 14, '61. Vet.;wnd. and pris. Germantown, Mar. 13, '63; M.O. Jul. 26, '65.
Richardson, Lorenzo D.; Menekaunee. Enl. Oct. 14, '61. M.O. Nov. 5, '64, term exp.
Roberts, Richard; Auburn. Enl. Sep. 14, '62. Wnd. and pris. Atlanta; M.O. Jul. 16, '65.
Sawyer, John; Two Rivers. Enl. Oct. 9, '61. Trans. to Co. H, Nov. 6, '61.
Shappery, Louie; Peshtigo. Enl. Oct. 15, '61. Died Jan. 2, '64, Vicksburg, Miss. diesease.
Sheahan, John D.; Fredonia. Enl. Nov. 27, '61. Vet., Corp; M.O. Jul. 16, '65.
Sheffein, Henry; Oconto. Enl. Oct. 26, '61. Vet., Corp.; M.O. Jul. 16, '65.
Sherman, James C.; Menekaunee. Enl. Oct. 14, '61. Vet.; M.O. Jul. 16, '65.
Shoults, Seymour; Maxville. Enl. Jan. 23, '64. From Co. G, 25th Wis. Inf.; M.O. Jul. 16, '65.
Sinclair, John; Durand. Enl. Jan. 23, '64. From Co. G, 25th Wis. Inf. M.O. Jul. 16, '65.
Smiley, William C.; Burnside. Enl. Feb. 1, '64. From Co. G, 25th Wis. Inf.; M.O. Jul. 16, '65.
Smiley, James B.; Burnside. Enl. Feb. 1, '64. From Co. G, 25th Wis. Inf.; M.O. Jul. 16, '65.
Smith, James D.; Menekaunee. Enl. Oct. 14, '61. M.O. Nov. 5, '64, term exp.
Smith, William B.;Oconto. Enl. Sep. 27, '61. Disch. May 27, '62, disability.

Stephens, Homer; Menekaunee. Enl. Sep. 18, '62. M.O. May 15, '65.
Thomas, David; Stiles. Enl. Feb. 22, '64. Killed in action, Jul. 21, '64, Atlanta, Ga.
Thomi, Mathis; Peshtigo. Enl. Sep. 30, '62. Died Aug. 22, '63. Madison, Wis.
Tourtillotte, John L.; Oconto. Enl. Oct. 23, '61. Trans to Co. H, Nov. 6, '61.
Turner, Levi; Hustisford. Enl. Oct. 14, '61. Vet., Corp., Sergt., 1st Sergt.; wnd. Atlanta; 1st Lieut., Nov. 21, '64, revoked Jan. 6, '65; 2nd Lieut., Jan. 6, '65, not mustered; disch. May 26, '65, wnds.
Ures, James; Oconto. Enl. Nov. 26, '61. M.O. Dec. 19, '64. term exp.
Ward, John; Peshtigo. Enl. Sep. 5, '62. Wnd. Atlanta; M.O. Jun. 6, '65
Washburn, Delos A.; Oconto. Enl. Sep. 27, '61. M.O. Nov. 5, '64, term exp.
Webster, Homer; Durand. Enl. Jan. 21, '64. From Co. G, 25th Wis. Inf.; M.O. Jul. 16, '65.
Welch, Stephen, Muskegon. Enl. Sep. 27, '61. Vet.; M.O. Jul. 16, '65.
Whitcomb, William W.; Pensaukee. Enl. Dec. 28, '61. M.O. Jul 16, '65
Whitney, Franklin L.; Pensaukee. Enl. Oct. 22, '61. Corp.; disch. May 1, '62, disability.
Whitney, Alonzo; Pensaukee. Enl. Oct. 19, '61. Died Jan. 4, '63, LaGrange, Tenn.
White, Joseph; Rubicon. Enl. Sep. 27, '61. Trans. to Co. H, Nov. 5, '61.
Williams, John; Little Chute. Enl. Sep. 28, '61. Died Jul. 16, '63, Vicksburg, Miss. disease.
Wilson, Henry W.; Pensaukee. Enl. Dec. 28, '63. Corp.; M.O. Jul 16, '65.
Wilson, Edwin P.; Wheatland. Enl. Feb. 27, '64. Wnd. Jonesboro; died Jan. 13, '65, Chattanooga, Tenn., wnds.
Wright, Charles M.; Maxville. Enl. Jan. 4, '64. From Co. G, 25th Wis. Inf.; M.O. Jul. 16, '65.
Young, Edward B.; Marinette. Enl. Oct. 14, '61. Vet., Musician; M.O. Jul. 16, '65.
Yourd, Francis; Oconto. Enl. Feb. 13, '64. M.O. Jul. 16, '65.

ROSTER OF COMPANY "G"

OFFICERS

Captains

DANIEL HOWELL; Grand Rapids. Rank Oct. 5, '61. Enl. Aug. 31, '61; resigned Mar. 10, '63.
W. WALLACE BOTKIN; Grand Rapids. Rank Mar. 10, '63. Enl. Sep. 9, '61; 2nd Lieut., Oct. 5, '61; 1st Lieut. May 11, '62; Prom. Lieut. Col. 42nd Wis. Inf., Jul. 29, '64.
WARREN P. LANGWORTHY. Madison. Rank Aug. 17, '64. Enl. Sep. 6, '61; 1st Sergt.; 2nd Lieut., May 11, '62; commanding Exp. to Fed. Fleet announcing Sherman's occupation of Savannah; 1st Lieut., Mar. 10, '63; M.O. Jul. 16, '65.

First Lieutenants

CHARLES M. WEBB; Grand Rapids. Rank Oct. 5, '61. Enl. Sep. 9, '61; res. May 1, '62.
HARLAN P. BIRD; Menekaunee. Rank Aug. 17, '64. From Sergt. Maj; 2nd Lieut. Mar. 10, '63; wnd. Picket Line, Jun. 18, '63. Vicksburg; A.A.A.G., 1st Brig. 3rd Div. 17th A.C.A.A.Q.M. to 17th A.C.; Actg. Ord. Officer 3rd Div. 17th A.C.; M.O. Jul 16, '63.

Second Lieutenants

FRANK H. PUTNEY; Grand Rapids. Rank Aug. 17, '64. Enl. Sep. 12, '61; Vet., Sergt, 1st Sergt.; Actg. Adjutant; A.A.I.G., 1st Brig. Gen. Ewing; wnd. Atlanta; M.O. Jul. 16, '65.

Enlisted Men

Albert, Ole; Strong's Prairie. Enl. Nov. 5, '61. Vet.; in Capt. Langworthy's Exp. to Fed. Fleet announcing Sherman's occupation of Savannah; M.O. Jul. 16, '65.
Allen, Taylor F.; Delafield. Enl. Oct. 14, '61. M.O. Jul. 16, '65.
Anderson, Hans; Cataract. Enl. Nov. 18, '61. Vet.; M.O. Jul. 16, '65.
Arvidson, Louis P.; Rudolph. Enl. Oct. 2, '61. Died Jun. 26, '62, in Camp on Obion River, Tenn.
Atchinson, Harrison H.; Cataract. Enl. Oct. 1, '61. Vet., Corp.; wnd. Jul. 15, '64 and Aug. 12, '64; M.O. Jul. 16, '65.
Baker, George W.; Grand Rapids. Enl. Sep. 18, '61. Vet., Corp.; wnd. Atlanta; M.O. Jul. 16, '65.
Baker, Gerd; Rudolph. Enl. Oct. 14, '61. Vet.; killed in action Jul. 22, '64, Atlanta, Ga.
Baker, Florence; Prescott. Enl. Sep. 27, '61. From Co. A, Dec. 31, '61; Vet.; M.O. Jul. 16, '65.
Bangs, Luther W.; Grand Rapids. Enl. Sep. 11, '61. Died Mar. 12, '63, Camp Butler, Tenn., disease.

Bangs, Samuel; Milwaukee. Enl. Feb. 16, '64. M.O. Jul. 16, '65.
Barrett, Albert J.; Prescott. Enl. Sep. 25, '61. From Co. A; Vet.; trans. to Co. A, Feb. 1, '64.
Bart, Joseph; Scott. Enl. Oct. 13, '64. M.O. Jul. 16, '65.
Belanger, Alfred; Grand Rapids. Enl. Dec. 30, '63. M.O. Jul. 16, '65.
Bennett, Orson W.; Hazel Green. Enl. Nov. 12, '61. Vet.; disch. Jan. 22, '64 to accept prom. in U.S.C.T.
Benson, Jacob. Grand Rapids. Enl. Sep. 18, '61. Died Apr. 20, '62, Lawrence, Kan.
Bernier, Armenegiel; Grand Rapids. Enl. Jan. 4, '64. M.O. Jul. 16, '65.
Boughton, Hart; Madison. Enl. Nov. 19, '61. Disch. Aug. 3, '62. disability.
Brager, Henry; Two Creeks. Enl. Oct. 15, '64. M.O. Jul. 16, '65.
Brandon, Charles; Pra. du Chien. Enl. Jan. 11, '64. From Co. I, 25th Wis. Inf.; M.O. Jul. 16, '65.
Brown, Nichols D.; Wausau. Enl. Sep. 16, '61. Vet., Corp., Sergt.; in Capt. Langworthy's exp. to Fed. fleet, announcing Sherman's occupation of Savannah; wnd. Atlanta; M.O. Jul. 16, '65.
Brown, William H.; Grand Rapids. Enl. Jan. 5, '64. M.O. Jul. 16, '65.
Buck, Benjamin, Jr.; Milwaukee. Enl. Feb. 16, '64. Pris. Atlanta; absent sick at M.O. of Regt.
Butler, George H.; Wausau. Enl. Sep. 23, '61. Vet., Corp., Sergt.; wnd. Jul. 5, '64.; M.O. Jul. 16, '65.
Butler, William P.; Grand Rapids. Enl. Sep. 24, '61. Disch. Jun. 7, '62
Burr, Thomas T.; Seneca. Enl. Oct. 4, '61. Disch. Sep. 8, '62, disability.
Burr, John; Grand Rapids. Enl. Sep. 9, '61. Wnd. Jul. 22, '64, Atlanta,; M.O. Oct. 30, '64, term exp.
Calkins, Nelson P.; Wausau. Enl. Sep. 16, '61. Disch. Nov. 2, '63, disability.
Carpenter, William M.; Stevens Point. Enl. Oct. 9, '61. Corp., Sergt., 1st Sergt.; M.O. Oct. 30, '64, term exp.
Chase, Hiram; Pra. du Chien. Enl. Jan. 11, '64. From Co. I, 25th Wis. Inf.; M.O. Jul. 16, '65.
Cooper, George S.; Pra. du Chien. Enl. Jan. 4, '64. From Co. I, 25th Wis. Inf.; M.O. Jul. 16, '65.
Cotey, Joseph L.; Grand Rapids. Enl. Sep. 16, '61. Deserted Nov. 1, '61
Cowan, Garret F.; Grand Rapids. Enl. Oct. 4, '61. Sergt.; disch. Jul. 19, '62, disability.
Crampton, Oscar; Wausau. Enl. Oct. 17, '61. Died Apr. 6, '62, Lawrence, Kan.
Dabos, P. William; Casco. Enl. Apr. 26, '64. M.O. Jul. 28, '65; see unassigned recruits, 9th Wis. Inf.
Dale, Wilber P.; River Falls. Enl. Sep. 23, '61. From Co. A; trans. to Co. A, May 1, '62.
Dipple, Carl W.; Madison. Enl. Dec. 12, '61. Trans to Band.
Dodge, William; Wausau. Enl. Sep. 23, '61. Vet.; M.O. Jul. 13, '65.
Duesler, James; Grand Rapids. Enl. Sep. 18, '61. Vet., Corp.; M.O. Jul. 16, '65.

Dugan, Alvin B.; Grand Rapids. Enl. Sep. 23, '61. M.O. Oct. 30, '64, term exp.
Eaton, Alanson; Grand Rapids. Enl. Sep. 27, '61. Sergt.; disch. Jul. 19,'62, disability.
Elliot, Joseph; Saratoga. Enl. Oct. 12, '61. Vet.; M.O. Jul. 16, '65.
Elliott, Benjamin A.; Saratoga. Enl. Oct. 3, '61. Vet.; M.O. Jul. 16, '65.
Ellington; John; Stevens Point. Enl. Oct. 11, '61. Vet.; M.O. Jul. 16, '65.
Ensign, John; Saratoga. Enl. Oct. 17, '61. Musician; disch. May 28, '62.
Farrannacei; Paul. Marshfield. Enl. Feb. 29, '64. M.O. May 15, '65.
Farrell, Charles; Grand Rapids. Enl. Jan. 20, '62. M.O. Jul. 16, '65.
Feltis, John; Wausau. Enl. Sep. 24, '61. M.O. Dec. 19, '65.
Femling, Frederick; Saratoga. Enl. Oct. 3, '61. Vet.; M.O. Jul 16, '65.
Fontain, Henry; Grand Rapids. Enl. Jan. 2, '64. Died Apr. 30, '65, Newbern, N.C.
Fox, Sylvanus L.; Stanton. Enl. Sep. 25, '61. Wagoner; M.O. Oct. 30, '64, term exp.
Freeman, Alonzo; Jamestown. Enl. Dec. 15, '63. From Co. I, 25th Wis. Inf.; M.O. Jul. 16, '65.
Freeman, Fortunatus; Jamestown. Enl. Dec. 15, '63. From Co. I, 25th Wis. Inf.; M.O. Jul. 16, '65.
Fritchey, George; Grand Rapids. Enl. Dec. 22, '63. Died Dec. 19, '64, Chattanooga, Tenn., disease.
Getts, Albert; Campbell. Enl. Oct. 3, '64. M.O. Jul. 16, '65.
Gibbs, William N.; Grand Rapids. Enl. Sep. 14, '61. Vet.; M.O. Jul. 16, '65.
Gibson, Joseph; Campbell. Enl. Oct. 31, '64. M.O. Jul. 16, '65.
Gilmore, Hiram; Pra. du Chen. Enl. Jan. 11, '64. From Co. I, 25th Wis. Inf.; M.O. Jul. 16, '65.
Gilson, Orvin; Grand Rapids. Enl. Dec. 31, '63. M.O. Jul. 16, '65.
Gongaware, Frederick; Pra. du Chien. Enl. Jan. 11, '64. From Co. I, 25th Wis. Inf.; absent sick at M.O. of Regt.
Gray, Edward; Manassas, VA. Enl. Nov. 14, '61. Musician; M.O. Dec. 20, '64, term exp.
Grignon, Ignace; Grand Rapids. Enl. Jan. 4, '64. Wnd. Jul. 22, '64; trans to V.R.C., Apr. 1, '65.
Hall, Rufus H.; Grand Rapids. Enl. Sep. 20, '61. Vet., Corp.; wnd. Aug. 26, '64; M.O. Jul. 16, '65.
Hanks, Burnis N.; Saratoga. Enl. Jan. 21, '64. Absent sick at M.O. of Regt.
Harkness, Francis; Rudolph. Enl. Sep. 23, '61. Died Aug. 6, '63, Vicksburg, Miss., disease.
Heath, Abram; Cataract. Enl. Oct. 1, '61. Trans. to V.R.C., Nov. 9, '63; M.O. Nov. 5, '64. term exp.
Himle, Nelson; Rudolph. Enl. Oct. 17, '61. Vet.; M.O. Jul. 16, '63.
Hines, George A.; Centralia. Enl. Jan. 4, '64. M.O. Jul. 16, '65.
Hudson, Josiah K.; Prescott. Enl. Oct. 22, '61. Disch. Apr. 15, '62, disability.
James, George; Madison. Enl. Dec. 21, '61. Deserted Oct. '62.

Jeffrey, Stephen; Grand Rapids. Enl. Sep. 19, '61. Vet.; M.O. Jul 16, '65.
Johnson, Abner A.; Cataract. Enl. Oct. 16, '61. Vet.; wnd. Jul. 22, '64; M.O. Jul. 16, '65.
Jones, John, 1st; Grand Rapids. Enl. Sep. 18,'61. Vet. M.O. Jul. 16, '65.
Jones, John, 2nd; Grand Rapids. Enl. Oct. 2, '61. M.O. Oct. 30, '64, term exp.
Kerstine, Sebastian; Wausau. Enl. Sep. 16, '61. Vet.; M.O. Jul. 16, '65.
Keyes, Patrick; Pra. du Chien. Enl. Jan 11, '64. From Co. I, 25th Wis. Inf.; M.O. Jul. 16, '65.
King, John; Mauston. Enl. Nov. 18, '61. Died Mar. 23, '63, Memphis, Tenn., disease.
Knudsen, Iver; Ettrick. Enl. Sep. 21, '64. Drafted; M.O. May 31, '65.
Lang, George L.; Grand Rapids. Enl. Sep. 14, '61. Vet., Corp., Sergt.; wnd. Jul. 21, '64, Atlanta; disch. May 17, '65. disability.
Lanscher, William; Kewaunee. Enl. Oct. 14, '64. M.O. Jul. 16, '65.
Lefler, Henry; Farmington. Enl. Oct. 12, '64. M.O. Jul. 16, '65.
Lester, Benjamin; Jamestown. Enl. Jan. 27, '64. From Co. I, 25th Wis. Inf.; M.O. Jul. 16, '65.
Letson, Albert H.; Prescott. Enl. Oct. 8, '61. Disch. Jul. 19, '62. disability.
Linguist, Charles J.; Rudolph. Enl. Oct. 2, '61. Vet., Corp.; in Capt. Langworthy's exp. to Fed fleet announcing Sherman's occupation of Savannah; wnd Jul. 22, '64; M.O. Jul. 16, '65.
Little, William; Watertown. Enl. Oct. 6, '64. Never reported to Co.
Long, George; Pra. du Chien. Enl. Jan. 11, '64. From Co. I, 25th Wis. Inf.,; M.O. Jul. 16, '65.
Mann, Azro; Stevens Point. Enl. Oct. 5, '61. Corp.; Prom. 2nd Lt. 8th Battery Dec. 31, '61.
McConnell, Charles; Highland. Enl. Oct. 11, '64. M.O. Jul. 16, '65.
McClaughry, Thomas B.; Wausau. Enl. Sep. 19, '61. Vet.; wnd. Jul. 22, '64, Atlanta; M.O. Aug. 7, '65.
Melburg, Frederick; Grand Rapids. Enl. Oct. 26, '61. Deserted Nov. 1, '61.
Mercier, Andre; Grand Rapids. Enl. Oct. 12, '61. Vet.; wnd. Aug. 21, '64, Atlanta; M.O. Jul. 16, '65.
Merry, Bruce; Milwaukee. Enl. Feb. 2, '64. M.O. Jul. 16, '65.
Miller, James D.; Mosinee. Enl. Oct. 8, '61. M.O. Oct. 30, ' 64, term exp.
Millenbach, Frederick W.; Seneca. Enl. Sep. 19, '61. Disch. Jan. 23, '62, disability.
Morrison, James; Grand Rapids. Enl. Sep. 10, '61. M.O. Dec. 22, '64, term exp.
Mosier, Festus D.; Grand Rapids. Enl. Sep. 23, '61. Sergt.; deserted Jul. 1, '63.
Moses, Joseph; Grand Chute. Oct. 4, '64. Never reported to Co.
Muffley, Franklin C.; Jamestown. Enl. Jan. 16, '64. From Co. I, 25th Wis. Inf.; M.O. Jul. 16, '65.
Mundy, Samuel J.; Seneca. Enl. Oct. 12, '61. Corp.; M.O. Jul. 16, '65.

Newton, Benjamin B.; Grand Rapids. Enl. Dec. 29, '63. Killed in action, Jul. 21, '64, Atlanta, Ga.
Nelson, Thomas H.; Stoughton. Enl. Nov. 15, '61. Vet.; In Capt. Langworthy's exp. to Fed. fleet announcing Sherman's occupation of Savannah; wnd. Kenesaw; M.O. Jul. 16, '65.
Nilson, Ole C.; Stevens Point. Enl. Oct. 8, '61. Died Oct. 2, '63, Natchez, Miss., disease.
Nielson, Knuit; Wausau. Enl. Sep. 24, '61. Vet.; M.O. Jul. 16, '65.
Oleson, Hilga; Wilton. Enl. Oct. 6, '64. Never reported to Co.
Oleson, Charles; Starks. Enl. Oct. 8, '64. M.O. Jul. 16, '65.
Oleson, Andrew; Stevens Point. Enl. Oct. 8, '61. Vet., Corp.; in Capt. Langworthy's exp. to Fed. fleet announcing Sherman's occupation of Savannah; wnd. Kenesaw; M.O. Jul. 16, '65.
Oleson, Ole O.; Prescott. Enl. Oct. 13, '61. Vet., Corp.; killed in action, Jul. 8, '64, Nickajack Cr., Ga.
Osborn, John; Grand Rapids. Enl. Jan. 5, '64. M.O. May 22, '65.
Page, Lucius S.; Christiana. Enl. Jan. 23, '64. M.O. Jun. 30, '65.
Park, John M.; Stevens Point. Enl. Oct. 16, '61. M.O. Dec. 19, '65.
Patterson, Alvin A.; Platteville. Enl. Jan. 25, '64. From Co. I, 25th Wis. Inf.; absent sick at M.O. of Regt.
Pealky, Joseph H.; Seneca. Enl. Feb. 2, '64. M.O. Jul. 16, '65.
Phillips, Norman P.; Grand Rapids. Enl. Dec. 27, '63. Wnd. Sep. 5, '64, Marietta, Ga.; M.O. May 29, '65.
Pohl, John; Rudolph. Enl. Oct. 2, '61. Vet.; wnd. Aug. 4, '64; M.O. Jul. 16, '65.
Polenski, Augustus; Seneca. Enl. Jan. 20, '64. M.O. Jul. 16, '65.
Pomeroy, George; Cataract. Enl. Oct. 1, '61. Corp., Sergt.; M.O. Oct. 30, '64, term exp.
Pope, John; Wausau. Enl. Oct. 5, '61. Vet.; M.O. Jul. 16, '65.
Porter, Ambrose; Wausau. Enl. Sep. 23, '61. Vet.; pris. Dec. 7, '64. M.O. Jul. 16, '65.
Pratt, Marcus S.; Grand Rapids. Enl. Oct. 12, '61. Vet., Corp.; M.O. Aug. 15, '65.
Pratt, Warren P.; Grand Rapids. Enl. Jan. 4, '64. Absent sick at M.O. of Regt.
Rathbun, Nathan F.; Dexter. Enl. Oct. 12, '61. Vet., Corp., Sergt.; wnd. Jul. 9, '64, Nickajack Cr.; M.O. Jul. 16, '65.
Rice, Lyman; Milwaukee. Enl. Feb. 6, '64. M.O. Jul. 16, '65.
Robarge, Louis; Wausau. Enl. Sep. 19, '61. Vet.; M.O. Jul. 16, '65.
Robarge, Joseph; Wausau. Enl. Sep. 16, '61. Vet.; killed in action, Aug. 12, '64, Atlanta, Ga.
Robert, Eugene; Wausau. Enl. Sep. 24, '61. Vet.; run over by cars, May 3, '64, Effingham, Ill., leg amp.; disch. Apr. 23, '65, disability.
Rockstad, John C.; Prescott. Enl. Oct. 7, '61. Vet.; M.O. Jul. 16, '65.
Rockstad, Ole C.; Prescott. Enl. Oc.t 7, '61. Died Aug. 10, '63, St. Louis, Mo., disease.
Salsbury, Harrison; Dexter. Enl. Sep. 29, '64. M.O. May 31, '65.
Salter, Stephen B.; Grand Rapids. Enl. Sep. 19,'61. M.O. Dec. 19, '63
Sanford, William; Milwaukee. Enl. Feb. 6, '64. M.O. Jul. 16, '65.
Scott, William; Eau Plaine. Enl. Oct. 9, '61. Vet.; M.O. Jul. 19, '65.

Scott, Jacob; Eau Plaine. Enl. Oct. 9, '61. M.O. Oct. 30, '64. term exp
Shaughnessy, George; Wausau. Enl. Sep. 16, '61. Vet.; died Jun. 25, '64, Big Shanty, Ga., disease.
Shearer, Andrew; Madison. Enl. Nov. 12, '61. Vet.; M.O. Jul. 16, '65.
Simenson, Martin; Stevens Point. Enl. Oct. 8, '61. Vet., Corp; wnd. Aug. 6, '64; M.O. Jul. 16, '65.
Single, Charles A.; Wausau. Enl. Sep. 16, '61. Trans. to 8th Wis. Battery, May 19, '62.
Smith, Edward A.; Grand Rapids. Enl. Sep. 16, '61. Died Jul. 4, '63, Vicksburg, Miss., disease.
Smith, Joseph W.; Seneca. Enl. Sep. 16, '61. Vet.; M.O. Jul. 16, '65.
Smith, Edwin F.; Milwaukee. Enl. Feb. 26, '64. Died Mar. 31, '64, Madison, Wis., disease.
Snyder, Allen L.; Grand Rapids. Enl. Dec. 21, '63. M.O. Jul. 16, '65.
Snyder, Stephen H.; Grand Rapids. Enl. Dec. 29, '63. Vet. Recruit; M.O. May 22, '63.
Straight, Joel N.; Woodland. Enl. Oct. 17, '61. From Regtl Band; trans. to V.R.C., Nov. 9, '63.
Stilson, William P.; Rudolph. Enl. Oct. 11, '61. Vet.; M.O. Jul. 16, '65
Streeter, Roselle; Jefferson. Enl. Sep. 24, '61. M.O. Oct. 30, '64, term exp.
Sullivan, Thomas; Kickapoo. Enl. Oct. 4, '64. Died Dec. 30, '64, Savannah, Ga., disease.
Swancey, William; Jamestown. Enl. Dec. 18, '63. From Co. I, 25th Wis. Inf.; M.O. jul. 27, '65.
Swart, James; Pra. du Chien. Enl. Jan. 11, '64. From Co. I, 25th Wis. Inf.; M.O. Jul. 16, '65.
Switzer, John; Willow Springs. Enl. Oct. 10, '64. M.O. Jul. 16, '65.
Taylor, Ebenezer M.; Wausau. Enl. Oct. 5, '61. Died Oct. 17, '63, Natchez, Miss.
Thompson, Louis N.; Portland. Enl. Sep. 10, '64. Drowned while bathing, May 9, '65, Virginia.
Ticknor, Elias H.; Wausau. Enl. Oct. 5, '61. Vet., Sergt., 1st Sergt.; in Capt. Langworthy's exp. to Fed. fleet announcing Sherman's occupation of Savannah; wnd. Jul. 22, '64; M.O. Jul. 16, '65.
Twedell, Edward; Hazel Green. Enl. Dec. 28, '64. From Co. I, 25th Wis. Inf.; M.O. Jul. 16, '65.
Tuttle, Mathew P.; Seneca. Enl. Sep. 16, '61. Disch. May 27, '62, Leavenworth, Kan.
Villandro, Augustus; Saratoga. Enl. Jan. 14, '64. M.O. Jul. 16, '65.
Wakeley, Newbold L.; Rudolph. Enl. Jan. 4, '64. M.O. Jul. 16, '65.
Wakeley, Franklin; Rudolph. Enl. Jan. 4, '64. Died Dec. 23, '64, Madison, Ind.
Wakeley, Otis D.; Saratoga. Enl. Oct. 14, '61. Vet., M.O. Jul. 16, '65.
Wakeley, Daniel; Saratoga. Enl. Oct. 4, '61. Vet., Corp., Sergt.; M.O. Jul. 16, '65.
Waldo, Orrin; Saratoga. Enl. Oct. 13, '61. Vet.; accidentally killed by cars, Jun. 8, '65, Clarksville, Va.
Wall, John W.; Jamestown. Enl. Feb. 20, '64. From Co. I, 25th Wis. Inf.; M.O. Jul. 16, '65.

Warren, Clarence M.; Grand Rapids. Enl. Sep. 18, '61. Vet., Corp.; wnd. Jul. 22 and 28, '64; M.O. Jul. 16, '65.
Wasson, George W.; Elk Grove. Enl. Jan. 22, '64. From Co. I, 25th Wis. Inf.; M.O. Jul. 16, '65.
Welty, David W.; Wausau. Enl. Oct. 8, '61. M.O. Oct. 30, '64, term exp.
Whipple, Efflugar E.; Grand Rapids. Enl. Oct. 17, '61. Disch. May 28, '62, disability.
Wile, William; Milwaukee. Enl. Feb. 2, '64. M.O. Jul. 16, '65.
Wiley, John W.; Prescott. Enl. Oct. 8, '61. Disch May 28, '62, disability.
Woods, Theodore; Pra. du Chien. Enl. Jan. 11, '64. From Co. I, 25th Wis. Inf.; M.O. Jul. 16, '65.

ROSTER OF COMPANY "H"

OFFICERS

Captains

MILO C. PALMER; Green Bay. Rank Oct. 23, '61. Enl. Sep. 3, '61; res. Aug. 7, '63. disability.
CARLTON B. WHEELOCK; Green Bay. Rank Sep. 12, '63. Enl. Sep. 30, '61; 1st Sergt.; 1st Lieut., Aug. 9, '62; prom. Major, Jan. 6, '65.
EPHRAIM BLAKESLEE; La Valle. Rank Apr. 11, '65. From 1st Sergt. Co. B; 2nd Lieut., May 11, '62; 1st Lieut., Jan. 21, '64; det. in com'd. of Co. E, from Aug. 15, '64, to Jan. 1, '65; M.O. Jul. 16, '65.

First Lieutenants

NATHAN A. C. SMITH; Green Bay. Rank Oct. 23, '61. Enl. Oct. 8, '61; res. Aug. 4, '62, disability.
WILLIAM R. BOUTON; Green Bay. Rank Apr. 11, '65. Enl. Sep. 30, '61; Vet., Corp., Sergt., 1st Sergt.; 2nd Lieut., Jan. 21, '64; det. as acting R.Q.M. for Nov. and Dec.,'64; M.O. Jul. 16, '65.

Second Lieutenants

CHARLES O. LOVETT; Green Bay. Rank Oct. 23, '61. Enl. Oct. 1, '61; res. May 5, '62.
JAMES LENNON; Sevastopol. Rank Apr. 11, '63. Enl. Oct. 1, '61; Vet., Sergt., 1st Sergt.; M.O. Jul. 16, '65.

Enlisted Men

Adams, Alexander; Holland. Enl. Oct. 4, '64. M.O. Jul. 16, '65.
Addison, Thomas L.; Green Bay. Enl. Sep. 23, '61. Disch. Apr. 30, '62, disability.

Allen, Charles H.; Harmony. Enl. Oct. 7, '64. Died May 6, '65, Newbern, N.C., disease.
Allquer, Alpheus; Marinette. Enl. Sep. 16, '62. From Co. F; M.O. May 31, '63.
Arnd, Edward W.; Green Bay. Enl. Oct. 8, '61. Disch. Mar. 17, '63, disability.
Arnold, Ira E. S.; Green Bay. Enl. Oct. 24, '61. Vet.;M.O. Jul. 16, '65
Askinett, Peter; Howard. Enl. Feb. 4, '64. Killed in action, Jul. 21,'64, Atlanta, Ga.
Aspenwall, John; Weyauwega. Enl. Sep. 30, '64. Wnd., Bentonville; right arm amputated; M.O. Jun 5, '65.
Athey, Charles W.; Fort Howard. Enl. Nov. 19, '61. Disch. May 28, '62., disability.
Bannan, James; Sturgeon Bay. Enl. Oct. 14, '61. From Band; Vet.; trans. to V.R.C., Apr. 1, '65; M.O. Jul. 23, '65.
Baptist, Arnold F.; Nassawaupee. Enl. Apr. 14, '64. M.O. Jul. 16, '65.
Beaulieu, Harrison H.; Milwaukee. Enl. Feb. 12, '64. Killed in action, July 13, '64. Atlanta, Ga.
Beaulieu, John H.; Oconto. Enl. Jan. 19, '64. Supposed pris.; absent at M.O. of Regt.
Beation, Richard F.; Casco. Enl. Apr. 4, '64. M.O. Aug. 2, '65.
Beighl, Fawait R.; Sylvan. Enl. Sep. 23, '61. From Co. I; Vet., Musician; M.O. Jul. 16, '65.
Betts, James N.; Preble. Enl. Feb. 24, '64. M.O. Jul. 16, '65.
Bigsby, George W.; Ridgeway. Enl. Dec. 14, '63. Trans to Co. K, Mar. 1, '64.
Bilderback, John E.; Potosi. Enl. Dec. 19, '63. From Co. H, 25th Wis. Inf.; M.O. Jul. 16, '65.
Bowers, Henry; Marinette. Enl. Sep. 11, '62. From Co. F; trans. to Co. A, Oct. 26, '62.
Boyd, W. H. C.; Green Bay. Enl. Oct. 2, '61. Corp.; disch. May 30, '62, disability.
Bradley, Mortimer; Sturgeon Bay. Enl. Oct. 10, '61. Disch. Jun. 7, '62, disability.
Broillard, Peter; Green Bay. Enl. Nov. 21, '61. Died May 6, '62, Lawrence, Kan., disease.
Bromley, Van Buren; Green Bay. Enl. Oct. 8, '61. Corp.; disch. Oct. 30, '63, by order.
Brooker, Eleazer; Potosi. Enl. Jan. 2, '64. From Co. H, 25th Wis. Inf.; M.O. May 16, '65, of Regt.
Brooks, James A.; Green Bay. Enl Oct. 10, '61. M.O. Nov. 4, '64, term exp.
Brown, Daniel; Big Suamico. Enl. Oct. 8, '61. Died Oct. 215, '63, Natchez, Miss.
Brown, Thomas M.; Fort Howard. Enl. Oct. 14, '61. Vet., Corp., Sergt., 1st Sergt.; M.O. Jul. 16, '65.
Brundridge, Hiram A.; Wilton. Enl. Oct. 12, '64. From Co. H, 25th Wis. Inf.; M.O. 1Jul. 16, '65.
Buckmaster, William; Marinette. Enl. Sep. 25, '61. From Co. K; M.O. Nov. 4, '64, term exp.
Bursell, Thomas; Green Bay. Enl. Sep. 23, '61. Disch. Jan. 20, '63, disability.

Busha, John; Green Bay. Enl. Nov. 24, '61. Vet.; M.O. Jul. 16, '65.
Busha, Michael; Green Bay. Enl. Oct. 10, '61. Disch. Apr. 29, '62, disability.
Cady, John L.; Green Bay. Enl. Oct. 5, '61. Disch. Jun. 14, '62, by order.
Campbell, Lelon; Clifton. Enl. Sep. 20, '64. Drafted; died Feb. 8, '65, Nashville, Tenn., disease.
Campbell, Robert R.; Green Bay. Enl. Oct. 16, '61. Vet., Corp.; prom. Sergt. Major, Jan. 1, '65.
Chatterson, Joshua. Green Bay. Enl. Oct. 15, '61. Vet.; M.O. Jul. 16, '65.
Clark, William; Green Bay. Enl. Oct. 8, '61. Vet., Corp.; M.O. Jul. 16, '65.
Coats, John; ? Enl. Nov. 8, '63. Died Jan. 24, '64, Natchez, Miss., disease.
Codington, Levi; Big Suamico. Enl. Oct. 18, '61. M.O. Nov. 4, '64, term exp.
Colburn, Eleazer J.; Green Bay. Enl. Dec. 28, '63. M.O. Jul. 16, '65.
Connolly, Patrict; Big Suamico. Enl. Oct. 24, '61. Disch. Apr. 9, '63, disability.
Coryell, Edward C.; Johnstown. Enl. Feb. 13, '65. Died Apr. 27, '65, Madison, Wis., disease.
Cox, Jesse; Mineral Point. Enl. Feb. 4, '64. Wnd. Atlanta; M.O. Jul. 16, '65.
Crocker, Samuel E.; Harrison. Enl. Dec. 29, '62. From Co. H, 25th Wis. Inf.; M.O. Jun. 27, '65.
Cross, Jacob; Sturgeon Bay. Enl. Oct. 10, '61. Vet.; M.O. Jul. 16, '65.
Crouch, Robert; Potosi. Enl. Jan. 4, '64. From Co. H, 25th Wis. Inf.; M.O. Jul. 16, '65.
Crow, John D.; Potosi. Enl. Jan. 4, '64. From Co. H, 25th Wis. Inf.; M.O. Jul. 16, '65.
Curtis, Joseph S.; Green Bay. Enl. Jan. 1, '62. Vet., Corp.; prom. 2nd Lieut. Co. E, 42nd Wis. Inf., Jul. 29, '64.
Daggett, Samuel M.; Big Suamico. Enl. Oct. 8, '61. Sergt.; disch. May 30, '62, disability.
Daggett, Charles M.; Big Suamico. Enl. Oct. 8, '61. Disch. Aug. 28, '62, disability.
Dakin, Paul; Green Bay. Enl. Sep. 30, '61. Corp., Sergt.; prom. 2nd Lieut. Co. F, 32nd Wis. Inf., Sep. 22, '64.
Davis, Charles; Milwaukee. Enl. Oct. 15, '64. M.O. Jul. 16, '65.
Deckner, William; Casco. Enl. Mar. 12, '64. M.O. Jul. 16, '65.
Deheck, John. Marinette. Enl. Sep. 16, '62. From Co. F; M.O. May 31, '65.
Desbrow, Jerome; Green Bay. Enl. Oct. 23, '61. M.O. Nov. 4, '64, term exp.
Dickenson, George W.; De Pere. Enl. Oct. 12, '61. M.O. Nov. 4, '64, term exp.
Druen, William H.; Windsor. Enl. Jan. 5, '64. From Co. H, 25th Wis. Inf.; M.O. Sep. 22, '65.
Dunlap, James; Casco. Enl. Apr. 4, '64. Wnd. Atlanta; M.O. Jul. 16, '65.

Du Rochie, William; Preble. Enl. Feb. 3, '64. Wnd. and pris., Atlanta; supposed to have died in Rebel Prison.
Enderby, William R.; Green Bay. Enl. Oct. 9, '61. Vet., Corp.; wnd.; M.O. Jul. 16, '65.
Falk, John; (Served as John Selway.)
Fanin, Michael; Green Bay. Enl. Oct. 16, '61. Vet.; M.O. Jul. 16, '65
Feldhausen, Mathias; Wrightstown. Enl. Oct. 6, '64. Wnd. Bentonville, N.C.; M.O. May 15, '65.
Fellows, William; Madison. Enl. Sep. 27, '62. From Co. F; Corp.; disch. Sep. 25, '65, to accept prom.
Ford, Silas N.; Cottage Grove. Enl. Jan. 4, '64. Disch. Oct. 5, '64, disability.
Forsyth, Jerome; Green Bay. Enl. Oct. 2, '61. Died Mar. 30, '62, Leavenworth, Kan., disease.
Fox, Michael; Pensaukee. Enl. Sep. 28, '64. M.O. May 31, '65.
Frazier, Samuel E.; Excelsior. Enl. Feb. 20, '65. M.O. Jul. 16, '65.
Garvie, Michael; Oconto. Enl. Jan. 12, '64. Wnd. Atlanta; absent wnd. at M.O. of Regt.
Gothe, John F.; Fort Howard. Enl. Oct. 21, '61. Deserted Oct. 19, '62.
Gram, Andrew; Green Bay. Enl. Oct. 8, '61. Corp.; M.O. Nov. 4, '64, term exp.
Gribner, Henry; Fond du Lac. Enl. Dec. 5, '61. Died Jul. 23, '63, on Hosp. Boat "Nashville," Vicksburg, Miss., disease.
Grignon, Alexander; Green Bay. Enl. Oct. 30, '61. Vet.; M.O. Jul. 16, '65.
Gunn, John; Green Bay. Enl. Oct. 5, '61. Corp.; wnd. Sep. 2, '64; died Sep. 26, '64, Marietta, Ga., wnds.
Hale, Lewis; Fort Howard. Enl. Oct. 21, '61. Deserted Oct. 5, '62.
Hansen, Lewis E.; Wrightstown. Enl. Feb. 8, '64. M.O. Jul. 16, '65.
Hanzlik, Wenzel J.; Milford. Enl. Feb. 15, '65. M.O. Aug. 9, '65.
Harder, Frank; Green Bay. Enl. Oct. 2, '62. Vet., Corp., Sergt.; M.O. Jul. 16, '65.
Harris, Enoch; Harmony. Enl. Oct. 3, '64. M.O. Jul. 16, '65.
Harris, Henry; Sturgeon Bay. Enl. Sep. 15, '61. Vet., Corp.; prom 2nd Lieut. Co. F, 43rd Wis. Inf., Aug. 10, '64.
Harris, Joseph, Jr.; Sturgeon Bay. Enl. Sep. 28, '61. Vet., Corp.; prom 2nd Lieut. Co. K. 36th Wis. Inf., Feb. 15, '64.
Harvey, Nathan C.; Woodland. Enl. Dec. 24, '63. Corp.; M.O. Jul. 16, '65.
Hayden, George W.; Fort Howard. Enl. Oct. 8, '61. Vet., Corp.; M.O. Jul. 16, '65.
Howett, Richard J.; Potosi. Enl. Jan. 3, '64. From Co. H, 25th Wis. Inf.; M.O. Aug. 16, '65.
Hogarty, Michael; Green Bay. Enl. Dec. 12, '61. Vet.; M.O. Jul. 16, '65.
Hollingshead, Elijah; Excelsior. Enl. Feb. 20, '65. M.O. Jul. 16, '65.
Howard, Charles; Portage. Enl. Dec. 16, '63. Deserted Mar. 18, '64.
Howard, John; Adrian. Enl. Oct. 13, '64. From Co. H, 25th Wis. Inf.; M.O. Jul. 3, '65, O. of Regt.
Huck, Daniel; Little Suamico. Enl. Oct. 23, '61. M.O. Nov. 4, '64, term exp.

Hubbard, Daniel J.; Frnklin. Enl. Feb. 23, '64. Wnd. Atlanta; absent wnd. at M.O. of Regt.
Hubbard, Hiram H.; Fort Howard. Enl. Oct. 17, '61. Disch. Aug. 28, '62, disability.
Jackson, James A.; Delavan. Enl. Feb. 21, '64. Wnd. Atlanta; M.O. Jul. 16, '65.
Jepson, Charles H.; Green Bay. Enl. Dec. 28, '63. M.O. Jul. 16, '65.
Jepson, Joseph; Green Bay. Enl. Oct. 3, '61. Sergt.; died Jul. 30, '63. Benton Barracks, Mo., disease.
Johnson, Samuel S.; Green Bay. Enl. Oct. 8, '61. Corp.; disch. May 26, '62, disability.
Jones, Michael; Green Bay. Enl. Nov. 24, '61. Vet.; wnd. Atlanta; M.O. Jul. 16, '65.
Jones, John D.; Marinette. Enl. Sep. 24, '62. From Co. F; trans. to Co. A, Oct. 21, '62.
Jostin, Joseph; Green Bay. Enl. Oct. 15, '61. Vet.; M.O. Jul. 16, '65.
Jump, William; Fort Howard. Enl. Oct. 17, '61. Vet.; M.O. Jul. 16, '65
Keeler, Henry A.; Green Bay. Enl. Sep. 30, '61. Vet.; killed in action Jul. 21, '64, Atlanta, Ga.
Kish, Henry; Seldon. Enl. Oct. 6, '64. M.O. Jun. 30, '65.
Kronberg, Elias; Sturgeon Bay. Enl. Oct. 30, '61. Deserted May 27, '62.
Krouse, Peter; Big Suamico. Enl. Oct. 15, '61. Vet., Corp.; M.O. Jul. 16, '65.
Lawrence, Charles J.; Fort Howard. Enl. Oct. 30, '61. Vet.; M.O. Jul. 16, '65.
Loudenklos, John Peter; Casco. Enl. Apr. 4, '64. M.O. Jul. 16, '65.
Lusha, Charles G.; Oconto. Enl. Feb. 29, '64. M.O. Jul. 16, '65.
Mack, Le Roy; Kewaunee. Enl. Oct. 8, '61. Vet.; wnd. Kenesaw; disch. Jun. 29, '65, wnds.
Maxfield, James L.; Oconto. Enl. Oct. 22, '61. Vet.; absent without leave at M.O. of Regt.
McBride, John; Green Bay. Enl. Oct. 1, '61. Vet., Corp.; M.O. Jul. 16, '65.
McKaller, Arthur; Green Bay. Enl. Oct. 23, '61. Wagoner; trans. to V.R.C., Nov. 9, '63.
McMonagal, David; Big Suamico. Enl. Oct. 8, '61. Sergt.; deserted Mar. 7, '64.
McMonagal, William; Green Bay. Enl. Oct. 30, '61. Disch. Aug. 4, '62, disability.
McNamee; Hugh; Wequaoc. Enl. Oct. 30, '61. Disch. Apr. 29, '62, disability.
Miller, Henry; Preble. Enl. Jan. 23, '64. Wnd. Kenesaw; disch. Jan. 24, '65, wnds.
Mitchell, James; Marinette. Enl. Sep. 16, '62. From Co. F; died Mar. 3, '63, Camp Butler, Tenn., disease.
Mitchell, William R.; Green Bay, Enl. Oct. 10, 61. Musician; M.O. Nov. 4, '64, term exp.
Mitchell, Silas N.; Hampden. Enl. Feb. 28, '65. M.O. Jul. 16, '65.
Mitchell, Blish; Green Bay. Enl. Mar. 20, '62. Vet.; M.O. Jul. 16, '65.
Morris, George P.; Green Bay. Enl. Oct. 12, '61. Prom. Com. Sergt., 1st Batt. 2nd Wis. Cav., Jan. 9, '62.

Moshaquette, Lewis; Preble. Enl. Jan. 21, '64. M.O. Jul. 16, '65.
Neeley, William; Green Bay. Enl. Oct. 5, '61. Disch. May 28, '62, disability.
Neilson, Neils; Sturgeon Bay. Enl. Sep. 30, '61. Died Jun. 25, '62, Troy, Tenn., disease.
Olive, Maxime; Peshtigo. Enl. Oct. 15, '61. Trans. to Co. F, Jan. 1, '62.
Pallado, Joseph; Wrightstown. Enl. Oct. 14, '61. Vet., Corp.; M.O. Jul. 16, '65.
Parson, George; Harmony. Enl. Oct. 13, '64. M.O. Jul. 7, '65.
Peterson, Christian; New Denmark. Enl. Oct. 21, '61. Vet.; wnd.; M.O. Jul. 16, '65.
Peterson, John; New Denmark. Enl. Oct. 21, '61. Vet.; M.O. Jul. 16, '65.
Peterson, Peter; Green Bay. Enl. Sep. 30, '61. Vet.; wnd. Atlanta; disch. Jun. 29, '65, wnds.
Phillips, George M.; Green Bay. Enl. Oct. 30, '61. Vet.; M.O. Jul. 16, '65.
Pickering, David; Oakland. Enl. Feb. 28, '65. M.O. Jul. 16, '65.
Pickering, Milo; Buena Vista. Enl. Feb. 20, '65. M.O. Jul. 16, '65.
Pilligor, Michael; Wrightstown. Enl. Dec. 14, '63. M.O. Jul. 16, '65.
Price, John W.; Woodland. Enl. Dec. 17,'63. M.O. Jul. 16, '65.
Pung, John; Marinette. Enl. Sep. 16, '62. From Co. F; killed in action, Jul. 21, '64, Atlanta, Ga.
Remington, David; Depere. Enl. Oct. 17, '61. Vet.; M.O. Jul. 16, '65.
Ritter, John P.; Green Bay. Enl. Oct. 1, '61. Trans. to V.R.C., Jan. 15, '64.
Roe, Richard; Green Bay. Enl. Oct. 2, '61. Vet.; wnd. Jul. 21, '64; pris. Jan. 28, '65, Salkahatchie, S.C.; M.O. Jun. 30, '65.
Roe, James Y.; Green Bay. Enl. Oct. 2, '61. Vet.; wnd.; M.O. Jul. 16, '65.
Rogers, Jacob; Tomah. Enl. Sep. 30, '64. Died Feb. 5, '65, Nashville, Tenn., disease.
Rossiter, William; Fort Howard. Enl. Oct. 30, '61. Vet., Corp., Sergt.; M.O. Jul. 16, '65.
Sager, George C.; Depere. Enl. Oct. 1, '61. Vet.; M.O. Jun. 27, '65.
Salveson, Ole R., Sturgeon Bay. Oct. 10, '61. Vet.; M.O. Jul. 16, '65.
Sandford, Eliphalet; Nassawaupee. Enl. Apr. 14, '64. Died Aug. 10, '64, Marietta, Ga., disease.
Sawyer, John; Manitowoc. Enl. Oct. 9, '61. Vet.; deserted Oct. 28, '64
Scholl, Joseph; Potosi. Enl. Jan. 2, '64. From Co. H, 25th Wis. Inf.; M.O. May 10, '65.
Shedaker, Christian. Big Wuamico. Enl. Oct. 10, '61. Killed in action, Sep. 4, '64, Lovejoy, Ga.
Sherman, David B.; West Point. Enl. Jan. 2, '64. Wnd. Jun. 15, '64; M.O. Jul. 16, '65.
Sherwood, Albert H.; Sturgeon Bay. Enl. Sep. 28, '61. Vet.; M.O. Jul. 16, '65.
Simpson, Joseph F.; Charlestown. Enl. Oct. 14, '64. M.O. Jul. 16, '65.
Smith, Henry C.; Green Bay. Enl. Dec. 28, '63. Vet. Recruit; pris.; M.O. Jun. 24, '65.

Smith, Albert H.; Big Suamico. Enl. Oct. 8, '61. Vet., Corp.; M.O.
Jul. 16, '65.
Smith, Joseph; Wheatland. Enl. Feb. 19, '64. Wnd. Kenesaw; M.O.
Jul. 16, '65.
Smith, Thomas; Green Bay. Enl. Oct. 8, '61. Corp.; trans. to V.R.C.,
Nov. 10, '63; M.O. Nov. 4, '64, term exp.
Solway, John; Sevastopol. Enl. Apr. 13, '64. M.O. Jul. 16, '65.
Stanberg, Abner; Johnstown. Enl. Feb. 13, '65. M.O. Jul. 16, '65.
Starks, William; Weyauwega. Enl. Oct. 8, '64. Dropped as deserter,
Jun. 27, '65.
Straight, Joel N.; Woodland. Enl. Oct. 17, '61. Trans. to Band,
Jan. 1, '62.
Strope, William; Fort Howard. Enl. Oct. 10, '61. Vet.; M.O.
Jul. 16, '65.
Tabor, John C.; Woodland. Enl. Dec. 24, '63. M.O. Jul. 16, '65.
Tabor, Robert N.; Woodland. Enl. Dec. 17, '63. M.O. Jul. 16, '65.
Taylor, Abram; Fort Howard. Enl. Oct. 1, '61. Corp.; Disch. May 30,
'62, disability.
Taylor, Jacob; Green Bay. Enl. Oct. 23, '61. Corp.; M.O. Nov. 4, '64,
term exp.
Ten Eyck, Tenadore; Green Bay. Enl. Oct. 12, '61. Corp.; prom. Capt.
18th U.S. Inf., Feb. 19, '62.
Thompson, Joseph; Green Bay. Enl. Oct. 23, '61. Vet., Corp., Sergt.;
M.O. Jul. 16, '65.
Ticko, Samuel; Preble. Enl. Jan. 27, '64. Dropped as a deserter, Jun.
29, '65.
Tonnard, Joseph; Dykesville. Enl. Oct. 14, '61. Died Aug. 10, '63, on
Hosp. Boat "Nashville," near Vicksburg, Miss., disease.
Tourtellotte, John L.; Stiles. Enl. Oct. 23, '61. Vet., trans. to
V.R.C., Apr. 13, '65; M.O. Aug. 1, '65.
Tracy, Francis U.; Boscobel. Enl. Sep. 7, '61. From Co. K; trans. to
Co. K, Jun. 28,'63.
Turner, Robert; Potosi. Enl. Dec. 28, '63. From Co. H, 25th Wis. Inf.;
M.O. Jul. 21, '65.
Vaughn, Alonzo; Hickory Grove. Enl. Nov. 13, '63. Trans to Co. K,
Mar. 1, '64.
Walch, John; Green Bay. Enl. Sep. 30, '61. Disch. Oct. 6, '62.
disability.
Walch, Lewis; Green Bay. Enl. Dec. 12, '63. M.O. Jul. 16, '65.
Walch, Francis; Green Bay. Enl. Sep. 30, '61. Vet.; M.O. Jul. 16, '65.
Warren, Lewis E.; Sturgeon Bay. Enl. Sep. 28, '61. Vet., Corp.; 2nd
Lieut. Co. G, 53rd Wis. Inf., not mustered; M .O.
May 11,'65.
Warren, Julius; Sturgeon Bay. Enl. Feb. 16, '64. Wnd. Atlanta; M.O.
Jul. 16, '65.
Watkins, Samuel; Big Suamico. Enl. Oct. 14, '61. Died Aug. 29, '62,
Humboldt, Tenn., disease.
Weiderhold, George; Paris. Enl. Oct. 6, '64. From Co. H, 25th Wis.
Inf.; M.O. Jul. 16, '65.
Whitcomb, Walter S.; Green Bay. Enl. Sep. 30, '61. Vet., Corp.,
Sergt.; M.O. Jul. 16, '65.
White, Joseph; Oconto. Enl. Sep. 27, '61. Vet.; M.O. Jul. 16, '65.

Wilkins, Charles; Preble. Enl. Jan. 29, '64. M.O. Jul. 16, '65.
Woodman, Charles; Madison. Enl. Mar. 31, '63. From Co. H, 25th Wis. Inf.; M.O. May 24, '65.
Woody, Joseph H.; Woodland. Enl. Dec. 19, '63. M.O. Jul. 16, '65.
Wright, Benjamin F.; Caledonia. Enl. Jan. 30, '64. M.O. Jul. 16, '65.
Wright, Rufus M.; Sturgeon Bay. Enl. Feb. 16, '64. Corp., wnd. Sep. 2, '64, Lovejoy's Station; M.O. May 26, '65.

ROSTER OF COMPANY "I"

OFFICERS

Captains

HARTWELL L. TURNER; Viola. Rank Sep. 30, '61. Enl. Sep. 5, '61; res. Apr. 12, '62.
VAN S. BENNETT; Viola. Rank Mar. 19, '62. Enl. Sep. 2, '61; 1st Lieut., Sep. 30, '61; M.O. Nov. 7, '64, term exp.
FRANCIS HOYT; Prescott. Rank Jan. 6, '65. From 2nd Lieut. Co. A; 1st Lieut, Mar. 19, '62. M.O. Jul. 16, '65.

First Lieutenant

ELI McVEY; Whitestown. Rank Jan. 6, '65. Enl. Sep. 28, '61; Vet., Sergt., 1st Sergt.; 2nd Lieut., Nov. 21, '64; M. O. Jul. 16, '65.

Second Lieutenants

JEROME S. TINKER; Viroqua. Rank Oct. 7, '61. Enl. Sep. 15, '61; res. Mar. 20, '62.
LEVI M. BRESEE; Madison. Rank Mar. 19, '62. From Com. Sergt.; A.D.C., 3rd Brig., 4th Div., 17th A.C.; prom. Adj., Jul. 30, '63.
SELMA RODGERS; Viola. Rank Jul. 30, '63. Enl. Sep. 23, '61; 1st. Sergt.; M.O. Nov. 1, '64. term exp.
IRWIN GRIBBLE; Kickapoo. Rank Feb. 11, '65. Enl. Sep. 20, '61; Vet., Sergt., 1st Sergt.; M.O. Jul. 16, '65.

Enlisted Men

Adams, James; Harmony. Enl. Oct. 9, '61. Disch. Mar. 17, '63, disabiltiy.
Adams, James F.; Goole. Enl. Feb. 27, '64. M.O. Jul. 16, '65.
Allbee, Horace; Highland. Enl. Dec. 21, '63. From Co. B, 25th Wis. Inf.; M.O. Jul. 16, '65.
Allen, Eugene; Hull. Enl. Oct. 1, '64. M.O. Jun. 27, '65.
Ashbaugh, Bartlett; Prescott. Enl. Oct. 18, '61. From Co. A; Vet.; prom. Hosp. Steward, Jan. 1, '65.

Baldwin, Eugene; Kickapoo. Enl. Oct. 7, '61. Vet., Corp.; killed in action, Feb. 4, '61, Bolton, Miss.
Balcom, James; Kinnickinnick. Enl. Oct. 11, '61. From Co. A; M.O. Oct. 23, '64, term exp.
Barclay, Angus; Forest. Enl. Oct. 22, '61. Vet.; M.O. Jul. 16, '65.
Bartle, Peter F.C.; Lima. Enl. Mar. 5, '64. From Co. B, 25th Wis. Inf.; M.O. Aug. 16, '65.
Baumann, Frank; Milwaukee. Enl. Sep. 30, '64. M.O. May 31,'65.
Beighl, Faeralt R.; Sylvan. Enl. Sep. 23, '61. Trans. to Co. H. Jan. 1, '62.
Bell, John; Milwaukee. Enl. Oct. 3, '64. M.O. Jul. 16, '65.
Bender, Emanuel P.; Forest. Enl. Sep. 23, '61. Trans. to V.R.C., Nov. 9, '63.
Bender, Jonas C.; Forest. Enl. Sep. 25, '61. Vet., Corp., Sergt.; absent sick at M.O. of Regt.
Benn, Jacob; Kickapoo. Enl. Feb. 23, '64. Wnd. Atlanta; M.O. Jul. 16, '65.
Benjamin, Silas; Sylvan. Enl. Sep. 23, '61. Vet., Corp., Sergt.; pris. Atlanta; M.O. Jul. 16, '65.
Beslin, Irvin; Viroqua. Enl. Oct. 27, '63. Wnd. Big Shanty; M.O. Jul. 16, '65.
Blair, James A.; Muscoda. Enl. Feb. 2, '64. From Co. B, 25th Wis. Inf.; M.O. Jul. 16, '65.
Blaisdell, Nathaniel; Diamond Bluff. Enl. Sep. 25, '61. From Co. A; trans to Co. A. May 23, '64.
Bochtier, Joseph; Lake. Enl. Oct. 12, '64. M.O. Jul. 16, '65.
Bockover, John D.; Orion. Enl. Feb. 22, '64. From Co. B, 25th Wis. Inf.; M.O. Jul. 16, '65.
Bolzell, Elias; Mineral Point. Enl. Oct. 11, '64. M.O. Jul. 16, '65.
Bon, Samuel P.; Kickapoo. Enl. Sep. 25, '61. Vet., Corp., Sergt., 1st Sergt.; wnd. Lovejoy Station; M.O. Jul. 16, '65.
Booth, William S.; Avoca. Enl. Mar. 8, '64. From Co. B, 25th Wis. Inf.;M.O. Jul. 16, '65.
Brewer, Rensaelaer; Marshall. Enl. Sep. 23, '61. M.O. Oct. 28, '64, term exp.
Brisbin, William O.; Muscatine. Enl. Oct. 2, '61. From Co. a; M.O. Oct. 29, '64, term exp.
Brock, John C.; Patch Grove. Enl. Dec. 24. '63. From Co. B, 25th Wis. Inf.; M.O. May 29, '65.
Brooks, Caleb T.; Wellington. Enl. Sep. 20, '64. Drafted; died Jul. 8, '65, Fairfax Seminary Hospital, disease.
Bryant, Thomas F.; Viroqua. Enl. Sep. 30, '61. Vet., Corp.; M.O. Jul. 16, '65.
Button, Myron M.; La Crosse. Enl. Oct. 14, '64. M.O. Jun. 30, '65.
Byington, Orin; Highland. Enl. Jan. 12, '64. From Co. B, 25th Wis. Inf.; M.O. Jul. 16, '65.
Campbell, Andrew J.; Summit. Enl. Sep. 19, '64. Drafted; M.O. May 31, '65.
Carter, John W.; Viroqua. Enl. Sep. 30, '61. Disch. Jan. 1, '62, disability.
Carver, Robert F.; Muscoda. Enl. Dec. 12, '63. From Co. B, 25th Wis. Inf.; M.O. Jul. 16, '65.

Caruthers, John; River Falls. Enl. Sep. 23, '61. From Co. A; trans. to
Co. A, May 23, '64.
Cassady, Thomas J.; Manitowoc. Enl. Jan. 8, '62. Died Jan. 23, '63,
Bolivar, Tenn., disease.
Churchill, George W.; Kickapoo. Enl. Oct. 7, '61. Vet., Corp.; wnd.
Lovejoy's Station, Ga.; M.O. Jul. 16, '65.
Churchill, James; Sugar Grove. Enl. Mar. 31,'64. M.O. Jul. 16, '65.
Clark, Francis B.; Kickapoo. Enl. Sep. 25, '61. Disch. Apr. 18, '62,
disability.
Clark, Emery L.; Kickapoo. Enl. Sep. 23, '61. Vet., Corp.; M.O.
Jul. 16, '65.
Clason, William L.; Wauzeka. Enl. Jan. 5, '64. From Co. B, 25th Wis.
Inf.; M.O. Jul. 16, '65.
Clift, Lasl; Forest. Enl. Sep. 23, '61. Corp.; disch. Jun. 15, '62,
disability.
Clift, Windsor P.; Forest. Enl. Jan. 2, '63. Corp.; M.O. Jul. 16, '65.
Coggon, Lancelot; Forest. Enl. Sep. 17, '61. Died Jul. 6, '63,
Vicksburg, Miss., disease.
Colvin, Dalias; Highland. Enl. Jan. 12, '64. From Co. B, 25th Wis.
Inf.; M.O. Jul. 16, '65.
Cook, William C.; Sylvan. Enl. Oct. 5, '64. Died Dec. 16, '64,
Savannah, Ga., disease.
Core, John; Orion. Enl. Feb. 24, '64. From Co. B, 25th Wis. Inf.;
absent sick at M.O. of Regt.
Cornwell, Albert; Milwaukee. Enl. Oct. 6, '64. M.O. Jul. 14, '65.
Cox, Daniel; Webster. Enl. Oct. 8, '61. Disch. Jan. 1, '62, disability.
Craig, John; Muscoda. Enl. Mar. 20, '64. From Co. B, 25th Wis. Inf.;
M. O. Aug. 15, '65.
Dale, Wilber P.; River Falls. Enl. Sep. 23, '61. From Co. A; M.O. Oct.
28, '64, term exp.
Darnell, Elias; Forest. Enl. Sep. 23, '61. Corp.; died Aug. 22, '62,
Humboldt, Tenn., disease.
Dascey, George; Viroqua. Enl. Sep. 30, '61. Corp.; pris, Atlanta; died
Sep. 25, '64, Andersonville, Ga., wnds.
David, Marquis P.; Port Andrew. Enl. Jan. 20, '64. From Co. B, 25th
Wis. Inf.; M.O. Jul. 16, '65.
David, Darius P.; Port Andrew. Enl. Jan. 23, '64. From Co. B, 25th
Wis. Inf.; absent pris. at M.O. of Regt.
Davis, John; Atlanta (?). Enl. Aug. 1, '63. M.O. Jul. 16, '65.
Day, George W.B.; Bristol. Enl. Nov. 5, '61. Vet.; pris. Jun. 3, '64,
Rome, Ga.; absent par. pris. at M.O. of Regt.
Dean, Cassius C.; Dodgeville. Enl. Feb. 18, '64. From Co. B, 25th
Wis. Inf.; M.O. Jul. 16, '65.
Dean, Thomas; Perry. Enl. Feb. 20, '64. Wnd. Jul. 21, '64, Atlanta;
died Jul. 22, '64, near Atlanta, Ga., in 3rd Div. Hosp.,
wnds.
Dean James W.; Stark. Enl Sep. 23, '61. Vet.; deserted May 1, '64.
Degarmo, Cushing; Liberty. Enl. Sep. 23, '61. Vet.; wnd, Atlanta;
died Sep. 20, '64, Rome, Ga., wnds.
DeJean, George; Kildare. Enl. Oct. 1, '64. M.O. Jul. 5, '65.
Dewitt, Eliphaz; Medina. Enl. Oct. 14, '64. Died Jan. 3, '65,
Savannah, Ga., disease.

Dobson, Thomas L.; Forest. Enl. Sep. 23, '61. Disch. May 9, '62, disability.
Dobson, William J.; Forest. Enl. Sep. 23, '61. Died Feb. 20,'62, disease.
Dosch, Edmund; Orion. Enl. Dec. 22, '63. From Co. B, 25th Wis. Inf.; M.O. May 20, '65.
Dowell, William; Viola. Enl. Nov. 1, '61. Vet., Corp.; M.O. Jul. 16, '65
Downey, Eli; Viola. Enl. Feb. 19, '64. M.O. Jul. 16, '65.
Drake, Henry S. G.; Red Wing. Enl. Feb. 27, '64. M.O. Jul. 16, '65.
Dupee, Henry H.; Reedstown. Enl. Sep. 25, '64. Wnd. Jul. 21, '64; died Aug. 10, '64, Marietta, Ga., wnds.
Emenson, Steener; Preston. Enl. Sep. 21, '64. Drafted; M.O. May 31, '65.
Eno, Edgar; Forest. Enl. Oct. 4, '61. Vet., Corp.; M.O. Jul. 16, '65.
Everett, George; Viroqua. Enl. Oct. 7, '61. Vet.; M.O.Jul. 16, '65.
Farmer, Alpheus D.; Summit. Enl. Sep. 19, '64. Drafted; M.O. May 31, '65.
Fetterly, Jerome; Forest. Enl. Sep. 23, '61. M.O. Oct. 28, '64, term exp.
Fleming, Martin; Clinton. Enl. Sep. 22, '64. Drafted; M.O. May 31, '65.
Foreman, Rudolph; Kickapoo. Enl. Oct. 14, '61. Vet., Corp.; M.O. Jul. 16, '65.
Foster, Benjamin F.; Troy. Enl.Sep. 23, '61. Vet.; killed in action, Aug. 17, '64, Atlanta, Ga.
Foster, George J.; Mauston. Enl. Sep/ 23, '61. Sergt.; M.O. Oct. 28, '64, term exp.
Francis, Russell; Sylvan. Enl. Sep. 23, '61. Musician; trans to Co. F, Jan. 1, '62.
Geran, James; Milwaukee. Enl. Oct. 10, '64. Absent without leave at M.O. of Regt.
Gillis, David G.; Albany. Enl. Mar. 30, '64. From Co. B, 25th Wis. Inf.; trans. to V.R.C. Apr. 21, '65; disch. Jun. 6, '65, disability.
Granger, Rawson; Alma. Enl. Oct. 12, '64. Pris. Jan. 30, '65, Pocotaligo; absent pris. at M.O. of Regt.
Gray, Martin; Blue River. Enl. Dec. 21, '63. From Co. B, 25th Wis. Inf.; absent at M.O. of Regt.
Griffin, Charles; Tomah. Enl. Sep. 20, '64. drafted; M.O. May 21, '65.
Halgerson, Alva; Preston. Enl. Sep. 21, '64. Drafted; M.O. May 20, '65.
Hancock, George W.; Webster. Enl. Oct. 8, '64. M.O. Jul. 16, '65.
Hard, Francis C.; West Bend. Enl. Oct. 6, '61. From Co. I; disch. Dec. 15, '63, to acc. prom. in 6th Miss. C. T.
Harries, Thomas; Muscoda. Enl. Mar. 30, '64. From Co. B, 25th Wis. Inf.; M.O. Jul. 16, '65.
Hawkins, John; Franklin. Enl. Oct. 6, '64. Pris. Feb. 21, '65, near Columbia, S.C.; M.O. May 2, '65.
Hays, Alexander; Christana. Enl. Jan. 25, '64. Died Mar. 4, '64, Madison, Wis., disease.
Henthorn, John; Sylvan. Enl. Sep. 30, '61. Died Oct. 6, '64, Marietta, Ga., disease.

Hill, Lorenzo; Forest. Enl. Feb. 20, '64. M.O. May 22, '65.
Hogenson, Ole; Greenville. Enl. Mar. 29, '64. From Co. B, 25th Wis. Inf.; M.O. Jul. 27, '65.
Honey, Henry G.; Forest. Enl. Sep. 23, '61. Disch. May 31, '62, disability.
Hope, George W.; Diamond Bluff. Enl. Oct. 30, '61. From Co. A; trans to Co. A, May 31, '64.
Hoyt, Albert J.; Highland. Enl. Feb. 1, '64. From Co. B, 25th Wis. Inf.; M.O. Jul. 16, '65.
Hubbard, Jonas; Forest. Enl. Sep. 21, '64. Drafted; M.O. May 31, '65.
Hull, Henry H.; Franklin. Enl. Nov. 18, '61. Vet., Corp.; M.O. Jul. 16, '65.
Hulbert, Ansel; Orion, Enl. Feb. 10, '64. From Co. B, 25th Wis. Inf.; M.O. May 20, '65.
Hutchinson, Joshua; Reedstown. Enl. Sep. 23, '61. Vet., Corp., Sergt.; M.O. Jul. 16, '65.
Jeffries, James; Union. Enl. Sep. 28, '61. Disch. Mar. 27, '62, disability.
Jennings, David; Christiana. Enl. Jan. 23, '64. M.O. Jul. 16, '65.
Jennings, Jared; Liberty. Enl. Sep. 21, '64. Drafted; M.O. May 31, '65
Jenness, Thomas L.; Clinton. Enl. Oct. 9, '61. Corp.; M.O. Oct. 28, '64, term exp.
Jordan, Timothy S.; Union. Enl. Sep. 21, '64. Drafted; M.O. May 31, '65.
Kanable, Jeremiah S.; Forest. Enl. Feb. 20, '64. M.O. Jul. 16, '65.
Kellogg, Ranson; Kickapoo. Enl. Sep. 23, '61. Vet., Corp.; M.O. Jul. 16, '65.
Kellogg, Luman S.; Kickapoo. Enl. Sep. 23, '61. Vet.; M.O. Jul. 16, '65.
Kellogg, Lewis D.; Kickapoo. Enl. Sep. 23, '61. M.O. Oct. 28, '64, term exp.
Keepers, Lewis M.; Dayton. Enl. Oct. 23, '61. Vet.; wnd. Atlanta; died Aug. 9, '64, Marietta, Ga., wnds.
Keepers, James M.; Eagle. Enl. Jan. 25, '64. From Co. B, 25th Wis. Inf.; M.O. Jul. 16, '65.
Keepers, Hays J.; Richland Centre. Enl. Dec. 14, '61. Vet.; M.O. Jul. 16, '65.
Keyes, Stephen P.; Strong's Prairie. Enl. Nov. 5, '61. Vet.; M.O. Jul. 16, '65.
Leach, Hiram; Peshtigo. Enl. Oct. 15, '61. From Co. F; trans. to Co. F, Sep. 8, '63.
Leavitt, William H.H.; Hartland. Enl. Feb. 8, '64. M.O. Jul. 16, '65.
Leavitt, Nathan W.; Hartland. Enl. Feb. 8, '64. Died Feb. 14, '65, Savannah, Ga., disease.
Leighty, Robert M.; Viroqua. Enl. Oct. 9, '61. Musician; trans. to Co. C, Jan. 1, '62.
Lewis, James; Excelsior. Enl. Feb. 11, '64. From Co. B, 25th Wis. Inf.; M.O. Jul. 16, '65.
Libby, Warren; Hammond. Enl. Sep. 23, '61. From Co. A; trans. to Co. A, May 28, '64.
Lind, Ova; Harmony. Enl. Oct. 8, '61. Vet.; killed in action, Feb. 4, '64, Bolton, Miss.

Lincoln, John; (?) Enl. Aug. 1, '63. M. O. Jul. 16, '65.
Logue, George T.; Muscoda. Enl. Dec. 14, '63. From Co. B, 25th Wis.
    Inf.; M.O. Jul. 16, '65.
Logue, Adam J.; Muscoda. Enl. Jan. 5, '64. From Co. B, 25th Wis.
    Inf.; M.O. Jul. 16, '65.
Logue, John S.S.; Muscoda. Enl. Dec. 23, '63. From Co. B, 25th Wis.
    Inf.; M.O. Jul. 16, '65.
Logue, John M.; Muscoda. Enl. Feb. 10, '64. From Co. B, 25th Wis.
    Inf.; M.O. May 12, '65.
Mace, James E.; Sylvan. Enl. Sep. 23, '61. Musician; disch. May 19,
    '64, disability.
Malette, Sylvester M.; Sylvan. Enl. Oct. 31, '61. Vet.; wnd. Aug. 16,
    '64; M.O. Jul. 16, '65.
Marshall, George L.; Rockbridge. Enl. Oct. 28, '61. Died Nov. 25, '62,
    Bolivar, Tenn., disease.
Marsh, Joel G.; Milwaukee. Enl. Oct. 12, '64. M.O. Jul. 16, '65.
Masterson, Michael; Clinton. Enl. Oct. 9, '61. Pris. Atlanta; M.O.
    Oct. 28, '64, term exp.
McClurg, Seth; Christiana. Enl. Jan. 8, '64. M.O. Jun. 12, '65.
McHugh, Peter; Kewaskum. Enl. Oct. 21, '61. From Co. D; trans. to
    Co. D, Jan. 1, '64.
McKinny, Robert C.; Excelsior. Enl. Jan. 9, '64. From Co. B, 25th
    Wis. Inf.; M.O. Jul. 16, '65.
McMillan, John; Prescott. Enl. Sep. 21, '61. From Co. A; M.O. Nov.
    8, '64, term exp.
McVey, Allen; Whitestown. Enl. Sep. 30, '61. Wnd. Atlanta; M.O.
    Oct. 31, '64, term exp.
Milner, Hamilton S.; Orion. Enl. Dec. 29, '63. From Co. B, 25th Wis.
    Inf.; M.O. Jul. 16, '65.
Moody, Horace; Waukesha. Enl. Sep. 28, '64. M.O. May 31, '65.
Moon, Lafayette; Sylvan. Enl. Sep. 23, '61. Vet.; killed in action,
    Jul. 21, '64, Atlanta, Ga.
Moon, John W.; Sylvan. Enl. Feb. 26, '64. M.O. Jul. 16, '65.
Moore, James; Stark. Enl. Sep. 21, '64. Drafted; M.O. May 31, '65.
Moore, James; Sun Prairie. Enl. Sep. 29, '62. Died Apr. 4, '64, Sun
    Prairie, Wis., disease.
Moore, Warner C.; Muscoda. Enl. Dec. 7, '63. From Co. B, 25th Wis.
    Inf.; M.O. Jul. 16, '65.
Moore, John A.; Viroqua. Enl. Oct. 24, '64. M.O. Jul. 16, '65.
Moran, Joseph; Sharon. Enl. Oct. 12, '64. M.O. Jul. 16, '65.
Mower, William D.; Milwaukee. Enl. Oct. 17, '64. M.O. Jul. 16, '65.
Munger, Israel E.; Barton. Enl. Sep. 24, '61. Vet.; M.O. Jul. 16, '65.
Munyon, John; Franklin. Enl. Nov. 18, '61. Died Apr. 5, '64,
    Vicksburg, Miss., disease.
Murray, Lewis E.; Whitestown. Enl. Sep. 23, '61. Vet.; wnd.
    Decatur; M.O. Jul. 16, '65.
Murray, John A.; Whitestown. Enl. Sep. 23, '61. Disch. Mar. 27, '62,
    disability; re-enl. Apr. 29, '64; M.O. Jun. 8, '65.
Murray, William H.; Vienna. Enl. Aug. 31, '62. Killed in action,
    Feb. 4, '61, Bolton, Miss.
Neal, Lemuel; Sun Prairie. Enl. Sep. 29, '62. M.O. May 31, '65.
Neely, Peter; Kickapoo. Enl. Oct. 5, '61. Vet.; M.O. Jul. 16, '65.

Ogden, William; Sylvan. Enl. Sep. 23, '61. Corp.; disch. Aug. 4, '62, by order.
Osmer, William D.; Whitestown. Enl. Sep. 23, '61. Vet., Corp.; trans to V.R.C., Oct. 17, '64; M. O. Jul. 24, '65.
Ostrander, Oscar; Bristol. Enl. Jan. 25, '64. M.O. Jul. 16, '65.
Ostrander, Conrad; Whitestown. Enl. Sep. 23, '61. Died Aug. 16, '63, Bristol, Wis., disease.
Ostrander, Horace; Viola. Enl. Sep. 23, '61. Trans to Co. E, Jan 4, '64.
Payn, Emery J.; Star. Enl. Sep. 23, '61. Vet., Corp., Sergt.; M.O. Jul. 16, '65.
Perrigo, William; Port Andrew. Enl. Jan. 20, '61. From Co. B, 25th Wis. Inf.; absent sick at M.O. of Regt.
Pettygrove, Neal; Avoca. Enl. Jan. 16, '64. From Co. B, 25th Wis. Inf.; M.O. Jul. 16, '65.
Porter, William H.; Trenton. Enl. Sep. 17, '61. From Co. D; trans. to Co. D, Jan. 18, '62.
Powell, Moses; Stark. Enl. Sep. 23, '61. Corp.; disch. Jan. 1, '62, disability.
Privett, Joseph C.; Orion. Enl. Jan. 5, '64. From Co. B, 25th Wis. Inf.; M.O. Jul. 16, '65.
Pugh, Wallace B.; Reedstown. Enl. Sep. 25, '61. Vet., Corp.; M.O. Jul. 16, '65.
Purcell, James K.; Richwood. Enl. Feb. 16, '64. From Co. B, 25th Wis. Inf.; M.O. Jul. 16, '65.
Richards, George C.; Franklin. Enl. Sep. 30, '61. Corp.; died Jul. 8, '63, Vicksburg, Miss., disease.
Rider, Benjamin F.; Christiana. Enl. Jan. 30, '64. M.O. Jul. 16, '65.
Rider, Haskell; Ontonagon. Enl. Oct. 22, '61. From Co. A; M.O. Oct. 28, '64, term exp.
Robinson, Bryant; Lanesfield, TN. Enl. Aug. 1, '63. M.O. Jul. 16, '65.
Robinson, Samuel J.: Richland. Enl. Dec. 29, '63. From Co. B, 25th Wis. Inf.; M.O. Jul. 16, '65.
Salmon, Cutler; Muscoda. Enl. Jan. 16, '64. From Co. B, 25th Wis. Inf.; M.O. Jul. 16, '65.
Sample, Milton; Viroqua. Enl. Mar. 16, '64. Killed in action, Jun. 30, '64, Kenesaw Mountain, Ga.
Sanford, Ephraim; Kickapoo. Enl. Mar. 17, '62. M.O. Jul. 16, '65.
Sanford, David; Kickapoo. Enl. Feb. 20, '64. Died Apr. 116, '64, Cairo, Ill., disease.
Savage, Albert J.; Sylvan. Enl. Aug. 14, '62. M.O. May 31, '65.
Shafer, Henry A.; Forest. Enl. Sep. 23, '61. Vet.; wnd. Atlanta; disch. May 25, '65, wnds.
Sheasby, John; New Centerville. Enl. Oct. 7, '61. Vet., Corp.; M.O. Jul. 16, '65.
Silbaugh, James; Christiana. Enl. Jan. 5, '64. Killed in action, Mar. 11, '65, Fayetteville, N.C.
Skinnen, Thomas; Christiana. Enl. Jan. 17, '64. Pris. Jul. 21, '64, Atlanta; absent pris. at M.O. of Regt.
Smith, Samuel; Christiana. Enl. Jan. 5, '64. Disch. Apr. 7, '65, disability.

Snow, Willis S.; Richland Centre. Enl. Sep. 23, '61. Wagoner; disch. Apr. 18, '62, by order.
Snow, Jerome B.; Fort Atkinson. Enl. Sep. 23, '61. Vet., Sergt.; M.O. Jul. 16, '65.
Sommars, David B.; Forest. Enl. Sep. 23, '61. Vet., Corp.; wnd. Jul. 21, '64, Atlanta; left arm amputated; disch. Dec. 9, '64, wnds.
Sommars, John B.; Forest. Enl. Sep. 23, '61. Vet.; wnd. Atlanta; trans to V.R.C., Apr. 24, '65; M.O. Jul. 29, '65.
Sommars, Amos P.; Forest. Enl. Feb. 23, '64. Trans to V.R.C., Dec. 21, '64; M.O. Jul 18, '65.
Squires, Stephen; Delton. Enl. Nov. 20, '62. Trans. to Co. E. Jan. 1, '62.
Stacks, Daniel D.; Polk. Enl. Oct. 9, '61. From Co. D; trans to Co. D, Jan 1, '64.
Strong, Henry F.; Trenton. Enl. Oct. 3, '61. Vet.; wnd. Aug. 31, '64, Jonesboro; right arm amputated; disch. Apr. 8, '65, wnds.
Styles, Leonard C.; River Falls. Enl. Oct. 4, '61. From Co. A; M.O. Oct. 31, '64, term exp.
Sutherland, John W.; Readstown. Enl. Aug. 30, '62. M.O. May 31, '65.
Sutton, Christopher C.; Richwood. Enl. Dec. 15, '63. From Co. B, 25th Wis. Inf.; M.O. May 20, '65.
Tate, William L.; Leeds. Enl. Jan. 23, '64. M.O. Jul. 16, '65.
Teal, Horatio J.; Stark. Enl. Sep. 23, '61. Vet., Corp.; M.O. Jul. 16, '65.
Tenny, David; Sylvan. Enl. Sep. 23, '61. Died Jul. 12,'63, Vicksburg, Miss., disease.
Tenny, Edwin B.; Sylvan. Enl. Sep. 23, '61. Corp.; trans to V.R.C., Nov. 9, '63.
Thayer, William H.H.; Forest. Enl. Sep. 23, '61. Disch. apr. 23, '62, by order.
Thompson, James C.; Sylvan. Enl. Aug. 14, '62. Died Dec. 21, '62, Jackson, Tenn., Gen. Hosp., disease.
Thorp, John A.; Spring Valley. Enl. Nov. 6, '61. Vet.; died Jun. 5, '64, Rome, Ga., disease.
Thorp, Abner; Spring Valley. Enl. Nov. 6, '61. Died May 6, '62, Quincy, Ill., disease.
Ticknor, Charles H.; Prescott. Enl. Sep. 21, '61. From Co. A; disch. Sep. 20, '64, disability.
Tompkins, Andrew J.; Stark. Enl. Oct. 7, '61. Died Feb. 12, '62, Weston, Mo., disease.
Toptine, James C.; Kickapoo. Enl. Feb, 23, '64. Died Aug. 20, '64, Marietta, Ga., disease.
Toptine, Charles A.; Sylvan. Enl. Sep. 23, '61. Musician; died Dec. 23, '62, Bolivar, Tenn., disease.
Tyler, Ashbel B.; Forest. Enl. Sep. 17, '61. Died Nov. 23, '62, disease.
Van Voorhees, Wm W.; Kickapoo. Enl. Oct. 4, '64, M.O. Jul. 16, '65.
Vroman, Frank; Gilmanton. Enl. Oct. 15, '64. M.O. Jul. 22, '65.
Waldeck, James M.; Highland. Enl. Jan. 16, '64. From Co. B, 25th Wis. Inf.; M.O. Jul. 16, '65.

Walker, William H.; Hartland. Enl. Feb. 8, '64. M.O. Jul. 16, '65.
Warner, George D.; Sharon. Enl. Oct. 1, '64. Absent sick at M.O. of Regt.
Welles, John; River Falls. Sep. 30, '61. From Co. A; M.O. Oct. 28, '64, term exp.
Welker, John D.; Forest. Enl. Sep. 23, '61. Vet.; M.O. Jul. 16, '65.
Wempner, Henry; Forest. Enl. Sep. 23, '61. Vet.; wnd. Jul. 21, '64, Atlanta; died Jul. 26, '64, Atlanta, 3rd Div. Hosp., wnds.
Wempner, Augustus C.; Forest. Enl. Oct. 28, '61. Died Sep. 22, '63, St. Louis, Mo., disease.
West, Asabel W.; Forest. Enl. Sep. 23, '61. Vet.; wnd. Atlanta; died Aug. 1, '64, Marietta, Ga., wnds.
Willoughby, William; Richland. Enl. Dec. 14, '63. From Co. B, 25th Wis. Inf.; M.O. Jul. 16, '65.
Willett, Albert W.; Salem. Enl. Feb. 25, '64. From Co. B, 25th Wis. Inf.; M.O. Jul. 21, '65.
Wilsey, George W.; Highland. Enl. Jan. 16, '64. From Co. B, 25th Wis. Inf.; M.O. Jul. 16, '65.
Winters, Joel; Viroqua. Enl. Oct. 7, '61. Vet., Corp.; M.O. Jul. 16, '65
Wise, George W.; Viola. Enl. Sep. 23, '61. Corp.; disch. Jun. 24, '62, disability.
Whipple, John N.; Prescott. Enl. Sep. 23, '61. From Co. A; trans. to Co. A, May 31, '64.
Woodruff, William J.; Akan. Enl. Nov. 6, '61. Vet., Corp.; M.O. Jul. 16, '65.
Wright, William; Richwood. Enl. Jan. 25, '64. From Co. B, 25th Wis. Inf.; M.O. Jul. 16, '65.
Yakey, Samuel D.; Christiana. Enl. Jan. 5, '64. Died May 17, '65, in field, Virginia, disease.
Young, Andrew; Port Andrew. Enl. Dec. 21, '63. From Co. B, 25th Wis. Inf.; M.O. May 10, '65.

ROSTER OF COMPANY "K"

OFFICERS

Captains

DANIEL R. SYLVESTER; Castle Rock. Rank Oct. 19, '61. Enl. Sep. 7, '61; M.O. Nov. 11, '64, term exp.
ALMON N. CHANDLER; Marietta. Rank Jan. 6, '65. Enl. Sep. 7, '61; 1st Lieut., Oct. 19, '61; A.D.C.; killed in action Jan. 14, '65, Pocotaligo, S.C.
GEORGE R. PYLE; Clifton. Enl. Feb. 11, '65. Enl. Sep. 21, '61; Vet, Sergt., 1st Sergt.; 2d Lieut., Nov. 21, '64; 1st Lieut., Jan. 6, '65; M.O. Jul. 16, '65.

First Lieutenant

FRANKLIN PHILBRICK; Marietta. Rank Feb. 11, '65. Enl. Aug. 31, '61; Vet., Corp., Sergt., 1st Sergt.; 2d Lieut., Jan. 6, '65; M.O. Jul. 16, '65.

Second Lieutenants

ISAAC WALKER; Hickory Grove. Rank Oct. 19, '61. Enl. Sep. 7, '61; died Sep. 17, '62, at his home in Wisconsin.
GEORGE D. CLARK; Seneca. Rank Sep. 18, '62. Enl. Sep. 7, '61; 1st Sergt.; M.O. Oct. 30, '64, term exp.
GEORGE BROWN; Boscobel. Rank Feb. 11, '65. Enl. Aug. 31, '61; Vet., Corp., Sergt., 1st Sergt.; M.O. Jul. 16, '65.

Enlisted Men

Andrew, Henry; Platteville. Enl. Feb. 29, '64. From Co. E, 25th Wis. Inf.; M.O. Jul. 16, '65.
Barsness, Peter E.; Vermont. Enl. Oct. 13, '64. M.O. Jul. 16, '65.
Bartle, Charles C.; Kendall. Enl. Feb. 1, '64. From Co. E, 25th Wis. Inf.; M.O. Jul. 16, '65.
Bearse, James M.; Seneca. Enl. Nov. 8, '61. Vet.; M.O. Jul. 16, '65.
Bell, Enoch N.; Marietta. Enl. Oct. 19, '61. Disch. Apr. 18, '62.
Bigsby, George W.; Ridgeway. Enl. Dec. 14, '63. From Co. H; wnd. Jul. 28, '64, Atlanta; trans. to V.R.C., Apr. 24, '65; M.O. Jul. 19, '65.
Black, James L.; Platteville. Enl. Dec. 20, '63. From Co. E, 25th Wis. Inf.; M.O. Jun. 9, '65.
Blanchard, William W.; Marion. Enl. Oct. 31, '61. Wagoner; died Sep. 26, '63, Natchez, Miss., disease.
Blandin, Laison; Marietta. Enl. Aug. 31, '61. M.O. Oct. 30, '64, term exp.
Blandin, Naman; Madison. Enl. Aug. 15, '62. Died Jan. 16, '64, on steamer "Planet," disease.
Bolster, Andrew J.; Madison. Enl. Dec. 23, '63. Wnd. Jul. 21, '64; trans. to V.R.C. Apr. 1, '65.
Bonny, George; Marietta. Enl. Sep. 7, '61. Vet.; M.O. Jul. 16, '65.
Bonny, Edwin A.; Pra. du Chien. Enl. Aug. 30, '62. Died Feb. 12, '63, Camp Butler, Tenn., disease.
Brunnemer, John T.; Fennimore. Enl. Nov. 23, '61. Vet.; M.O. Jul. 16, '65
Buckmaster, William; Marinette. Enl. Sep. 25, '61. Trans. to Co. H., Oct. 16, '62.
Bullock, Silas; Platteville. Enl. Dec. 28, '63. From Co. E, 25th Wis. Inf.; M.O. Jul. 16, '65.
Bunnell, Benjamin H.; Wauzeka. Enl. Jan. 15, '64. M.O. Jul. 16, '65.
Bushnell, Daniel W.; Platteville. Enl. Dec. 12, '63. From Co. E, 25th Wis. Inf.; M.O. Jul. 16, '65.
Butler, Richard; Platteville. Enl. Dec. 22, '63. From Co. E, 25th Wis. Inf.; M.O. Jul. 16, '65.

Carver, Charles; Hickory Grove. Enl. Sep. 8, '61. Vet.; wnd. Atlanta; absent, wnd. at M.O. of Regt.
Chandler, Andrew; Lancaster. Enl. Jan. 4, '64. M.O. Jul. 16, '65.
Chandler, Daniel O.; Boscabel. Enl. Dec. 4, '61. Vet.; M.O. Jul. 16, "65
Chapman, Orson; Marietta. Enl. Sep. 21, '61. Corp.; disch. Jan. 1, '62
Clark, James; Seneca. Enl. Sep. 26, '61. Vet., Corp.; M.O. Jan. 16, '65.
Clark, Caleb B.; Fennimore. Enl. Nov. 15, '64. Killed in action, Jul. 22, '64, Atlanta, Ga.
Clevestine, Christian; Elk Grove. Enl. Jan. 30, '64. From Co. E, 25th Wis. Inf.; M.O. Jul. 16, '65.
Close, Ambrose F.; Madison. Enl. Dec. 14, '61. Fet., Corp., Sergt.; died Feb. 27, '64, Pearl River, Miss., disease.
Cook, Joseph; Marietta. Enl. Sep. 3, '61. Disch. Oct. 17, '62, disability.
Cummins, James; Elk Grove. Enl. Jan. 23, '64. From Co. E. 25th Wis. Inf.; M.O. Jul. 16, '65.
Curry, William A.; Boscobel. Enl. Oct. 23, '61. Vet.; M.O. Jul. 16, '65.
Davenport, Phillip; Rolling Ground. Enl. Aug. 17, '62. M.O. May 31, '65.
Dean, Manly M.; Ellenboro. Enl. Feb. 27, '64. From Co. E, 25th Wis. Inf.; M.O. Jul. 16, '65.
Dean, John S.; Ellenboro. Enl. Feb. 29, '64. From Co. E, 25th Wis. Inf.; M.O. Jul. 16, '65.
Dempsey, George P.; Fennimore. Enl. Sep. 7, '61. Vet., Corp.; disch. Nov. 28, '64, disability.
Dilley, Ira T.J.; Sladesburg. Enl. Sep. 21, '61. Vet.; M.O. Jul. 16, '65.
Doncaster, Joseph; Pra. du Chien. Enl. Aug. 30, '62. Disch. Apr. 25, '63, disability.
Dowling, Hugh; Crawford. Enl. Oct. 17, '61. M.O. Dec. 23, '64, term exp.
Doyle, Thomas D.; Walworth. Enl. Nov. 14, '61. Deserted Jan. 1, '62.
Earle, George; Fennimore. Enl. Sep. 15, '61. Disch. Jun. 10, '62.
Erickson, Andrew; Wauzeka. Enl. Jan. 22, '64. Died Mar. 24, '64, Cairo, Ill., disease.
Ewing, James M.; Richmond. Enl. Oct. 17, '64. Died Apr. 27, '65, Beaufort, S.C., disease.
Fairchilds, Isaac; Platteville. Enl. Dec. 26, '63. From Co. E, 25th Wis. Inf.; M.O. Jul. 16, '65.
Ferrell, John T.; Marietta. Enl. Aug. 31, '61. Vet., Corp., Sergt.; M.O. Jul. 16, '65.
Ferrell, Stephen S.; Marietta. Enl. Sep. 7, '61. Corp.; disch. Oct. 1, '62, disability.
Fisher, Edmund; Bowerville. Enl. Aug. 18, '62. Pris. Grand Gulf; M.O. May 31, '65.
Fisher, Austin; Marion. Enl. Dec. 17, '61. Vet.; M.O. Jul. 16, '65.
Frank, Robert; Lewiston. Enl. Oct. 12, '64. M.O. Jul. 16, '65.
Fry, Isaiah; Fennimore. Enl. Nov. 24, '63. Trans. to V.R.C., Mar. 15, '65; disch. Jun. 6, '65, disability.
Fuller, Fedora A.; Marietta. Enl. Sep. 21, '61. Vet.; absent sick at M.O. of Regt.

Fuzzard, George H.; Scott. Enl. Oct. 4, '61. Vet., Corp.; M.O. Jul. 16, '65.
Fuzzard, John; Clayton. Enl. Jan. 28, '64. M.O. Jul. 16, '65.
Gagnon, Lewis; Marietta. Enl. Nov. 8, '61. Vet.; deserted May 1, '64.
Geasland, Henry H.; Oregon. Enl. Jan. 12, '64. From Co. E, 25th Wis. Inf.; M.O. Jul. 16, '65.
Gehantek, Joseph; Maple Grove. Enl. Oct. 13, '64. Absent sick at M.O. of Regt.
Girdler, Frank B.; Marietta. Enl. Oct. 1, '61. M.O. Oct. 30, '64, term exp.
Grace, Alexander J.; Boscobel. Enl. Oct. 23, '61. Vet.; pris. Jul. 23, '64; M.O. Jul. 16, '65.
Graves, Joseph; Hall. Enl. Oct. 8, '64. Never reported to Co.
Green, Demetrius; Rolling Ground. Enl. Aug. 30, '62. Pris. Grand Gulf; M.O. May 31, '65. by order.
Greenhaigh, James E.; Clifton. Enl. Dec. 20, '63. M.O. Jul. 16, '65.
Gregory, George W.; Platteville. Enl. Dec. 29, '63. From Co. E, 25th Wis. Inf.; M.O. Jul. 16, '65.
Grass, John P.; Jefferson. Enl. Oct. 1, '64. M.O. May 27, '65.
Guist, Bradford; Crawford. Enl. Nov. 27, '61. M.O. Nov. 26, '64, term exp.
Hill, Charles N.; Oregon. Enl. Jan. 4, '64. From Co. E, 25th Wis. Inf.; Corp.; M.O. Jun. 22, '65, by order.
Haney, Patrick; Platteville. Enl. Dec. 25, '63. From Co. E, 25th Wis. Inf.; absent wnd. at M.O. of Regt.
Hanson, Peter E.; Sharon. Enl. Oct. 10, '64. M.O. Jul. 16, '65.
Hanson, Mathias; Milwaukee. Enl. Oct. 8, '64. M.O. Jul. 16, '65.
Havens, Henry B.; Marion. Enl. Dec. 2, '61. Disch. May 23, '62.
Hayne, Lewis; Boscobel. Enl. Sep. 21, '61. Sergt.; disch. Mar. 18, '63, disability.
Hoar, Joseph R.; Linden. Enl. Dec. 10, '61. Vet.; M.O. Jul. 16, '65.
Hopkins, Jacob; Fennimore. Enl. Dec. 7, '61. Disch. Feb. 7, '63, disability.
Hooverson, Hoover; Clayton. Enl. Oct. 2, '61. Vet., Corp.; M.O. Jul. 16, '65.
Howard, Samuel; Wingville. Enl. Dec. 6, '61. Vet., Corp.; absent sick at M.O. of Regt.
Irwin, Benjamin J.; Freeman. Enl. Oct. 12, '61. Vet.; M.O. Jul. 16, '65.
Iverson, Albert; Clifton. Enl. Feb. 15, '64. M.O. May 10, '65.
Johnson, Alfred; Kendall. Enl. Feb. 2, '64. From Co. E, 25th Wis. Inf.; M.O. Jul. 16, '65.
Johnson, Lewis; Freeman. Enl. Aug. 30, '62. M.O. May 31, '65.
Johnson, Henry; Freeman. Aug. 30, '62. M.O. May 31, '65.
Kane, Benjamin; Troy. Enl. Jan. 4, '64. From Co. E, 25th Wis. Inf.; M.O. Jul. 16, '65.
Kane, William D.; Adams Co. Enl. Nov. 17, '61. Deserted Jan. 1, '62.
Kast, Henry C.; Marietta. Enl. Sep. 30, '61. Disch. Jan. 1, '62.
Kast, James W.; Marietta. Enl. Sep. 30, '61. Died Oct. 27, '63, Madison, Wis., disease.
Kast, William F.M.; Pra. du Chien. Enl. Aug. 30, '62. Trans. to V.R.C., Nov. 9, '63; disch. Nov. 6, '64, disability.

Kelly, Lloyd; Marietta. Enl. Sep. 28, '61. Disch. Oct. 1, '62, disability.
Keil, Levi S.; Elk Grove. Jan. 25, '64. From Co. E, 25th Wis. Inf.; M.O. Jul. 16, '65.
Killson, John; Wonewoc. Enl. Sep. 19, '64. Drafted; died Feb. 17, '65, Nashville, Tenn., disease.
Knudtson, Halga; Ettrick. Enl. Sep. 21, '64. Drafted; died Jan. 22, '65, Dalton, Ga.
Larson, Lewis; Freeman. Enl. Aug. 29, '62. Died Mar. 31, '64, Madison, Wis., disease.
Lewis, John B.; Marietta. Enl. Oct. 1, '61. Corp.; M.O. Oct. 30, '64, term exp.
Long, William H.; Platteville. Enl. Dec. 24, '63. From Co. E, 25th Wis. Inf.; M.O. Jul. 16, '65.
Lull, Hoyt M.; Fennimore. Enl. Nov. 11, '63. Corp.; M.O. Jul. 16, '65.
Lysne, Thomas J.; Freeman. Enl. Aug. 30, '62. M.O. May 31, '65.
Malog, John; Marietta. Enl. Nov. 2, '61. Vet.; M.O. Jul. 16, "65.
Martin, Benjamin F.; Boscobel. Enl. Oct. 15, '61. Vet.; M.O. Jul. 16, '65.
Marston, George H.; Glen Haven. Enl. Dec. 19, '63. Wnd. Sep. 2, '64; absent wnd. at M.O. O. Regt.
Marston, Samuel R.; Mount Hope. Enl. Oct. 10, '61. Disch. Oct. 17, '62, disability.
Markham, Eben W.; Castle Rock. Enl. Jul. 26, '62. M.O. May 31, '65.
Maynard, Caleb, Jr.; Utica. Enl. Oct. 2, '61. Vet.; wnd. Aug. 12, '64, Atlanta; Trans. to V.R.C., Apr. 24, '65.
Mead, James B.; Blue River. Enl. Sep. 14, '61. Wnd. Vicksburg; disch. Aug. 21, '63, wnds.
Mellison, George; Marietta. Enl. Oct. 3, '61. Vet., Sergt.; wnd. Jul. 23, '64; M.O. Jul. 16, '65.
Miller, Albert F.; Henrietta. Enl. Oct. 15, '64. M.O. Jul. 16, '65.
Miller, Lafayette; Hickory Grove. Enl. Jul. 26, '62. Died Dec. 26, '62, Lumpkins' Mill, Miss., disease.
Mills, Robespiere; Rolling Ground. Enl. Dec. 7, '61. M.O. Dec. 22, '64 term exp.
Montague, George E.; Marietta. Enl. Sep. 7, '61. Corp.; M.O. Oct. 31, '64, term exp.
Moore, Edward H.; Fennimore. Enl. Jan. 4, '64. From Co. E, 25th Wis. Inf.; M.O. Jul. 16, '65.
Munns, Henry A.; Fennimore. Enl. Dec. 7, '63. Wnd. Jul. 21, '64; died Jul. 27, '64, Atlanta, Ga., wnds.
Munns, George; Castle Rock. Enl. Sep. 28, '61. Vet., Corp., Sergt.; M.O. Jul. 16, '65.
Munson, Newton; Clifton. Enl. Dec. 29, '63. Died Sep. 22, '64, Rome, Ga., disease.
Nash, Aaron; Castle Rock. Enl. Sep. 7, '61. Vet.; wnd. Vicksburg; M.O. Jul. 16, '65.
Nash, Ole T.; Towerville. Enl. Aug. 28, '62. Wnd. Jul. 21, and Aug. 23, '64; M.O. May 31, '65.
Newcomb, Elon; Crawford. Enl. Dec. 7, '61. Died Mar. 26, '62, disease
Nichols, John; Kendall. Enl. Feb. 4, '64. From Co. E, 25th Wis. Inf.; M.O. Jul. 16, '65.

Nordby, Ole Oleson; Vermount, WI. Enl. Oct. 15, '64. M.O. Jul. 16, '65.
O'Connor, John; Rising Sun. Enl. Sep. 22, '61. Vet., Corp., Sergt.; M.O. Jul. 16, '65.
Oleson, John; Towerville. Enl. Jan. 5, '64. M.O. Jul. 16, '65.
Oleson, Lewis; Rising Sun. Enl. Oct. 12, '61. Vet., Corp.; M.O. Jul. 16, '65.
Ostrander, Hiram; Marion. Enl. Nov. 16, '61. Vet.; M.O. Jul. 16, '65.
Palmer, Andrew; Boscobel. Enl. Nov. 23, '61. Died Jun. 28, '63, Vicksburg, Miss. disease.
Peckham, Solomon C.; Fennimore. Enl. Nov. 18, '61. Corp.; died Oct. 12, '63, Vicksburg, Miss., disease.
Peterson, Peter; Towerville. Enl. Oct. 2, '61. Vet.; Corp., Sergt.; M.O. Jul. 16, '65.
Peterson, Ole C.; Towerville. Enl. Jan. 26, '64. M.O. Jul. 16, '65.
Pinkham, Joseph; Rolling Ground. Enl. Nov. 27, '61. Vet.; M.O. Jul. 16, '65.
Pinkham; Caleb; Rolling Ground. Enl. Oct. 18, '61. Vet.; M.O. Jul. 16, '65.
Potter, Abijah P.; Kendall. Enl. Feb. 8, '64. From Co. E, 25th Wis. Inf.; absent sick at M.O. of Regt.
Randall, Henry; Mifflin. Enl. Nov. 28, '61. Deserted Dec. 29, '62.
Redman, Madison A.; Boscobel. Enl. Oct. 15, '61. Trans. to V.R.C., Nov. 9, '63.
Rein, John; Blue Mounds. Jan. 6, '62. Trans to Co. C, Jan. 3, '64.
Reynolds, Hiram H.; Marietta. Enl. Aug. 31, '61. Vet.; M.O. Jul. 16, '65.
Ricks, Reuben; Boscobel. Enl. Oct. 21, '61. Vet., Corp.; M.O. Jul. 16, '65.
Ricks, James B.; Boscobel. Enl. Oct. 31, '61, Vet.; M.O. Jul. 16, '65.
Rob, John G.; Marietta. Enl. Sep. 18, '61. Sergt., 1st Sergt.; disch. Sep. 19, '64, disability.
Robison, James B.; Oregon. Enl. Jan. 16, '64. From Co. E, 25th Wis. Inf.; M.O. Jul. 16, '65.
Rogers, Edwin; Marietta. Enl. Sep. 28, '61. Disch.; re-enl. Mar. 29, '64; disch. Oct. 30, '64, disability.
Rogers, Commodore; Stoughton. Enl. Oct. 1, '61. Corp.; disch. Apr. 25, '63, disability.
Rounds, Chauncey; Horicon. Enl. Oct. 1, '61. Musician; died Aug. 21, '63, Vicksburg, Miss., disease.
Sampson, Albert S.; Mifflin. Enl. Sep. 7, '61. Sergt.; prom. 1st Lieut. Co. K, 33rd Wis. Inf., Sep. 29, '62.
Schofield, Hiram; Boscobel. Enl. Nov. 16, '61. Vet.; M.O. Jul. 16, '65.
Schofield, Henry E.; Fennimore. Enl. Dec. 3, '64. M.O. Jul. 16, '65.
Schofield, Frank; Wingville. Enl. Apr. 20, '64. M.O. Jul. 16, '65.
Seright, Andrew; Sterling. Enl. Aug. 30, '62. M.O. May 31, '65.
Seltz, August; La Crosse. Enl. Sep. 19, '64. Drafted; M.O. Jul. 16, '65
Shaver, George P.; Stockbridge. Enl. Sep. 30, '64. M.O. May 31, '65.
Shields, Thomas; Boscobel. Enl. Jan. 6, '62. M.O. Jan. 11, '65. term exp.
Simons, William; Kendall. Enl. Jan. 27, '64. From Co. E, 25th Wis. Inf.; M.O. Jul. 16, '65.

Slates, Thomas; Rome Corners. Enl. Dec. 10, '61. Vet.; M.O. Jul. 16, '65.

Slates, William; Marietta. Enl. Sep. 29, '61. M.O. Oct. 30, '64, term exp.

Smith, Enos W.; Beetown. Enl. Oct. 19, '64. M.O. Jul. 16, '65.

Spicer, George E.; Pra. du Chien. Enl. Oct. 4, '64. Never reptd to Co.

Squire, George W.; Marietta. Enl. Oct. 5, '61. Corp., Sergt.; M.O. Oct. 30, '64, term exp.

Stanover, Frederick; Platteville. Enl. Dec. 22, '63. From Co. E, 25th Wis. Inf.; absent sick at M.O. of Regt.

Stevens, Jornay; Madison. Enl. Jan 6, '62. Disch. May 9, '62.

Stevens, Gustavus A.; Mifflin. Enl. Sep. 21, '61. Died Aug. 19, '64, Vicksburg, Miss., disease.

Stevens, Adelbert V.; Castle Rock. Enl. Sep. 21, '61. Vet., Corp., Sergt., 1st Sergt.; M.O. Jul. 16, '65.

Stevens, James H.; Clifton. Enl. Dec. 29, '63. M.O. Jul. 16, '65.

Steckel, Englebert; Liberty. Enl. Oct. 14, '64. Absent sick at M.O. of Regt.

Stuart, John S.; Boscobel. Enl. Dec. 31, '61. Disch. Mar. 27, '62.

Sutherland, John G.; Marietta. Enl. Oct. 3, '61. Died Aug. 20, '63, Natchez, Miss., disease.

Taylor, George C.; Ridgeway. Enl. Dec. 22, '63. M.O. Jul. 16, '65.

Taylor, Charles L.; Hickory Grove. Enl. Nov. 21, '63. Died Apr. 12, '64, Vicksburg, Miss., disease.

Thompson, Charles H.; Castle Rock. Enl. Oct. 12, '61. Died Aug. 1, '62, Humboldt, Tenn., disease.

Torgerson, Torger; Freeman. Enl. Dec. 11, '63. Wnd. Jul. 21, '64, M.O. Jul. 16, '65.

Tracey, Francis U.; Boscobel. Enl. Sep. 7, '61. Trans. to Co. H, Oct. 16, '62; rejoined Jun. 28, '63; died Aug. 24, '63, St. Louis, Mo., disease.

Trout, Hiram P.; Belmont. Enl. Jan. 9, '64. From Co. E, 25th Wis. Inf.; M.O. Jul. 16, '65.

Tuffley, George; Boscobel. Enl. Oct. 15, '61. Corp.; M.O. Oct. 30, '64, term exp.

Tuffley, Thomas H.; Boscobel. Enl. Sep. 14,'61. Vet.; M.O. Jul. 16,'65

Vaughn, Alonzo; Hickory Grove. Enl. Nov. 13, '63. From Co. H; died Feb. 26, '65, Jefferson Barracks, Mo., disease.

Walker, Sylvester; Castle Rock. Enl. Oct. 12, '61. Died May 24, '62, Lawrence, Kan., disease.

Wannemaker, Chas. H.; Columbus, KY. Enl. Apr. 15, '63. From Co. E, 25th Wis. Inf.; M.O. Jun. 3, '65.

Watt, Andrew J.; Boscobel. Enl. Nov. 4, '61. Killed in action, Jul. 22, '64, Atlanta, Ga.

Watt, James A.; Clifton. Enl. Oct. 14, '61. M.O. Nov. 16, '64, term exp.

Wayne, Lewis; Marietta. Enl. Sep. 7, '61. Sergt.; disch. Mar. 1, '63, disability.

Wayne, Nathaniel L.; Boscobel. Enl. Sep. 7, '61. Vet.; M.O. Jul. 16, '65.

Wayne, William G.; Marietta. Enl. Oct. 1, '61. M.O. Oct. 30, '64, term exp.

Wayne, Samuel P.; Marietta. Enl. Oct. 1, '61. M.O. Oct. 30, '64, term exp.
Wayne, Frank; Boscobel. Enl. Sep. 28, '61. M.O. Oct. 30, '64. term exp.
Weitenhiller, Charles; Elk Grove. Enl. Jan. 27, '64. From Co. E, 25th Wis. Inf.; M.O. Jul. 16, '65.
Wettleson, William O.; Dekorra. Enl. Oct. 7, '64. M.O. Jul. 16, '65.
Wheeler, Hiram H.; Hickory Grove. Enl. Nov. 5, '63. Wnd. Atlanta; M.O. May 26, '65.
Wheeler, George H.; Hickory Grove. Enl. Nov. 12, '63. M.O. Jul. 16, '65.
Wheeler, Alfion W.; Hickory Grove. Enl. Nov. 5,'63. M.O. Jul. 16,'65.
Wheeler, William; Lancaster. Enl. Oct. 22, '61. Vet.; M.O. Jul 16, '65.
Wilcox, Franklin; Marietta. Enl. Sep. 28, '61. M.O. Oct. 30, '65, term exp.
Willis, Richard; Castle Rock. Enl. Oct. 12, '61. Disch. Mar. 12, '63, disability.
Willsey, Franklin; Marietta. Enl. Oct. 28, '61. M.O. Oct. 30, '64, term exp.
Wilkins, Arvine C.; Madison. Enl. Jan. 1, '62. Vet., Corp.; M.O. Jul. 16, '65.
Winchester, William W.; Reedsburg. Enl. Nov. 12, '61. Musician; disch. Mar. 12, '63, disability.
Winship, Nathaniel; Castle Rock. Enl. Sep. 7, '61. Vet., Corp., Sergt.; M.O. Jul. 16, '65.
Wood, Frank A.; Wingville. Enl. Dec. 7, '63. M.O. Jul. 16, 65.
Wood, Ed; Fennimore. Enl. Sep.7, '61. M.O. Oct. 30, '64, term exp.
Wood, Isaiah; Wauzeka. Enl. Jan. 22, '64. Died Apr. 22, '64, Vicksburg, Miss., disease.
Zeller, William; Madison. Enl. Dec. 23, '63. Trans. to V.R.C., Dec. 20, '64; M.O. Mar. 7, '65.

ROSTER OF RECRUITS NOT ON COMPANY ROLLS

Bailey, John; ? Enl. ? M.O. Jun. 3, '65. as of Co. I.
Burns, James; Wheatland. Enl. Feb. 29, '64.
Davis, Nathan; Milford. Enl. Feb. 27, '65. M.O. Jun. 10, '65.
Everson, Gunder; Glyde. Enl. Oct. 6, '64.
Gill, Henry; Oak Grove. Enl. Feb. 25, '64.
Helgerson, Helga; ? Enl. Sep. 19, '64. Drafted; M.O. Jul. 25, '65.
Murphy, John; Wheatland. Enl. Feb. 26, '64.
Root, John; Mineral Point. Enl. Jan. 6, '65
Steel, Henry; Mineral Point. Enl. Jan. 6, '65.
Stevens, Frank; Marinette. Enl. Nov. 22, '62. Never reported.
Thatcher, John H.; Milwaukee. Enl. Feb. 24, '64.
Wilson, Thomas; Mineral Point. Enl. Jan. 6, '65.
Winchell, Samuel; Iowa Co. Enl. Aug. 18, '62. Never reported.

INDEX

Abbeville, MS, 19
Acworth, GA, 70
Adairsville, GA, 78
Augusta RR, 58
ALBERT, Ole, 89
ALLEN, Tom 16,33
Alligator Swamp, 39
Altoona Pass, 78
Army of the Potomac, 102,103
Army of Tennessee, 15,69
Athens, AL, 42
Atlanta, GA, 42,49,58,59,67, 74,75,77,79,81,82
Averysboro, NC, 97
Baker's Creek, 37,38
Baraboo, WI., 4
Baton Rouge, 21
Beaufort, SC, 89,92
Beauregard, Gen., 94
"Belgian Rifles", 8
BENNETT, Ed, 73,78
BENNETT, H. H., 34
Bentonville, NC, 97
Big Black River, MS, 26,38
Big Shanty, GA, 43,47,49,78
Black River, LA, 32
BLAIR, Gen. Frank P., 43,44, 46,47,51,99,100
BLAKESLEE, Lt.Ephraim,75
BLODGET, Albert, 16
BLYTH, G.L, 21,22
Bolivar, MS, 18
Branchville, SC, 93
BRIGGS, Charley, 2
BROUGHTON, Clem.,64,70,71
BROWN, Col., 91
BROWN, Sergt. N.D., 89
Brush Mountain, 49
BRYANT, Col. George E,5-7,9, 12,17,18,21,23,32,40,66,67,69, 72,74,79
Burlington & Quincy RR, 9
CAESAR, 18,19
Cairo, IL, 38,39,40,41,43,46
Cairo & New Orleans RR, 18
Camp Butler, TN,20,23
Camp Halleck, KS. 12
Camp, James, 64

Camp Leach, TN. 15
Camp Randall, WI, 4,5,7,9, 40,41,58
Canton, MS, 38
Cape Fear Riv., NC, 96
Cartersville, GA, 45,78
Carthage, LA, 25
CARY, Dr. Luther H., 5
CHALMERS, Gen., 21
Champion's Hill, MS, 26,37
CHANDLER, Capt.Almon,92
Charleston, NC, 94
Charlotte, NC, 90
Chattahoochee Riv.,53,58,77
Chattanooga, TN,51,77,79,82
Cheraw, NC., 94-96
Chicago, IL, 3,40,41,107
Chicago No.West. RR, 9
Chickasawah, 39
City Point, VA, 99
CLEMENT, James M.,64,73
Clifton, TN, 43
Clinton, MS, 37
Coldwater Riv., 18,21,22
Collierville, TN, 19,20,23
Columbia, SC, 93
Columbus, KY., 15,14,37
Corinth, MS. 13,17,37
CORSE, Gen., 78
COSPES, Erastus, 2
COTTON, Wm., 73
CROCKER, Brig. Gen., 38,39
DARROW, Nathaniel,73,75,100
DAVIS, Gen., 85
Decatur, AL, 43
Decatur, GA, 58,59,79,81
Decatur, MS, 38,39
Delton, WI., 1,2
Douglasville, IL., 10
"Dutch Company", 2
Edwards Station, 37
18th Missouri Regt. 10
8th Wisconsin Battery, 13
11th Illinois Cavalry, 39
11th Illinois Regt. 29,37
11th Wisconsin Regt., 5,29
ENDERBY, William, 15
Enterprise, MS, 39

185

Etowah Riv., 45,51
Ezra Church, 73
FALKNER, Col. W.C., 22
Fayetteville, NC, 94,96
FIELDS, Charles, 64
15th Corps,73,74,76,79,81,
  82,85-87,93,97,99,100,101
15th Illinois Regt.,38
15th New York Regt. 91
15th Ohio Battery,21,22,
5th Ohio Cavalry, 21
53rd Indiana Regt.,31,39
1st Brigade, 43,58,69,74
FLUNO, Henry, 54
FORCE, Gen.,Manning,58,62,
  63,69,92
FORREST, Gen. N. B.38,41
Fort Leavenworth,KS.,11,12,13
Fort McAllister, GA 87
Fort Pillow, 41
Fort Pulaski, 90
Fort Riley, KS, 12,13
Fort Scott, KS., 11,12
41st Illinois Regt. 21,22,31
45th Illinois Regt., 60
FOSBINDER, Charley, 23
14th Corps, 81,82
4th Division, 31,58,59,65-67
Fredericksburg, VA, 102
FREER, Mr. 2,3
Furlough, 38
GADDIS, John, 43,46,73
Georgia Central RR, 85,87
Germantown Station, 20
GILLESPIE, John, Lt.1,3,4,59,
  60,62,64,75,103
Goldsboro, NC, 97
Gordon, GA, 85
Grand Gulf, MS, 25,26,28
Grand Junction, MS, 18
Grand Review, 97
GRANT, Gen. Ulysses S.,13,16,
  19,25,26,42,68,82,99
GRESHAM, Gen. Walter O.,33,
  34,38,54,58,59
GRIERSON, Col. B. F., 21,23,
  37,38
GRFFIN, John, 73
GRIFFIN, Michael, 64

HAGAMAN, E. H., 65
HALL, Col. 38
HALLECK,Gen.Henry W.,49,101
HAMPTON, Gen. Wade, 94-96
Hannibal, MO., 10
Hard Times, LA, 25
HARDEE, Gen. W.J., 47,87,89,
  94,97
Harrisonburg, LA, 32,33
HARVEY, Gov. Louis P., 8,12
HAYES, Maj., 21,22
Haynes' Bluff, MS, 25,26
Hebron, MS, 38
HENRY, Sergt. 65
Hernando, MS, 21,22,23
Hillsboro, MS, 37,38
Holly Springs, MS. 17,18,19
HOOD, Gen, John B.,70,73,
  77-79,94
HOWARD, Gen.Oliver O.,69,74,
  81,82,85,89,97
HOWELL, Capt. Daniel, 5
Humboldt, TN, 15,17
Huntsville, AL, 42,43
HURLBUT, Gen. 18,37
Illinois Central RR, 40
INGALLS, John, 75
Jackson, MS, 26,31,37,38
JOHNSON, Pres.Andrew,101,102
JOHNSON, Rufus, 54
JOHNSTON, Gen. Joe, 31,42,47,
  49,94,97,99,101
Jonesboro, GA, 76,77
Kansas Riv., 11
KEELER, Henry, 65
Kennesaw Range,47,49-52,77,78
Kilbourn City, GA, 45
KILPATRICK, Gen., 82,85,95
KINNEY, Lt. Alpheus, 75
Lafayette,GA, 79
Lafayette, TN, 19
La Grange, MS, 18,21
Lake Concordia, LA, 32
LANGWORTHY, Capt.Warren
  89,90,91
LAUMAN, Gen. J.G., 21,28,31
Lawrence, KS., 12
LAWSHA, Jacob, 64,65
LEE, Gen. Robt. E., 97,99,101

LEGGETT,Gen.,M.D.,37,58,89,91
Leggett's Hill, 64
LIBBY, Sergt., 65
LINCOLN, Pres. Abraham,91,99, 101,104
LINDSFELDT, Dr. F. St. Sure,5
LINNELL, Lt. Lewis, 75
LINQUIST, Chas., 89
LOEBER, Capt. Charles F., 5
LOGAN, Gen.John A.,99,100,107
Louisville, KY, 107
Luka, Battle of, 17
Lumpkins Mill, 19
Macon & Western RR, 85
Madison, WI, 2,4,5,40,108
MAGGIE, 33
Manchester, VA, 102
Manhatten, KS. 13
Marietta, GA, 43,49,52,58,75, 78,79
MASON, Rev. L. B., 5
MATHEWS, James, 73
MAXSON, Capt. Orrin F., 17
McCLERNAND, Gen.John A.25
McLEOD, Capt. Norman, 5
McPHERSON, Gen.James B.,18, 37,45,47,68,81
McVEY, Sergt., 50
Memphis, TN, 19,21,21,23,38
Memphis & Charleston RR.19,20
Memphis & Nashville RR, 15
Milledgeville, GA, 85
Millen, GA, 86,87
Meridian, MS, 31,37,38
MILES, James, 60,65
Milliken's Bend, LA, 25
Mississippi River, 24
Missouri Riv., 11
Mobile & Ohio RR, 15,37,39
Morton, MS, 37
Moscow, TN, 19
MOSIER, Wm. L., 64,65,73,75
"Mott's Ferry", 4
Mower's Div., 92
Natchez, MS, 32-35
NELSON, Thomas H., 89
NICHOLS, Maj.GeorgeW,85,93
9th Alabama Regt., 39
Nickajack Creek, 53,56

9th Wisconsin Regt., 10
Nonconnah, MS, 21
North Edisto, SC, 93
Norton, Capt. George C., 5
Obion River, 15
Ogeechee Riv. 89
Ohio Riv. 43
Okalona, 37,38
Olathe, KS. 11
OLESON, Andrew, 89
OLIVER, William, 7
Orangeburg, SC, 93
Oxford, MS., 19
Paducah, KY, 41,43
PALMER, Capt. Milo C., 5
Paola, KS., 11
Peach Tree Cr.,58
PEARSON, Col., 74
Pearl Riv., MS, 37
PEMBERTON, Gen.John, 26,30
Perry's Ferry, 22
Petersburg, VA, 99,100
Pine Mountain, 47,48
Pittsburg Landing, TN. 12
Pocahontas, MS 17
Pocotaligo, 92
POLK, Gen., 48
POOLE, Lt. Col. Dewitt, 5,22
Poolers Station, GA, 87
Port Gibson, MS. 26
Port Hudson, 30
PORTER, Adm. David, 25
PRICE, Capt. John M., 5
PRICE, Gen. Sterling, 17
PROUDFIT,Adj.Lt.Col.JamesK. 5,33,34,38,56,57,74,75,81,92, 93,99
Quincy, IL., 9
Quincy & Weston RR., 10
Quitman, MS, 38,39
Raleigh, NC,97,99,100
Raymond, MS, 26
Resaca, GA, 78
Richmond, VA,81,82,99,101,102
Roanoke Riv.,100
ROBINSON, Ed, 20,73
Rome, GA,45,78
ROOD, Hosea, 23,27,34,48,50, 53,59,64,65,68,70,73,75,81,83, 91,93,94,96,99,101,102,107

ROOT, Corp. J. W., 34
Roswell's Mills, 58
SAGER, George, 16
St. Louis, MO, 32
Salkehatchie Riv., 92
SANDERSON, Col. W.L., 48
Savannah, GA, 82,87,89,91,92
Savannah & Charleston RR,92
SCHOFIELD, Gen.John M.,97
2nd Illinois Cavalry, 20
2nd Iowa Cavalry, 21
17th Corps, 18,73,74,76,77,79
  81,82,85,86,92-94,97,99,100
7th Illinois Cavalry, 21
SEXTON, Qtr.Mstr. Andrew, 5
Shawneetown, KS., 11
Sherman, Wm. T.,25,26,31,37,
  42,43,48,68,73,75,79,81,87,89,
  91,93-97,99,101,102
  Farewell to Army, 105-107
16th Army Corps, 31,73
16th Wisconsin Regt.,47,58,60,
  61,69,87
6th Illinois Cavalry, 21
SLOCUM, Gen. Henry W.,82,
  85,87,97
SMITH, Gen. W. Sooy,21,23
SMITH, Gen. Wm.,37
Soldier's Home,40,107
Somerville, AL, 43
South Carolina RR, 94
Southern Mississippi RR, 37
SPEAR, Capt., 22,39
SQUIRES, Harlan, 9
STANTON, Edward M.,101
STEVENS, 'Billy', 60
STEVENS, Capt. Giles, 5
STOWELL, William, 64,70,71
STRONG, Maj. William, 5,17
STULTS, John, 64
STUTSON, Henry W., 64
SYLVESTER, Capt. D. H., 5
Tecumseh, KS. 13
Tennessee Riv.,43
Tensas River, 32
THAYER, Lt. James, 75
3rd Brigade,31,38
3rd Division,18,37,43,58,74
3rd Wisconsin Cavalry, 13
13th Army Corps, 31

13th Wisconsin Regt. 13
30th Illinois Regt.,60,69
31st Illinois,60,69,74,96
33rd Wisconsin Regt. 20,21
THOMAS, Gen.GeorgeH.,79,97
Thunderboldt Lndg, GA,92
TICKNOR, Elias, 89
TITUS, Daniel, 4,73
Topeka, KS. 13
Trinity, LA, 32
Troy, TN, 15
TRUELL, Edwin M., 64
TUBBS, Edwin, 7
TURNER, Capt. H. L., 5
12th Wisconsin Regt.,1,5,6,
  8,9,11,13,15,18,20-27,29,31,
  33,34,37-41,43,48,52,69,74,
  76-78,87,92,92,93,107
20th Corps,82,85,97
20th Illinois Regt.,60,69
28th Illinois Regt.,31
Union City, TN, 15
VANDERPOEL,Capt.Abraham
  1,3,5
VAN DORN, Gen., Earl, 17,19
"Veteran", 34
Vicksburg, MS, 25,26,30-33,
  37,38,40
VILLIPIGUE, Gen., 17
WALKER, Capt., 68
Walnut Cr.,85
Warrenton, MS, 25,28
Washita River, 32
Washington, D.C.,99,100,102
Waterford, MS. 19
Wateree Riv., NC, 94
Water Valley, 19
WEMPNER, H, 65
WHITCOMB,GeorgeBryant,7
Wilderness, Battle of, 102
Wilmington, NC, 94,96,97
Winnsboro, SC, 94
WOOD, Sergt. 65
WOODWARD, Dr. E. A., 5
WRIGHT, Orson, 64,77
Wyandotte, KS., 11
Yazoo River, MS, 25
Yocona Creek, MS, 19
Young's Point, 25

www.ingramcontent.com/pod-product-compliance
Lightning Source LLC
Chambersburg PA
CBHW071621170426
43195CB00038B/1740